JOHN CALVIN:
A Biography

BOOKS BY T. H. L. PARKER
Published by The Westminster Press

John Calvin: A Biography

English Reformers
  (The Library of Christian Classics) (Ed.)

Portrait of Calvin

JOHN CALVIN:
A Biography

T. H. L. Parker

THE WESTMINSTER PRESS
PHILADELPHIA

Published by The Westminster Press®
Philadelphia, Pennsylvania

PRINTED IN THE UNITED STATES OF AMERICA

Library of Congress Cataloging in Publication Data

Parker, Thomas Henry Louis.
  John Calvin, a biography.

  Bibliography: p.
  Includes index.
  1. Calvin, Jean, 1509–1564.
BX9418.P344   230′.4′20924 [B]   75-33302
ISBN 0-664-20810-X

For Mary

Preface

Four full-length lives of Calvin have appeared in English in this century. They are by Williston Walker (1906), H. Y. Reyburn (1914), R. N. C. Hunt (1933), and J. Mackinnon (1936). It would be hard to choose between them, for there is much to be learned from each. Reyburn's book has been unjustly neglected; no doubt it suffered from being published in the year that the Great War broke out. Reyburn made good use of the original sources and quotes liberally from them. Nevertheless, Williston Walker's *John Calvin* is a far stronger and more perceptive biography. Its recent reprinting is to be welcomed.

When the publishers asked me to write a new life of Calvin, I was happy to agree for several reasons. That almost forty years have elapsed since the last of the books just mentioned appeared is of more than ordinary significance, for they have been forty years of great change both in the world in general and in the Church in particular. Walker, Reyburn, and even Hunt were writing in a pre-Hitler world, that is, in a world which did not know at first hand what severe persecution means for the Church. It is not irrelevant to Calvin-studies that the Confessing Church turned so eagerly to Luther and Calvin, men who spoke the word needed for strengthening. One can no longer write about Calvin as if he had played no part in the 'German Church struggle'. Again, between the thirties and the seventies stands the Second Vatican Council. The changes and developments which have already taken place in the Roman Catholic Church have important bearings on the interpretation of Calvin. It is no accident that some of the most interesting and creative work on him in the last ten years or so has come from Roman Catholic scholars. Is it perhaps that, the old polemical spirit laid aside, they find that Calvin and they share to a remarkable extent the same world of thought? Yet another thing. Only in Mackinnon is the influence of Karl Barth discernible, and then to little purpose. But to treat of Calvin now without taking into account both Barth's criticisms of Calvin and also the new light he has shed on many of Calvin's doctrines would be to label oneself as hopelessly archaic. Obviously it was hardly the fault of the older writers on Calvin that they lived when they did. Their age gave them certain advantages which we might envy—notably that they lived in the same orderly world which Calvin inhabited and shared with him the same classical tradition. But to one living after Vatican II and after Karl Barth, they seem woefully weak interpreters of his theology—no doubt because they thought it was a thing of the past. Moreover, ignorant as they were of Calvin's preaching and Biblical work, they gave an unbalanced picture of Calvin by neglecting these central activities.

So far as hard facts go, the present book adds little or nothing to what is already known. But in one or two respects it may claim to be a bit different. Thus it draws more attention to Calvin's student days by portraying university life and studies more fully than has been done in previous lives. It also makes more of his Biblical work and of his preaching. But what is more important is the interpretation of Calvin. As I have been writing the book he has more and more taken on the character and stature of a doctor of the Catholic Church. A 'Reformer'? Yes, certainly, for it is the office of the doctors of the Church to reform the Church—and *ecclesia semper reformanda*. But not just 'Reformer' in its historical sense; not just the first of the Calvinists or the Calvinians or the 'Reformed' or the Presbyterians. Rather, at a time when the Western Church had become provincial, he was a doctor of the Catholic Church. Perhaps this will come through to the reader as strongly as I myself have felt it.

It remains to record my thanks. First, to Professor H. S. Offler of the University of Durham for his guidance—and cautions!—on that most difficult and intricate subject, the University of Paris in the early sixteenth century. I hope he will not be dissatisfied with the use I have made of his advice. I would also thank those among the staff of the Durham University Library who are concerned with Inter-Library Loan, for their patience and help. And finally, my thanks are due to the publishers' editors, both for their long-suffering as year has succeeded to year and also for the several valuable suggestions they have offered. If I make no other acknowledgments of help received, it is only in *direct* reference to this book. To record the indirect help and the help given over the years would extend our preface beyond all bounds.

Durham, October 1974   T. H. L. PARKER

Contents

Contents

Illustrations

(numbers 5 and 9 from copies in possession of the author, the others re-produced by kind permission of the Bibliothèque Publique et Universitaire de Genève)

Introduction

Our story is of a man of order and peace who was born into a world of conflict. A conservative by nature, by upbringing, by conviction, his ideas became among the most revolutionary in Europe. The order, aristocratic in tendency, which he prized and which he devoted his life to establishing, became one of the platforms for democracy in succeeding centuries. His theology was fundamentally so old-fashioned that it seemed a novelty. He himself, a lover of shaded paths and retired groves, was constrained to engage in a most difficult and arduous ministry among suspicious foreigners. And finally, he, the man who understood the need for unity better than any other in his century, was, before he died, to see not merely three major 'Churches' in Europe (one of which acknowledged him as its leader), but the religious dissensions breaking out into the first of the savage civil wars. He did not create the conflict. It was inherent in the culture, the theology, and the politics of his day. Indeed, no man who bore public office could avoid the conflict. He either carried it within himself or he saw his actions, perhaps even actions intended to resolve conflict, turn against themselves in a fatal ambiguity. Willi Pirckheimer, the humanist of Nüremberg, is one example, Guillaume Briçonnet another, Sir Thomas More a third. Attempts were made to exclude the conflict (the Council of Trent might be viewed in this light), but shutting the door did not drive the conflict from the door-step. The threat, if nothing else, still disturbed those within.

The world into which Calvin was born was already informed by the conflict which he was to embody to such a remarkable degree. But only the most discerning recognized the changes as revolution. To the ordinary folk the tenor of life was what it had been in their great-grandfathers' days. Between 1400 and 1500 there had occurred no such technological developments and consequent changes in life as have transformed the world in which I now write from the world into which my father was born exactly a hundred years ago. The early sixteenth century saw great changes in architectural style as the need for defence passed; the introduction of gunpowder revolutionized war and the printing press threw open the doors of knowledge; the horizon itself expanded dramatically as sea-discoverers went to new worlds. But the farmer, the peasant, the artisan, the housewife, and the child all went about their tasks in pretty much the same way as their distant forebears had done, affected only remotely by the printing press, gunpowder, or the Americas. In many respects, life was less unstable in 1500 than it had been in 1400. Only a few were aware of the significance of the tensions in their society and none at all could imagine the root and branch changes that would take place in the structure of the Church, the State, and society itself in the century which was just beginning.

None could imagine; but many could fear a vague threat to their existence. Curiously enough, it was the obscurantists who turned out to be right in their assessment of their world. The Christian humanists of the fifteenth century believed that they could achieve a synthesis between Christianity and the classical cultures of Greece and Rome, or, if that was going too far, that they could press the old philosophies into the service of the Gospel, and all this without disturbing the framework of society. But in the event their activities accelerated the secularization of Europe which the obscurantists were striving to halt. Again, the study of Greek was a thing to be desired to make one wise, not only in the classics, but also in the New Testament and the Greek fathers. But the instinct of the obscurantists was sound: Greek spelt the beginning of the end for the Latin Church. The Reformists also had no thought of schism when they proposed improvements in the organization of the Church. The obscurantists saw their fear come true that this was (as they might say) the thin end of the wedge. At the time of Calvin's birth in 1509, however, the latent suspicions had not crystallized as they did in the next ten years. The last major Church council had met seventy years previously at Basel. There had been demands for reform. The reforms granted had failed to match the needs of the Church and therefore to quieten the demands. Another council was to assemble in 1512; but the most astounding feature of this Lateran Council was its lack of urgency. It was the Roman Church's last chance before Luther burst on the scene with his amazing faculty for understanding the inward theological meaning of practical matters, with his daring and stubbornness in asserting and defending his convictions, and his brilliance and power as a writer.

Luther's reception by the world would not have been hard to foretell. It was to be expected that he would quickly attract a large number of disciples. His theology was Augustinian and a form of Augustinianism was the official faith of the Western Church; for many it needed no *sacrificium intellectus* or *sacrificium fidei* to side with Martin Luther. It was to be expected that many Churchmen would welcome his stand on indulgences, already a topic of controversy. It was to be expected also that the Christian humanists would hail him as a fellow-traveller and that he and his disciples would make use of their linguistic and textual tools for the better understanding of the Bible and the fathers. The old saying that Erasmus laid the egg and Luther hatched it out is an over-simplification, of course, but it expresses the real dependence of the Reformation on the so-called Christian renaissance. Above all, granted the ecclesiastical circumstances which obtained, the official reaction of the Church to Luther was to be expected.

In the late autumn of 1517 Luther attacked the sale of indulgences on theological and pastoral grounds, and called upon the Pope to dissociate himself from the abuses and to correct the system. The Pope first tried to settle the matter by arranging conversations between Luther and certain loyal theologians. The conversations, far from achieving their purpose, merely served to clarify Luther's thinking on the subject of authority, so that he moved from the authority of the Pope to the authority of Councils and finally to the authority of Holy Scripture. The magnitude of this shift in conscious allegiance can hardly be over-estimated. It meant that the Church was no longer, in effect, her own accuser and her own judge but stood under the objective accusation and judgment of God in the Scriptures. This had always been so theoretically. It now became in Luther's thinking practically and immediately the case. The consequence, inevitable upon the circumstances, was that the Pope excommunicated Luther. But excommunication can lead to one of two courses. Either the person repents and is received back into the Church. Or he can continue in his opinions and live outside the Church. This latter course would normally be circumvented by the action of the secular power; that is, he would be removed from society by imprisonment or death. A number of interacting political causes saved Luther from these fates and ensured his liberty of speech and action for the rest of his life. And the fact that most of his followers were willing to share his excommunication meant that loosely integrated communities of worshipping Christians had come into existence outside the Roman Church and were in due course to be formed into Protestant Churches.

In Switzerland a movement, perhaps independent of Luther, perhaps inspired by him, but in any case closely similar in aims and methods, proceeded under the leadership of Huldreich Zwingli and gained religious control in some of the great cities, notably Zürich, Basel, and Bern. This more radical type of reform spread then into parts of southern Germany and into the Rhineland as well as across the sea into England.

In Calvin's own land of France, no less than in the Netherlands, Germany, and England, the Christian humanists and the Reformists were in evidence before the emergence of Luther. There was a strong Erasmian movement in Paris in the fifteen-tens, and calls for reform had long been heard from good Churchmen. The Faculty of Theology in Paris exercised its traditional role of defender and spokesman of the Catholic Faith in France and moved into opposition both against the new learning and against reform. Its leaders were Jacques Barthélémi, Duchesne, and, foremost, Noël Bédier or Beda.

This last had been principal and still was the presiding spirit in the Collège de Montaigu. Pierre Bayle called him 'the greatest Clamourer, and the most mutinous and factious Man, of his Time'.[1] Violent, prejudiced, and stubborn, he wrote hardly a book that did not proclaim by its title that it was *contra* or *adversus* some other theologian or group—'On the one and only Magdalene *contra* Faber and Clichtoveus'; '*Contra* Faber's Commentaries on the Gospels and Epistles, and *contra* Erasmus' Paraphrases'; 'Apologia *adversus* secret Lutherans'. When Luther first came into prominence, his writings enjoyed a large popularity in Paris. Some even among the Faculty of Theology had lent a willing ear to the denunciation of abuses which had hurt Frenchmen no less than Germans. But when Luther had been condemned by the Pope in 1520, Bédier led a crusade to extirpate Lutheranism in France. On 15 April 1521 the Faculty endorsed Leo's condemnation in a document which was less concerned to put forward theological refutation than to call Luther impious, a schismatic, blasphemer against the Holy Ghost, an heresiarch, the heir of the Ebionites, Manichees, Arians, Cathari, Wycliffites, and Hussites, a pernicious enemy of the Church; the *Babylonian Captivity* was comparable only to the Koran and should be publicly burned. The condemnation was given practical effect four months later by the *Parlement* of Paris ordering the surrender of all writings by Luther.

Even before Luther, however, the Faculty had shown its loyalty to the Faith by condemning Erasmus' Greek New Testament and with it the study of Greek itself. After Luther had been dealt with, Bédier turned his attention to the Reformists and particularly to Lefèvre and Erasmus. Assuring Erasmus that he had at heart only his salvation, he informed him and Lefèvre that they were Arians, Sabellians, Donatists, Wycliffites, Hussites. They had made Luther possible. In Lefèvre's commentary on St Paul's epistles he found 143 Lutheran heresies. Erasmus, whose *Paraphrases of the New Testament* had been attacked, was well able to look after himself and retaliated with the 181 lies, 310 calumnies, and 47 blasphemies in Bédier's book which he had noted in passing, although there were, no doubt, many more. For him, Bédier was more a block of wood than a man.

It was the Biblical scholar Jacques Lefèvre d'Étaples (Latin, Faber Stapulensis), who provided the main native intellectual and spiritual stimulus for the Reformists.[2] Lefèvre was less the forerunner of the Reformation than a Renaissance heir of medieval mysticism. The mysticism was the faith by which Lefèvre lived, the key with which he unlocked the Scriptures. His commentaries on the New Testament (St Paul, 1512; the Gospels, 1522) are informed by the same mystical devotion to the person of Jesus Christ. At a first glance he seems to be on the way towards the Christocentricity of the Reformation, and it was not only the conservatives who connected him with Luther. Yet Lefèvre did not teach, and was not even moving towards, the Pauline and Lutheran doctrine of justification by faith alone. For him redemption comes through following the mystical path of purgation and illumination.

xiv

Not simply is sin to be purged but also the dominion of sense, of the lower self, that the man may be illuminated in the knowledge of God through contemplation. Thus will he attain to the blessedness of perfection in the kingdom of God. Purgation is the preparation for illumination and justification. When a man has passed through the stage of purgation, he will begin to know Christ, not simply 'according to the flesh', but spiritually. Along with all this, be it noted, went an unswerving, if critical, loyalty to the Church.

What was there in Lefèvre to supply spiritual energy for reform? Time was to show that there was remarkably little. But to a generation of Frenchmen who had seen their religious liberties destroyed and who longed for the purification of a Church all too obviously in need of reform, Lefèvre's summons to the pure Gospel and to Christ alone seemed the welcome alternative to Luther and Zwingli. Lefèvre was a Frenchman. His theology was apparently undogmatic and reasonable. But he also looked firm, his principles unmistakeable.

The active leader of the Reformist movement in France was not, however, Lefèvre, but his pupil Guillaume Briçonnet.[3] He was the son of a former minister of the crown who, after the death of his wife, had taken Orders and become a cardinal archbishop. Between them, this cardinal and his two sons held three abbacies, five bishoprics, and two archbishoprics. Guillaume Briçonnet was, then, no obscure person dragged into the light by circumstances and his convictions, but by birth, connections, and wealth a man who claimed authority as of right. Bishop of Lodève at an early age, he was chosen abbot of Saint-Germain-des-Près (in succession to his father) precisely to effect the reform of that ancient Parisian house. One of the inmates was Lefèvre himself. It was after Briçonnet's return from being envoy to Popes Julius II and Leo X that he took up residence in the diocese of Meaux, to which he had been appointed two years previously in 1516. He now set out to put into practice the ideas that he had learned from Lefèvre: the Bible was to be opened up to his people so that Jesus Christ, the centre of religion, might accomplish his saving work in them. The Jesus Christ in question was the Jesus Christ of medieval devotion. His saving work consisted in the mystical purgation of the soul. It was the bishop, 'an angel sent by Christ', who 'performs the angelic office of purging, illuminating, perfecting souls'. The Bishop of Meaux harnessed his considerable organizing ability to reforming his diocese according to this pattern of Biblicist, mystical, and conservative Churchmanship.

He began by dividing the diocese into twenty-six districts, to each of which was sent a preacher to give Lent and Advent sermons. From 1521 he imported a number of scholars and preachers, known for their reforming zeal, to help in his reforms. Among them were Lefèvre, Vatable, also of Saint-Germain-des-Près and later to become the Royal Reader in Hebrew at Paris, Gérard Roussel, who was to be Bishop of Oléron, Pierre Caroli, and Lefèvre's pupil Guillaume Farel, who will appear frequently in our story. The group's main activity in the early fifteen-twenties lay in making the Bible available and comprehensible through a number of French translations and through preaching and lecturing. Soon there were Biblical lecturers in four of the chief towns in the diocese. The friars, already antagonistic, attacked this concentration on the Bible as Lutheran.

Practical Church reform was slight. The customary abuses and excesses were denounced, the sale of Masses, the uncritical cult of the saints, the veneration of relics, and the like. If images depicting the earthly life of Christ were retained, representations of the Trinity were rejected. A timid revision of the liturgy was attempted. A few parts of the Mass were sung in French and the *Salve Regina* was omitted. One or two of the preachers went further than their bishop liked. Mazurier, for example, left out some of the prayers in the Burial Service, and Caroli levelled criticisms against the canon of the Mass. Farel, too, was acting against the spirit of the movement when in his pugnacious way he advocated taking on the opponents in public disputations.

Lefèvre and Briçonnet had surely not foreseen the outcome of their reforming zeal. Their programme had aimed at the purification of the Church through the renewal of its individual members. By 1523 the diocese was in a ferment. Not only were the friars minor in open revolt against Briçonnet but the preaching and lecturing had been accepted and believed by some among the lower classes who then expressed their beliefs in violent and unliturgical ways. There occurred the usual phenomena of groups splintering off from the Church, of iconoclastic outbursts, of the heckling of preachers. Reformism had got out of hand in Meaux.

Briçonnet tried to control the events he had unwittingly set in motion. In April 1523 he withdrew licences from a few of the more extreme preachers, among them Farel; the following October a diocesan synod condemned Luther's interpretation of Scripture and his views on marriage, and at the same time forbade the possession or reading of books by Luther. Briçonnet then sent a pastoral letter to the clergy in which he insisted on his evangelical intentions and condemned those who denied the existence of purgatory, the efficacy of prayers for the departed, and the legitimacy of the invocation of the Blessed Virgin and the saints. He repeated the condemnation of Lutheranism in March 1524. But by now he was so suspect to the obscurantists that no retractions could reinstate him as orthodox.

Meaux was a small arena for an active and powerful man. Briçonnet had ambitions of reform beyond his diocese; not only that other bishops might follow his example but also that the French Church might be reformed by an authoritative council. At the Councils of Constance and Basel and in the Pragmatic Sanction of Bourges in 1438 the authority of councils had been declared superior to that of the Pope. Some demands from the French had been met— the clergy were allowed a vote in the election of bishops, for example, and restrictions were placed on taxes payable to Rome. But the Sanction depended on royal approval and was in the event more often disregarded than observed until the concordat between Francis I and the Pope finally killed it in 1516. Now elections (Briçonnet's main concern in this wider context) were abolished; the King would nominate bishops, the Pope confirm his nomination. Royal control of the episcopate led inevitably in the sixteenth century to the appointment of ministers of the Crown at the Church's expense.

In France, the France consolidated after the defeat of dissident Burgundy, it was the King who ruled. He ruled the country, he ruled the University of Paris, he ruled the Church; and this government from the centre was generally active and effective. But kings may be wooed and won. The party that won Francis would, at least for his lifetime, win the Church. The Reformists started with some initial advantages. The King's mother might oppose their cause, but the King himself was not unfavourable, and in his sister they had their most powerful friend. She, Marguerite of Angoulême, later Duchess of Alençon, and at last Queen of Navarre, showed her convictions and religious desires in the Christ-mysticism which found expression in her genuine and technically accomplished poetry, in her stories of men and women who preserved their virtue under the most adverse circumstances, and in the desire for reform which made her the patroness and protectress of many Reformists and an object of odium to the Faculty of Theology.

For a time, while King and Pope were at odds, the sun shone. There was 'Gospel' preaching at the Court; theology became the fashionable topic of conversation; Francis himself was busy reading Lefèvre and made no difficulty about authorizing the publication of his French New Testament. But when in 1522 Marguerite tried to arrange talks between her brother and Briçonnet, now her spiritual adviser, the results were meagre. A conference was convened. But all it could do was to condemn Lutheran books and draw up a few decrees on the reformation of public morality. Lefèvre wrote disconsolately to Farel: 'One day God will grant us to see the clear light. But now, now, nothing but darkness.' [4]

In 1525 Francis was defeated at the Battle of Pavia and carried off to a Spanish prison, and a regency was set up under his mother and sister. Ecclesiastically it was Louise's anti-reform policy which got its way, and a sharp persecution followed. Lefèvre's French New Testament was condemned to the flames and its translator himself was, like others of his group, saved from prosecution only by flight. One young man, Joubert, was burned for his Lutheranism; Jean Leclerc, a linen-carder from the Meaux diocese, was burned at Metz; Jacques Pouent a year later suffered in Paris. Fortunately for the Reformists, Francis was out of action for little more than a year, and on his return he recalled and restored to honour some of the fugitives. But this happy state did not last long. Kings may be wooed, but they more effectively may be bought. Money was needed, for kings and their sons cannot be ransomed cheaply. The Church, like the nobility, was prepared to contribute generously—in exchange for the suppression of Lutheranism. Nevertheless, the reforming activity continued in Paris, in Lyon, in some other great cities. From its centre in Meaux, also, reform spread to a few other dioceses, notably Chalons. By the mid fifteen-twenties at the latest, there were 'Lutherans' in the Picard city of Noyon, the city to which we must now turn.

Chapter 1

Childhood and Youth

1. CHILD OF THE CHURCH

Calvin would sometimes speak of himself as 'merely a man from among the common people'. The plebeian level lay two generations back, with his grandfather, the first of the family that we meet. In those days they were called Cauvin and lived in Pont-l'Evêque, a village whose stone bridge spanned the Oise a couple of miles from Noyon, which it served as port. This mid fifteenth-century grandfather may well have been, as one account has it, a boatman (a vague enough term), or, as another suggests, a cooper, or both; for not only did the Oise, flowing into the Seine, provide a trade route to the north coast and to Paris, but it was at Pont-l'Evêque that the wine was shipped.

The Cauvins are said to have been long established in Pont-l'Evêque, but the last quarter of the century saw the break-up of the family as two or three of the boatman-cooper's sons moved out to try their fortunes elsewhere. Richard and Jacques (if these were indeed brothers and not, as is more probable, father and son) each set up as locksmith or blacksmith in Paris, the one near Saint-Germain-Auxerrois, the other in the rue de Renard, near Saint-Merry. The remaining son, Gérard, must have received a good enough education to enable him to attain a professional career. By 1480 he had migrated to Noyon, a small church-dominated city with a cathedral, two abbeys and four city parishes. Here he steadily prospered. The Cathedral Chapter made him its notary and *promoteur*; he became registrar to the ecclesiastical court; and to these offices were in time added those of notary apostolic and notary fiscal to the Bishop, who was also Count. Plainly he had climbed not a little way above boats and casks. With his respectability sealed by Bishop and Chapter, and as, no doubt, he got the name of a shrewd man of affairs, he was employed now by this, now by that, great local family. In 1497 he could successfully apply to be made *bourgeois*. About this time, when he must have been forty or more, he married Jeanne Le Franc, daughter of an inn-keeper of Cambrai who had now retired to Noyon. He had not only become *bourgeois* the year after Gérard but had also achieved a seat on the city council. From the fact that Jean Le Franc was taxed at four *livres* (twice as much as the average payment) and Gérard Cauvin at only fourteen *sous*,

1

we may infer that the marriage meant a financial advantage for him with something of social advancement for his bride.

Their house, after surviving the great fire of 1552, was gone by 1614. It stood at the corn-market, between la ruelle des Porcelets and what was then rue Fromentière but is now rue Calvin. Or speaking ecclesiastically, as one should do in Noyon, on one side of it stood the Cathedral of Nôtre-Dame, on the other the parish church of Sainte-Godeberte. It was in this church that their second son, Jean, was baptized, no doubt soon after his birth on 10 July 1509. His godfather was one of the cathedral canons, Jean des Vatines. The couple had three or four other children, all boys; Charles the eldest, Antoine, and François who died young, and perhaps an earlier Antoine who also died in infancy and surrendered his name to his brother-to-be. In about 1515, or perhaps a year or two earlier, Jeanne Cauvin died. Her widower soon remarried and by his second wife seems to have had two daughters, Marie and one whose name is unknown.

The boys thus lost their mother at an early age. Their upbringing was no doubt conventional in the late medieval manner. They would know whippings in plenty. They would be treated as undersized adults from whom was demanded early responsibility. They would face the peril of not only the dangerous childish illnesses but also the plagues which so many summers brought to ravage Noyon. They would become resigned to the physical discomforts of an age that had not learnt to look after itself. But with all this, there was the security of a stable society as one year followed another in predictable course. The home of these children who began their lives with the sixteenth century was watched over by the Cathedral on their right hand, Sainte-Godeberte on their left, two stone symbols of the permanence of the Church of God, two living centres of the all-pervasive activity of the Church of God in his world. The only glimpses Calvin gives of his childhood are of exciting little religious treats and feasts. There was the pilgrimage with his mother to Ourscamp Abbey, where he was allowed to kiss the holy relic, a fragment of the body of St Anne, the mother of Our Lady. There were the Christmas and Michaelmas celebrations in Sainte-Godeberte:

I remember seeing as a little boy what happened to the images in our parish church. On the feast of St Stephen [26 December] people decorated with chaplets and ribbons not only the image of the saint himself, but also those of the tyrants (to give them a common name) who stoned him. When the credulous women saw the tyrants dressed up like this, they took them for companions of the saint and burned a candle for each one. What is more, the same thing happened to St Michael's devil.[1]

What more natural, then, than that Gérard should intend the three boys for the priesthood? His influence with Bishop and Chapter would at least settle Charles and Antoine in life, perhaps launch Jean on a successful career. To help pay for their education, he procured grants from the Bishop in the form of chaplaincies and benefices. Part of the chaplaincy of the Cathedral altar of La Gésine (that is, the Nativity, and popularly called 'nostre Dame accouchée') would be handed down from Charles to Jean to Antoine like an outgrown jacket. The two older boys went to school at le Collège des Capettes, on the road to Pont l'Evêque. This prevented Charles from singing in the Cathedral choir, but the Chapter reimbursed him for his lost earnings. He was still at school in October 1522, a lad of at least fourteen for whom the university was apparently not considered. We may infer that he was not particularly intelligent. Of Jean's brilliance at school, on the contrary, Desmay relates the local tradition: 'There he betrayed a fine intelligence, a natural readiness to comprehend the humanities.'[2] Papire Masson agrees:

His childhood was spent in his own district among boys of his own age under a pedagogue and master of scholars; but he outstripped the others, thanks to his quick intelligence and excellent memory.[3]

The time came for Jean to be given a third share in the Chaplaincy of La Gésine. The minute in the Chapter registers has survived:

19 May, 1521. M. Jaques Regnard, secretary to the Reverend Father in God, Monseigneur Charles de Hangest, Bishop of Noyon, reported to the Chapter that the Vicars General of the said Monseigneur had given to Jean Cauvin, son of Gérard, aged twelve years, a portion of the Chapel of La Gésine, vacant by the absolute resignation of Master Michel Courtin.*[4]

At the age of twelve, therefore, Jean became a *clerc* and received the tonsure. To be in the employment of the Bishop was to have connections with a powerful family. 'Since the beginning of the sixteenth century the family of de Hangest, one of the most considerable in the district, had the chief say in ecclesiastical affairs. They had the disposal of the best livings and monopolized, so to say, the episcopal throne, which they occupied for three-quarters of the century.'[5] More than this, they had their own place in the wider life of France and in the royal court. The mother of the Bishop and his two brothers was a sister of Georges d'Amboise, the powerful cardinal minister of Louis XII. One of these brothers was head of the family at Noyon, Louis, seigneur de Montmor and Chaleranges, and *grand écuyer* to Anne de Bretagne. The other brother was Adrien, seigneur de Genlis and *grand échanson de France*. Gérard Cauvin not only won the Bishop's patronage for his son, but also established him in the family of the Montmors. What precisely this involved it would be hard to say. It would seem most probable that at Noyon he went to live with them and shared a tutor, though at Gérard's expense. With his customary brevity in autobiography, Calvin merely says in

* Who held it after Charles had exchanged it for La Madeleine in 1520.

the dedicatory letter to his first book: 'I owe you all that I am and have . . . As a boy I was brought up in your home and was initiated in my studies with you. Hence I owe to your noble family my first training in life and letters.'[6] The Montmor sons were Joachim, seigneur de Moyencourt, and Yves, seigneur d'Ivry (both killed in battle in 1537), and a third, whose name has not come down to us but who took refuge in Geneva in 1547. With their cousins, the children of Adrien de Hangest, Jean was also to have connections. They were Claude, abbé of Saint-Eloi, one of the two abbeys at Noyon, and Jean, canon of Evreux, who became Bishop and Count of Noyon in 1532.

We should not over-estimate the standing or the influence of the family. Even had things turned out differently for Jean, it is doubtful whether they would have greatly advanced his career in the Church. It does not seem to have been through them that he was introduced to the French court; and Bishop Jean de Hangest, best situated to help him, would have proved a frail reed, engaged as he was in a continual undignified war with the Cathedral Chapter. As it was, the de Hangests conferred on Jean Cauvin the boon of polite society. The mere member of the common people, the grandson of a boatman-cooper and of an inn-keeper, became polished, self-assured, independent, one not out of place at the tables of the great.

2. ARTS STUDENT

In perhaps 1520 or 1521,* Jean Cauvin went to Paris with the Montmors, either as members of the same college or living together under the surveillance of a common tutor. This early period, when he attended the Collège de la Marche, has not been generally well understood. Strictly speaking, he was not yet reading for the arts degree but was only preparing for it. Before the student could embark on theology, medicine, or law (these were the three 'superior' faculties), he had to pass through the arts faculty. But before he could undertake the arts course (which consisted entirely of philosophy natural and moral), it was necessary for him to acquire the skills of reading and speaking Latin with sufficient ease to follow a course conducted entirely in that language. This preliminary stage was known as the grammar course. The time spent on it did not count towards an arts degree. Hence, although it is correct to speak of Calvin going now to the University of Paris and becoming a member of one of its colleges, he had first to take the elementary grammar course. This is the straightforward explanation of our sources. Thus Beza 2: † 'he so profited that he left his fellow-students in the grammar course (*in grammatices curriculo*) behind and was promoted to dialectics and the study of the other so-called arts'.[7]

At the Collège de la Marche, then, we may take it that Jean Cauvin, aged

---

* See Appendix 1, p. 156, for my proposed re-dating.
† I shall refer to Beza's first life of Calvin as Beza 1, to his second as Beza 2.

about eleven, was studying 'grammar' in order to enter on the arts course and, after that, theology. But 'grammar' meant considerably more than learning *mensa* and *dominus* off by heart. According to Thurot,[8] the course was in three stages. In the first (which we may assume Jean had already behind him before he came to Paris), the child learned reading, writing and the elements of Latin grammar—this last probably from Donatus' textbook *de octo partibus*. The second stage carried the child through the bewilderments of grammatical irregularities and anomalies, as well as through syntax and prosody. The text-book now was the formidable *Doctrinale* of Alexander of Ville-Dieu which had held sway since it appeared about the year 1200. For some time, however, men of the New Learning had thought a change was needed. 'Do not waste your time on Alexander,' begged Sulpicius Verulanus, the Italian grammarian, 'he is too brief; he is too obscure; he omits many things, he insists on many false precepts.'[9] Many a medieval boy might have wondered what Sulpicius called long if he thought Alexander brief. These two thousand six hundred and forty-five lines of verse had, if possible, to be learned by heart, whether understood or not. Nor were they such stuff as kept children from their play and old men from the chimney corner:

Rectis *as*, *es*, *a* dat declinatio prima,
atque per *am* propria quaedam Hebraea,
dans *ae* diphthongon genetivis atque dativis.
am servat quartus; tamen *en* aut *an* reperimus,
cum rectus fit in *es* vel in *as*, vel cum dat *a* Graecus (29–33)

The preceptors at la Marche may well have agreed with another outburst by Sulpicius: 'Too long have all the teachers wasted their time with Alexander ... Him alone they know among the grammarians ... him they explain to the boys, with him they squander all their days. O unlucky boys! I could weep. I could cry. Let Alexander be contemned! Let him be rejected!'[10] Or they may have held with Erasmus' 'I reckon that Alexander is tolerable'.[11] Certainly, the fact that more than a hundred editions had been printed by 1500 and that the book was still being issued by Parisian printers shows that the *Doctrinale* was used extensively as late as the fifteen-twenties. By way of Alexander, or some such text-book, Jean Cauvin was painstakingly learning 'grammar', 'the door-keeper to all the other sciences, the aptest purifier of the stammering tongue, the servant of logic, the master of rhetoric, the interpreter of theology, the refreshment of medicine, and the praiseworthy foundation of the whole *quadrivium*'.[12]

The Latin teaching at La Marche left much to be desired, and matters reached a crisis at the time Jean entered the Collège. The trouble seems to have been that the lower masters were neglecting steady work on grammar and language structure and trying to get their pupils on too fast. The preceptor in charge of the top class therefore took over the fourth class for a year. Thus it was that Jean, a member of that class, had the inestimable boon of being taught by one of the greatest of Latin teachers, Mathurin Cordier, a man whose Latin grammar was still being used at the beginning of the nineteenth century. Almost thirty years later, in dedicating a book to Cordier, he reminded him of their first acquaintance:

When I was a child and had merely tasted the rudiments of Latin, my father sent me to Paris. There God's goodness gave you to me for a little while as preceptor, to teach me the true way to learn so that I might continue with greater profit. When you had charge of the first class (and what success you had!), you were faced with a troublesome problem. You saw that boys taught very ambitiously by other masters nevertheless lacked a solid foundation and had nothing but show, so that you had to start with them from scratch. You grew tired of it, and for that year descended to the fourth class. Well, such was your purpose, but for me this happy start to the study of Latin happened by the special blessing of God. I enjoyed your teaching only for a little space, since we were soon moved up by that stupid man who directed our studies according to his will, or rather his whim. Yet I was so helped by you that whatever progress I have since made I gladly ascribe to you.[13]

The third stage in the course consisted of elementary logic, studied by means of the *summulae*, an abridgment of Aristotle's *Organon*. If Jean Gerson's regulations as Chancellor of the University were still in force, the boys would have to learn the *summulae* by heart 'even if they do not at once understand them'.[14] Besides this and the Latin grammar and some Latin poetry (mainly classical, but perhaps some medieval), the preliminary course provided a sort of secretarial training in the writing of letters to persons of varying ranks. A certain amount of arithmetic was thrown in as well.

Soon, within a year perhaps, Jean Cauvin was adjudged capable of starting the arts course, *philosophia*. At this point he migrated from La Marche to Montaigu, a college of quite a different complexion, which would well suit a future theological student.[15] Forty years previously Montaigu had been reformed by its principal, Jean Standonck. He himself had been educated in the evangelical mysticism of the Brethren of the Common Life and was imbued with the spirit and aims of their founder, Gerard Groote. Influenced also by the examples of the older religious orders, he set out to make Montaigu into an educational monastery, a religious college, 'a community of poor clerks who, under the most severe rules, were preparing to become priests and "reformed" monks'.[16] The daily offices were recited, and not only were the great feasts of the Church observed but also the feasts of the Blessed Virgin, of the Evangelists and Apostles, of Sainte Catherine and Saint Nicolas and the patron Saint Spérat. There was a strict control of the moral life; pupils were taught to search their consciences in preparation for the regular public confession of sins; denunciation of one another was demanded and a weekly examination into behaviour was conducted. Is this perhaps the basis for the often quoted statement that Calvin was called 'the accusative case' by his fellow-students? [17] A perpetual fast was kept, in the sense that food was scanty and coarse. For the main meal the boys were given as much bread as they wanted with one-thirtieth of a pound of butter or some boiled fruit. The meat course seems always to have consisted of part of a herring or an egg and some vegetables. Theology students were in the enviable position of getting a whole herring or two eggs as well as cheese or fruit. They were also, unlike the others, allowed some wine, a third of a pint of the cheapest, topped up with water.

The students fell into three groups: the rich *pensionnaires* or *portionnistes* who ate at a common table; the also rich *caméristes* who lived *en chambre* in neighbouring houses and were fed at their own expense; and *less pauvres*, who lived in the college itself and seem to have occupied a position somewhat akin to that of sizars in unreformed Oxford and Cambridge. They had to do housework; they worshipped in a separate chapel; the arts students among them had to enter the lecture room before *les riches* and sit apart from them. And whereas the *pensionnaires* and *caméristes* were expected to cope with their fleas and lice themselves, *les pauvres* had to undergo a regular inspection.

The two rulers of Montaigu in Jean Cauvin's day were, effectively, Bédier and, nominally, Tempête, the one the most reactionary, the other the most irascible of men. Bédier was, and continued for some years to be, the leader of the conservative Paris theologians, the watchdog who barked his warning when he scented any stranger, who bit first and offered no apology afterwards. Guided by the criterion not of the creeds of Christendom, not even of the statements of medieval councils, but of the narrowly parochial, and thus inbred, theology of late medieval Paris itself, he fancied himself the champion of the Faith, fastening on any doctrines that were novel to him and settling the matter conclusively by calling them 'Lutheran'. Tempête, principal all the time that Calvin was at the college, carried a name apt enough for the dullest student to perpetrate a pun, even if he did not put it so well as Rabelais: '*Horrida tempestas montem turbavit acutum.* Tempête was a great whipper of schoolboys at the Collège of Montaigu.'[18] He called it furthermore 'that verminous college' where 'enormous cruelties and villainy' were practised. Indeed, a thoroughly Rabelaisian and highly unedifying episode occurred about the time of Calvin's entry. Montaigu and the Collège de Sainte-Barbe on the other side of rue Saint-Symphorien had one of their frequent quarrels. This street, alias rue des Chiens, was not only a Villonesque haunt of thieves and cut-throats, but was, excessively even for the Middle Ages, filthy and stinking, for the sewers from Montaigu discharged into it. At last the city council ordered that it should be paved, Montaigu and Sainte-Barbe jointly bearing the cost. Paved it therefore was. But the result now was that the sewage could not soak away. The slope of the paving carried it to Sainte-

Barbe. Sainte-Barbe, after vain expostulation, determined to act. The students were apparently supplied with tools and set about re-laying the pavement during the night to correct the slope. Alas! morning found the work still incomplete, and Montaigu awakened was exasperated at the sight of rue Saint-Symphorien again half-unpaved. The porters were ordered to lay in a store of stones in the upstairs rooms; and when that night Sainte-Barbe took up again their dawn-interrupted labours they were met by showers of missiles. A furious pitched battle ensued. Heads were broken, windows smashed, the chapel crucifix was damaged. The next day, after consultation between the principals, it was decided to construct a drain. This was early sixteenth-century Paris.

At Montaigu, it is generally agreed, Jean Cauvin was one of the privileged *riches*. A phrase of Colladon's suggests that he was a *camériste*: 'Then Calvin lived in the collège de Montaigu under a preceptor in class, a Spaniard; and also *en chambre* under a Spanish preceptor who afterwards became a Doctor in Medicine.'[19] But it is improbable that living out released him from the rigours of the discipline, and his daily life would follow something of this pattern:

Up at four o'clock for the morning office, followed by a lecture until six, when Mass was said. After Mass came breakfast, and then, from eight until ten, the *grande classe* with a discussion for the ensuing hour. Eleven o'clock brought dinner, which was accompanied by readings from the Bible or the life of a saint and followed by prayers and college notices. At twelve the students were questioned about their morning's work, but from one to two was a rest period with a public reading. Here our sources skip an hour, and it may be that the students were left free until the afternoon class claimed them from three until five. Now vespers were said, and after vespers a discussion on the afternoon class took place. Between supper, with its attendant readings, and bed-time at eight in winter or nine in summer there was time for further interrogation and for chapel. On two days a week opportunity was given for recreation. Students were permitted to play games or to be taken for a walk in the Pré-aux-clercs, the university recreation ground. Montaigu itself had a garden across the rue Saint-Symphorien but linked with its own buildings by a raised gallery on pillars; it seems, however, to have been for the use of the theologians only.

This then was Jean Cauvin's life at Montaigu for most of the year, beginning about October 1, the Feast of Saint-Rémy, and finishing perhaps in July, when, no doubt, he would go home to Noyon for the vacation. A few days were granted for holiday at Christmas and Easter, and there were, on the numerous saints' days, relaxations of the normal routine—or rather, on these days different activities were prescribed.

3. TRAINING IN PHILOSOPHY

We must remember, though, that he was a member not only of Montaigu but also of the University of Paris, and that he was studying first of all for his Bachelor of Arts degree. It would be foolish to pretend to certainty about the arts curriculum in Paris at that time. One has only to read the classical works on the subject to learn how bewildering the evidence, how conflicting the conclusions. Certainly we have the statutes and regulations, apparently hard facts. But the many admonitions to masters who had been a law unto themselves, the numerous concessions to cover the unusual cases, the stopping of loop-holes, warn against dogmatism. Certain it is, however, that the teaching must have been the same for Jean Cauvin as for every other student. The lectures were invariably commentaries on set books. Their form may have been either a straightforward explanation of the text (*expositio*) or the *quaestio* method of posing and answering questions suggested by the passage. Both forms were carefully regulated. The essence of *expositio* lay in making distinctions. The book was first divided into its main sections according to subjects. The first section was further divided according, let us say, to different aspects of its subject. The lecturer would at last be brought to a sentence, to a clause, to a phrase. He would deal with these primary units in order, forbidden by the regulations to proceed before expounding each point. The method of *quaestio* consisted in extracting from the parts of the document the most important problems and arguing for and against them.

The *quaestio* was a sort of one-man disputation. Disputations proper were the other part of the medieval teaching method. The modern 'essay' and written examination were, of course, unknown. In the *disputatio* the student was given a thesis or set of theses to defend publicly in opposition to a master. It would be carried on by means of the *quaestio*, or syllogistic, method. Anyone who wants to know what a *disputatio* was like may easily satisfy himself by reading, say, the disputation between Nicholas Ridley and others at Oxford.[20] The men of the New Learning might despise syllogistic reasoning as too stereotyped, but they found it very hard to rid themselves of this mental habit. The syllogisms that abound in Calvin's own writings testify to the thoroughness of his training at Paris. For the intelligent student the *disputatio* meant a continual creative involvement in the subject he was studying, a clear understanding, and above all, readiness in debate—'conference maketh a ready man'.

These regular disputations were a preparation for and were integrated with the 'determinations', the oral tests for degrees, which took place in the colleges and *pensions* between Martinmas (11 November) and Christmas and again at the end of January and into February. The 'determinant' was presented with sets of theses to defend on the books and subjects he had studied. This, like most examinations in prospect, sounds a formidable task, but the

9

standard was not high even for the master's degree. In 1503, for example, we find the rector complaining that 'ostlers, horse-boys, and cow-men are reaching this dignity of Master of Arts; they not only are ignorant of Aristotle, they have no knowledge even of Cato and the first elements'. The disputations were also necessarily part of the office of teaching. There was only one step from disputing with a master to being on the other side and disputing with a student. But long before this, from his first graduation as bachelor, the student would probably engage in teaching as a part of his own training. The lectures given by bachelors would cover metaphysics, ethics, rhetoric, and natural sciences, but not logic.

We have, therefore, to imagine Jean Cauvin, who has entered on his arts course at about the age of twelve or thirteen, attending the Latin lectures, learning to dispute, 'determining' for his baccalaureate in a couple of years and thereafter combining his studies with some teaching. After another year he will 'determine' for his licentiate and become Master of Arts at sixteen or seventeen (for which he would presumably need a concession from the regulation that masters must be at least twenty-one).

What books may we expect him to have read? We cannot give titles with certainty, but we can point to authors. The course consisted in understanding certain books. These books were representative of the medieval world-view and were, in their own spheres, authorities and not merely 'set texts'. They were accepted as authorities and where they differed from higher authorities (for example, Scripture) or among themselves, they had to be manipulated so that the discrepancy might be explained. The books of which we are particularly speaking were some of the works of Aristotle. It is true that certain medieval writings were also studied, but they lived in the light of Aristotle. Aristotle was read in Latin translations, of course, and most often it was Aristotle as transmitted by his Arabian or medieval commentators; but nevertheless, Aristotle whose sway, 'the longest tyranny that has ever been exercised', was only now beginning to draw to its end.[21] The reform of the arts curriculum in 1452 had stipulated the use of certain works, but the lists we have do not agree. We are therefore reduced to saying that no doubt the demand was still in force that the text of Aristotle should be expounded point by point, passage by passage, together with the opinions of his commentators. And presumably the chosen works of Aristotle covered the whole natural— that is, non-revelationary—knowledge to which man can attain. The natural sciences would be embraced in the *Physica*, supplemented perhaps by Boethius' *Arithmetica* and such works as Pierre d'Ailly's *de Sphaera*, John Pecham's *Perspectiva communis* (on optics), the first six books of Euclid, and Ptolemy's *Almagest*. For psychology there would be Aristotle's *de anima*, for ethics his Nicomachean Ethics, for natural theology his *Metaphysica*, and for logic part of his *Organon*.

It was logic that formed the back-bone of the arts course, and there can be little doubt that the logic that Jean Cauvin was taught was nominalist and terminist. But there were different types of terminism and we should only be able to point to one particular type if we knew who his teachers were. Beza tells us that he was taught by a Spaniard; he in Colladon's account becomes two Spaniards, of whom one later took his doctorate in Medicine. It has been conjectured that the Spaniard, or one of the Spaniards, was the terminist philosopher Antonio Coronel, who is known to have taught at Montaigu at this time. It is further conjectured that the Scottish theologian, John Major, who was a regent (i.e. professor) at Montaigu between 1525 and 1531, taught the young Calvin.[22] One or two writers even go so far as to assert that Major taught Calvin theology. The only foundation for the notion is that Major and Calvin were contemporary at Montaigu—although, if our dating is correct, and Calvin left Paris in 1525 or 1526, they could not have been contemporaries for long. What seems certain is that Calvin did not proceed beyond the arts course at Paris and therefore would not have attended any theological lectures that Major may have given. It is not impossible that Calvin went to Major's philosophy lectures.

Instead of indulging in unverifiable speculation about the identity of his teachers and therefore the precise type of logic that he was taught, it will surely be better to state the near certainty that the philosophy he learned was nominalist and terminist. By the beginning of the sixteenth century the so-called *via moderna* had begun to wear a distinctly old-fashioned look. But it was, in spite of rivals, still entrenched in the philosophy course at Paris. Terminist logic was, as the name suggests, concerned with the analysis of language, or rather, with the analysis of the relationship between language about objects, the mental conception of the object, and the object itself. It involved a linguistic exercise, at first very simple but then highly complicated, consisting chiefly in distinctions between several sorts of terms. Correspondingly, it had its own quite barbarous technical language—categorematic, syncatagorematic, absolute categorematic and connotative categorematic, *terminus prolatus, terminus scriptus, terminus conceptus,* first and second intentions and the like.

But terminist logic was really an attempt to understand the relationship between the knower and the known, and this was broken down into the relationship between the term which either signifies or stands in place of the object, the mental concept of the object mediated by the term, and the object itself. In such a formulation of the question two weak links in the chain of knowledge are apparent. The first is the validity of correspondence between the term and what it signifies or stands in place of. We must ask not only whether the term genuinely signifies what it is intended to signify, but also how far or even whether the term can stand for its object. The second is the validity of correspondence between the mental concept of the term and the term itself. The great problem, inherent in all forms of nominalism, therefore

11

was what guarantee there was that the mental concept genuinely corresponded to the object itself. To resolve the problem, attention was focused on the act of cognition, on the modes of knowing related to the types of terms.

Thus the effect of terminism was in the first place to make knowledge subjective, to concentrate on knowing and the mental concept at the expense of the object. This subjective philosophy was kin to the subjective religion of the late Middle Ages and both fostered it and was fostered by it. But secondly, subjectivism and scepticism go hand in hand. Do I know the object itself? That is, do I stand in true relationship with the object? Or, if it is possible to know only the term, does the term genuinely represent the object? Or am I, in this mysterious mechanism of the mind, only knowing the concept I have formed of the term which may not genuinely represent the object itself? Refer such thinking to religion, and theology in the true sense becomes impossible. All that can be done is to make a series of dogmatic assertions. It is small wonder that William of Ockham already in the fourteenth century had taken such doctrines as the existence of God and transubstantiation out of the province of philosophical theology and made them objects of implicit faith, that is, doctrines to be accepted on the word of the Church.

If, then, as seems most probable, the young Jean Cauvin was trained in terminist philosophy, a complete intellectual reversal would be necessary before he could confidently and joyfully understand that knowledge was relationship between subject and object, that the term genuinely stood for the object by inherent character, and that the intellect, far from moulding the object, is itself formed to the capacity of the knowledge of the object by the object itself.

Chapter 2

Orléans and Bourges

1. THE STUDY OF CIVIL LAW

In 1525 or 1526 Jean's life suffered a sudden change. Gérard had intended him from childhood for theology, that is, for the theological course at the university leading to the priesthood. The arts course was, as we have seen, a preparation for entry into one of the three 'superior' faculties. Now, when he had taken his licentiate in arts and his master's degree, his father changed his mind, withdrew him from Paris and sent him to the University of Orléans to study civil law.

The motive assigned by Calvin himself and by Beza 2 and Colladon is the simple but hardly elevated one that Gérard saw there was more money in a legal career. Few clergy would wish to deny the truth of this insight. But here a difficulty is posed: Gérard was himself a lawyer, within his limits successful and therefore shrewd enough in material matters relating to the two worlds he knew best, the Law and the Church; is it credible that only now at this late date he woke up to the fact that Law pays better than Church? Perhaps, however, it was not Gérard who changed so much as circumstances. Jean was destined for 'theology' as 'a very little boy'. How old is that? Surely not more than ten at the most, more probably seven or eight—in other words, somewhere between 1516 and 1519. And this is, in fact or in effect, before Martin Luther's impact on the Church. By 1525, with part of Germany successfully in revolt against Rome and with Reformation and Reformism active in Switzerland and France, the Church may well have seemed to a clear-sighted father to offer a less glittering prospect for his son. If reform got its way, what would become of the desirable plums? What chance would there be of a basket of plums for the pluralist?

In migrating to Orléans he moved not merely from one city or university to another, but to a new world.[1] Gone now the rigid restrictions over body, mind, and soul exercised by Montaigu. Orléans had no collegiate system, and, although the master or doctor who kept a student hostel was responsible for discipline, the intention was social order rather than the ruthless saving of possibly reluctant souls. There was but one faculty, that of Law, in which the Civil with five professors predominated over Canon Law with only three. But that it was devoted to law does not mean that it was secular. Like any other medieval university it was an integral part of the Christian society. Many of the masters were clerics, some of the students were destined for holy orders. We must suppose that Jean himself still wore the tonsure and was on his way to becoming an ordained lawyer, a breed common enough in the sixteenth century.

When Pantagruel in his itinerary through the universities of France visited Orléans, he found the students a sporting set, keener on tennis than on law.[2] The sixteen- or seventeen-year-old Jean was not, so far as we know, a tennis player. When as a *béjaune* (Scottish, bejant) he had paid his *bienvenue*, he set himself as a dutiful son to work hard at the new task which his father was demanding. Beza tells us that the poor health from which he later suffered is to be traced back to overwork now:

some still living, intimate friends with him then, bear witness that it was his habit to take a light supper and work until midnight; when he awoke the next morning he lay for a long time in bed meditating on and so to say digesting what he had read the night before—nor would he lightly allow this meditation to be interrupted. By these continual vigils he attained his substantial learning and preeminent memory, but it is also likely that he brought on that weakness of the stomach that was the cause of his various illnesses and at length of his early death.[3]

Since this training in law was of great importance in Calvin's development, it will not be out of place to speak of it rather fully.[4] The *Corpus Iuris Civilis* was undertaken in the reign of Justinian, between the years 529 and 534. It consisted in a thorough arrangement, modernization, and promulgation of previous Roman law and legal writings, and consisted of three works—in order of publication the *Codex*, the *Digesta*, and the *Institutiones*. The *Codex* or Code may be regarded as the heart of the *Corpus* inasmuch as it was the authoritative statement of Roman law. The *Digesta*, also known as the *Pandecta*, was a massive compilation under subjects of the more important statements of earlier Roman jurists, an historical commentary on the *Codex* without following its ordering. The *Institutiones* formed the elementary (but still authoritative) text-book for law-students. To these three must be added the *Novellae*, laws dealing with problems brought to light in the compiling of the *Digesta* or enacted subsequently to the publication of the *Corpus*.

In the Middle Ages this material had undergone some rearrangement. The *Digesta* was divided into the *Digestum vetus*, the *Infortiatum*, and the *Digestum novum*. The middle part suffered a further division, so that Book 35. 2–38 was known as the *Tres Partes*. When we hear, then, that for the baccalaureate at Orléans the *Codex* and the *Digestum vetus* were covered in 'ordinary' lectures, and the *Infortiatum*, the *Digestum novum*, the *Institutiones*, the *Tres partes*, and the *Authenticum* (i.e. a version of the *Novellae*) in 'extraordinary', we know that students were in theory taken through the *Corpus Iuris Civilis*.

In practice their contact with the *Corpus* was probably at second hand, or rather, third hand, by way of their lecturers' expositions of medieval glosses on the work. The process of commenting had been going on and augmenting throughout the Middle Ages. The earlier glosses had been condensed in the *Apparatus* of Accursus, which was still studied. But the most influential later school went under the name of Bartholus, a fourteenth-century jurist. It had arisen through the application to law of the dialectical method in use in theology.[5] In this school the *Corpus* was used as the basis for the understanding and revision of contemporary law. It was thus given a practical bias. Bartholus dominated the study of the law until the sixteenth century, and no doubt it was through his vast commentaries on the *Digesta* and *Infortiatum* that the 'civilians' at Orléans, among them Jean Cauvin, approached Roman law. Before this time, however, another change had occurred. As early as the first half of the preceding century certain humanists had gone straight to the *Corpus*, by-passing the medieval accretions. One effect of their method had been to remove the relevance of the *Corpus* to contemporary law and make it a literary and historical source-book; for they read it partly as a linguistic study, partly for the light it could throw on the history and social customs of ancient Rome. Thus, by the time Calvin was reading law, not only were there two opposing methods in law, but the modern school, through Valla, Politien, and Budé, had built up an imposing body of textual, linguistic, and historical studies of the 'Bible' of the civil law.

We can see what Calvin was working at during these years. The *Institutiones* starts out from a definition of the basic terms, *iustitia, iurisprudentia, ius naturale, ius civile* and *ius gentium,* and *lex.* Each of these terms has not only a legal but also a moral or ethical and even a theological significance. *Iustitia,* for example, 'is the constant and perpetual will that renders to every man his right'.[6] Jurisprudence 'is the knowledge of things divine and human, the science of the just and the unjust'.[7] Fundamentally, therefore, the jurist was concerned with a man's relationship with his fellows, and that, not only in a practical way, but also in regard to the forces making for unity or discord in society. Moreover, that it was civil law should not mislead us into thinking that it was therefore secular, non-religious law. Even before the Empire became Christian the connection between religion and law had been intimate. The *ius civile,* was, of course, the codification of law in a Christian state. Nor did the medieval view of society lend itself to a clear distinction between the secular and the religious. Hence civil law was studied on earth but very definitely under heaven. We may further note that the *ius civile* had a reference both to natural and also, to a limited extent, to revealed theology. Not only did the early part of the *Codex* deal with Church law in Rome, with chapters on church buildings, bishops, baptism, heretics, images, and the like, but the first chapter even provided a statement of the Nicaeno-Constantinopolitan doctrine of the Trinity. The student would therefore be expected to gain a knowledge of early Church doctrine and in particular of Christology, as well as some acquaintance with the early history of doctrine. It would seem then that Calvin's first theological studies took place not at Paris but at Orléans. But the philosophy of law and the theology occupied in extent only a small part of the *Corpus*. For much of the time he spent in Orléans, Calvin would be concerned with the innumerable material causes of man's dissensions with his neighbours—the disposal of rain-water, rights of way, leases, purchase and possession, marriage and divorce, inheritance—and the decisions which generations of Roman and medieval jurists had given in such disputes. All this was to come in useful in later life. And indeed, the way in which his friends made use of him in little bits of their personal or family business shows that even as a very young man there was a shrewd, practical side to his nature.

With the bachelor's degree behind him in about three years, he would be set on the path to the licentiate-in-laws, the goal of the course. More, he now had the right and the duty to lecture *extraordinarie* (these were the less important lectures, delivered by bachelors). That he lectured in arts at Paris we must assume; that he lectured in law at Orléans we may take as certain. In fact, he seems to have done more than lecture *extraordinarie*. The words of Beza and Colladon in telling us that he lectured have hardly been given their due weight. Beza 1 and Colladon say: 'in a little while he was regarded, not as scholar, but as one of the *docteurs ordinaires*, and he was more often teacher than hearer'.[8] And Beza 2: 'very often he stood in for the doctors themselves and was regarded as a teacher (*doctor*) rather than a hearer'.[9] From this it appears that Calvin gave lectures *ordinarie*. But there was no need for the biographers to treat this as such a marvel, for, although in one university regulation none but the *doctores actu ordinarie regentes* could deliver these lectures, in another this privilege was granted also to licentiates who were about to take their doctorate.[10] Nevertheless, it means that Jean was one of the outstanding students, in that he seems both to have lectured *ordinarie* for some considerable time and also to have been a natural choice for professors seeking a temporary substitute—something that the act of 1512 had regulated. The fact that in 1531 it was further ordered [11] that only *licenciés* could be substitutes suggests that previously bachelors, or at least a bachelor, had acted sufficiently often to demand the regulation.

The licentiate's course lasted for three years and marked the end of the student's career, for the doctorate was, strictly speaking, not a degree depending on conditions of time and study but a title conferred soon after the licentiate.[12] That Jean took his licentiate we know, for in legal documents of 1532 and 1536 he is referred to as *licencié-ès-loix*. But he does not appear to have proceeded doctor. Beza 1 and Colladon report that he was more than once offered a doctorate for nothing [13] (which fits in with the Orléans system) but that he refused. Beza 2 omits that he refused the honour.

2. FRIENDS AND RELATIVES

At Orléans Cauvin (but let us now drop the earlier version, as he himself begins to do) Calvin emerges from the deep shadow of his life in Paris; from a student known only by name he becomes a distinctive and recognizable figure. And that in spite of his curious habit of using pseudonyms. Sometimes he meets us as Charles d'Espeville, Espeville or Eppeville being a village from which the chaplaincy of La Gésine drew some rents and which belonged to the Hangests. They owned also Passel, a neighbouring village to Pont-l'Evêque, which supplied the name Passelius. Both these names are used in letters to and from him throughout his life. Sometimes now he becomes Martinus Lucanius, and later he will even publish some of his books under another anagram of his name, Alcuinus. But under all the pseudonyms Calvin is recognizable.

Recognizable, too, are many of his friends. Jean and Claude de Hangest, cousins of the Montmors, were fellow students and, Claude especially, members of his particular group. Calvin's earliest extant letters date only from 1530, but their recipients and most of the persons mentioned in them were from Orléans. There was Nicolas du Chemin, a licentiate-in-laws in whose *pension* he lodged in the rue du Pommier and whom he was to address as 'friend dearer than life itself'. François de Connan was son of a government official in Paris and himself achieved a high place in the Civil Service —his *Commentarii Iuris Civilis* was to procure him bright but fleeting fame. Philip Loré, being a bookseller of the city, was a good friend for an intending author to have and one who could keep him in touch with what was being published in other centres. But most of the early letters were written to François Daniel, a law student in his native Orléans. His family welcomed Calvin as a new member, and he was made privy to family secrets, used in family business.

The friends, whether Reformists or not, were, as students, liberal-minded. They were friendly with Sucquet, one of Erasmus' protégés, with Melchior Wolmar, with Nicolas Cop of Paris. Some of them would migrate eagerly to Bourges to hear a humanist lawyer. Some of them knew, or were learning, Greek. It may be that they were in secret sympathy with the Reformists. It may only be that they were attracted to the new learning. But whatever they were, they were certainly not obscurantist, opponents of all proposals for reform, of all fresh ideas. If, then, Calvin made and cultivated such friends in Orléans, we may be sure that, if he had ever been a typical son of Montaigu, an obscurantist in religion and in learning, he had ceased to be so after two or three years in his new university.

Two other friends there were who had already taken the decisive step into the ranks of the Reformation. The first was a kinsman of Calvin's, Pierre Robert, the son of Jehan Robert, a proctor in the church court of Noyon.

Little is known of this brilliant young man, the Henry Martyn of the French Reformation. One quality he shared with his cousin—the late night working, for which his friends nicknamed him Olivetanus, or Midnight Oil, a joke which in course of time became his surname. He was probably at Paris with Calvin. In 1528 he was, from fear of persecution in Orléans, to take refuge in the reformed city of Strasbourg. Beza 1 and Colladon make him responsible for Calvin's conversion: 'when he had been taught about true religion by a certain kinsman, Pierre Robert Olivetan, he began to devote himself to reading the Bible, to abhor superstitions, and so to separate himself from those rites'.[14] They seem to be mistaken in saying that this happened before the Orléans days, but it is by no means impossible that Pierre Robert may have been an influence, even the leading influence, in his conversion.

The other friend was Melchior Wolmar. Although thirteen years Calvin's senior, he was his contemporary in the Faculty of Arts in Paris. There in the determinations for the licentiate he was placed first out of a hundred candidates, and this in spite of the fact that he had given up nearly all his time to Greek and had published an annotated edition of two books of the *Iliad*. It was probably towards the end of their time in Orléans that he began to teach Calvin Greek, but before then arose the life-long friendship of which we can read in the manuscript greeting on the title-page of the British Museum copy of Calvin's St John: 'To Melior Wolmar, my particular friend, from Jean Calvin'. Wolmar had already, at Orléans, moved beyond the Reformism of his master Jacques Lefèvre into a commitment to the Reformation. According to some writers it was he who won Calvin for the evangelical faith. This also is not impossible.

Nor should we overlook the possibility that family troubles with the Noyon Church authorities contributed to the loosening of the ties. For while Jean was scorning delights and living laborious days at Orléans an unhappy dissension had developed between his father and the Cathedral Chapter. Some writers have seen the affair as a veiled persecution of one of Noyon's numerous 'Lutherans'. Others, with more reason, have suggested that Gérard, the Bishop's man, was caught in the cross-fire of the continual sniping between Bishop and Chapter. Others again regard it straightforwardly as a plain case of professional carelessness, or worse, on Gérard's part. As executor to the estates of first one chaplain and then also of another, he was asked by the Chapter to produce a statement of accounts by Saint Rémy's day 1526. On his failing to meet the request, he was censured. A year passed, and he was still in default. Another year of demands and another Saint-Rémy dead-line came and went. A month later, 2 November 1528, Gérard was excommunicated and an auditor was appointed.

It was not only the father who was in trouble. On 16 April 1526 both Jean and Charles were declared 'contumacious' because, as chaplains, they had failed to attend meetings of the full Chapter. Why Charles, who seems to have been living at Noyon all this while, was not present it is impossible to say. Jean's fault presumably lay in his not presenting, by proxy, a certificate from the Rector of the university that he was in residence. The following January they are again declared contumacious, now in company with others; but the nature of their fault is not mentioned. The rebuke is repeated in May. According to Desmay,[15] there formerly existed in the registers three entries relating that Jean was 'approché' in Chapter (the last two meetings being on 24 July and 7 August 1527—thus during his Long Vacation) before he received the benefice of Marteville. No reason for this action was assigned, but certain old canons, *les plus anciens*, told Desmay that they had seen a page in the registers blank save for the dread-full words *Condemnatio Joannis Calvini*; a non-entry which gave them and him, in the old phrase, furiously to think.

That Jean and Antoine were given benefices and chaplaincies presents no inconsistency. The living of Saint-Martin de Marteville, a village some twenty miles out of Noyon, to which Jean was appointed in September 1527, was not in the gift of the Chapter. Of La Gésine, now contributing to Antoine's upkeep, the Bishop was the patron. And Pont-l'Evêque was given to Jean by his fellow-student Claude de Hangest in his role as abbé of Saint-Eloi. For all their antagonism to the Cauvin brothers, the Chapter would be powerless to prevent their holding even chaplaincies within the Cathedral, even though they could certainly make their lives uncomfortable.

3. BOURGES AND A NEW START

Financed by the stipend of Saint-Martin de Marteville (less the stipend to the curate who performed all the duties), Calvin at about the age of eighteen or nineteen has 'determined' successfully for his bachelor's degree and has started out on the licentiate course, studying and lecturing on the *Corpus Iuris Civilis*. But early in 1529 he and his friends hear that an exciting new professor has just been secured for Bourges and decide to migrate there, a decision shared by students in many other cities.

As a university, Bourges had none of the ancient prestige of Orléans.[16] It had been founded, against opposition from Paris and Orléans, only in the fourteen-sixties and for half a century thereafter had failed to justify the hopes of its promoters. But in 1517 the Duchy of Berry had been given by the King to Marguerite of Angoulême and before long its capital, Bourges, had begun to feel her reforming influence. Not until 1527, however, were similar reforms to those imposed on Orléans in 1512 put into effect in the university. A side result was the attempt to invigorate the teaching by importing well-known professors, if possible 'the most approved professors in France'. One of the earliest recipients of a chair and certainly the most famous was the Italian jurist, Andreas Alciati.[17] Lured from Avignon to Bourges by promise of a munificent stipend with a one hundred per cent increment after a year, he was welcomed with extraordinary scenes of student and civic enthusiasm. His inaugural lecture, on a section from the Codex, *de verborum obligationibus,* was made the occasion for the opening of the *Grandes-Écoles* on Monday, 19 April. That this building had been until recently the City Hospital, which had now moved into fine new quarters, should not detract from the honour intended.[18]

Alciati was, if we are to believe his own account, a lawyer almost from childhood, his first book, on Greek words in the *Digesta,* written at the age of fifteen. Whether this is true or not, he was a figure of the first importance in the history of the development of law in the sixteenth century. Not only was he one of the great humanist lawyers, alive to textual criticism, interpreting the documents linguistically and historically, but he was also a practical lawyer and, like the Bartholists before him, went to the *Corpus* for help in contemporary problems. He may therefore be called a mediator between the old and the new methods. This led him, perhaps without his or his students' understanding why, to use some of the old methods in his teaching. And it is this that may lie behind the student unrest that he provoked at Bourges. We have it in his own flamboyant recital:

Either for the celebrity of our name, or from the novelty that is ever an enticement to the inquisitive, great nobles and scholars came from all over France and Germany. But when they had attended my lectures for a few months and had seen that I was walking in the same old rut as their native teachers, they began to drop away, led by some with greater authority. And they gave me their reason for it.[19]

Briefly, their reason was that they had heard great things of his brilliant learning and his modern methods, but none of this had appeared in his lectures. Instead, he was merely handing out the traditional material they had been used to, Bartholus and the like. 'When I saw that they were all in agreement and preferred teaching to phantasies, clarity to uncertainty, elegance to obscurity, Latin to barbarism, I fell in with their wishes.' [20]

The result, of course, was all that could be desired. Nevertheless, Henri Lecoultre may have been right in thinking that Alciati's account minimizes a quite serious student protest.[21] Among those dissatisfied with the master were, we may assume, Calvin and his group. And, however gratified they might be when Alciati at last spoke in his true person, a further discontent soon arose. Pierre de l'Estoile, the leading professor at Orléans, had criticized Alciati in his book *Repetitiones.*[22] The Italian had replied under a pseudonym, attacking l'Estoile and two Parisian lawyers. He had also written a book in which he had strongly disagreed with Budé's *De Asse.* All this had been a little earlier. Invited to Bourges, he was put in the awkward position of probably having to do with persons to whom he had been rude. He managed to stop the book against Budé going through the press, but he was too late with the other. Alciati might be a more brilliant lawyer than l'Estoile, but the loyalty of the Orléannais was quickened and by the middle of 1529 Nicolas du Chemin had replied with a counter-attack. His pamphlet was held over for a couple of years and then Calvin saw it through the press, adding a dedicatory preface. He himself was on l'Estoile's side and, despite some judicious praise where praise could not be withheld, critical of Alciati. Nor, when he came to mention Alciati in his own first book, were his criticisms softened. There is no reason to grant Alciati a strong influence on him, and such a gush as 'Nectar to Calvin it must have been, who thus discovered a new world, a world that was beautiful'[23] had better been left unuttered.

Whether Calvin was satisfied with his Italian professor or not, his stay of perhaps eighteen months in Bourges was of great importance, indeed, in one respect decisive, in his development. For, alongside his law studies he was learning Greek from Wolmar, also brought by Marguerite to teach in her university. Just as Calvin later dedicated a commentary to his great Latin master, so also to his Greek. In his letter of dedication he reminds Wolmar and tells us:

One of the most important things that happened to me was in those early days when I was sent by my father to learn civil law but, under your instigation and teaching, with the study of the laws mixed Greek [*Graecas literas*] of which you were then professor *summa cum laude*. Nor was it your fault that I did not make greater progress, for you were so kind that you would not have refused a helping hand to the end of the course; but the death of my father called me away at an early stage. To you it is, however, that I not a little owe it that I was at least taught the rudiments; and this was afterwards to be a great help to me[24]

This was a step not without significance at a time when Greek was still being linked with heresy. 'We are finding now a new language called *grège*. We must avoid it at all costs, for this language gives birth to heresies. Especially beware of the New Testament in Greek; it is a book full of thorns and prickles'.[25] Certainly this had been said some years before, but Greek still in 1530 represented the boundary between two worlds. The man who had learned Greek had sailed farther than Columbus from the old world of his birth and found a newer land. Calvin now had joined what du Bellay called 'the famed nation of the Gallogreeks'.

Law and Greek did not consume all his days. He was also doing some lecturing on rhetoric (presumably the course preparatory to arts) at the Augustinian convent where the future Reformer, Augustin Marlorat, was already or was shortly to become prior. More than this, it is said that 'he often preached in the stone pulpit which still stands in their ancient church',[26] and that he engaged in occasional preaching in villages—at Asnières, 'where his word sowed seeds which have never been stifled',[27] and at Linières, for some unexplained reason 'in a barn near the river' where nevertheless he had

21

among his auditors the local squire, Philbert de Beaujeu. The squire was taken with his preaching ('at any rate he tells us something new') but remained 'bon catholique'.[28] There seems something more here than the gossip of a tradition, for Philbert de Beaujeu was seigneur also of Meillan and it was at Meillan that Calvin was staying when he wrote the first of the letters that we have. Perhaps, as Doumergue suggests,[29] he was staying at the recently rebuilt château.

If the stories of his preaching are true, we meet a new aspect in Calvin. No doubt he could have preached had he been still a Roman Catholic, or had he been a humanist. But one must ask whether he would have had a compelling motive for doing so. If, however, one of the marks of an evangelical Christian is the urge to bear witness to his faith, to lead others to a like knowledge of the Redeemer, and if we are right in placing Calvin's conversion in 1529 or early 1530, then it is perfectly consistent that we should hear of him preaching while at Bourges. Indeed, we might go so far as to say that, were there sure evidence that he did not preach at this time, it would offer some indication that he was not yet an Evangelical.

At some time in 1529 or early 1530 Calvin was converted.* We do not know the circumstances. The identity of no agent, if agent there were, has won general credit. Calvin himself maintained a reticence about it—save for the one occasion in the Preface to his *Commentary on the Psalms*.[30]

Calvin is giving his credentials as an expositor of the Psalms. After mentioning as bonds of sympathy with the Psalmists the great troubles and conflicts for the Faith that he has undergone, he takes up specifically the similarity, as it seems to him, between the course of his own life and that of David, the shepherd boy so unexpectedly become king—or rather, for this is the crux of the comparison, David, the one whom God had chosen and therefore had taken from the sheepfold and raised to the throne. Calvin's life had similarly been changed and ordered by God's secret providence. He had been raised out of his obscure origins and made a minister of the Gospel. And this is how the decisive change came about. The plans in which he was destined for the priesthood were suddenly altered and he was put to the study of the law. This is the first disruption in his course, a quite normal, human change of plans. There now occurred a second disruption, and this a divine intervention in his life, overturning the second plan also. He was like a horse, led along by his father in a certain direction, unaware that he had a Rider on his back and a curbed bit in his mouth, until he knew himself pulled up short and turned on a fresh course. This is Calvin's conversion.

He is far from describing it in superlatives. The unexpected conversion is only a beginning, 'a mere taste of true godliness'. He did not immediately arrive at the complete theology later expressed in the *Institutio*; he did not

* See Appendix 2, p. 162.

immediately understand the whole ecclesiastical implication of his new faith; he did not forthwith cut himself off from all associations with the Church of his youth. All that happened was that his mind, wilful in its submission to other authorities, accepted now the sole authority of God. The wild ox tamed now knew his master; the sheep recovered heard his voice. Calvin was made teachable.

Like the Psalmist, he had been brought *de profundis*, out of an horrible pit, out of the miry clay. Beliefs and forms of worship which had been his since babyhood now appeared as superstitions, religion not God-given but arbitrarily devised by men. He had tasted true godliness, *pietas*, which is 'the reverential love of God to which we are drawn by a knowledge of his blessings'.[31] Many writers insist that Calvin's was no 'pietistic' conversion. If one knew what they meant by 'pietistic', one would be in a position to agree or disagree. As it is, the conversion that Calvin describes was, 'pietistic' or not, certainly 'pietastic': he received the first taste of *pietas*; he began to love and revere God as his Father; he was set on fire with a desire to increase in the knowledge and love of God.

One particular subject that he was now studying was the Eucharistic controversy among the Reformers. Nine or ten years had elapsed since Luther in his *Babylonian Captivity of the Church* (1520) rejected the doctrine of the sacrifice of the Mass and interpreted the Eucharist as the sacrament of God's promise, as the gift of Christ to be received by faith. Only recently, in October 1529, there had taken place the confrontation between Luther and Zwingli at Marburg. Calvin was now reading, it is thought, the *Babylonian Captivity* and two sermons of Luther's on the Eucharist translated from German into Latin and published in 1524 and 1527. Thirty years later he told an opponent that, when he was beginning 'to emerge from the darkness of Papacy and had conceived a weak taste for sound teaching', he read in Luther that the Zwinglians reduced the sacraments to bare and empty figures. This gave him such an animus against them that for a long time he would not even read their books. But one book we may be sure he was reading, and that with newly opened eyes, amazed that, well as he knew it, it seemed as if he had never read it before. Perhaps he made use of his improving Greek to read the New Testament in one of Erasmus' editions—the 1527 was the latest then, with the Greek and Erasmus' Latin translation in parallel colums. And no doubt he was frustrated that his lack of Hebrew compelled him to use the Vulgate for the Old Testament.

4. THE FIRST BOOK

We have Calvin therefore at Bourges, still a law student, but with the expulsive power of a new affection beginning to operate. He may have stayed there until the spring of 1531. More probably, he returned to Orléans for the academic year beginning in October 1530 and at this time took his licentiate. It was from Bourges, or rather from the village of Meillan some thirty miles to the south, that he wrote to François Daniel towards the end of the Long Vacation of 1530.[32] The letter is (or was at the time) amusing in its academic witticisms. He sends back a travelling raincloak he had borrowed, giving a learned little reference to Lampridius and to the Greek. He asks to be remembered to various friends, including Sucquet, to whom he has lent his *Odyssey*. Would Daniel please tell a white lie, say that Calvin needs it and then keep it? And he closes, 'Farewell, *amice incomparabilis*'.

Whether from Bourges or Orléans, in early March 1531 he was in Paris, perhaps to find a publisher for his own book, perhaps to make soundings about the prospects of further study in that university. While there he wrote a foreword to du Chemin's *Antapologia* against Alciati and saw it through the press. His intention of returning to Orléans was upset by news that his father was very ill and he went back to Noyon. Gérard, who must by now have passed his seventy years, was living with his second wife and perhaps one or both of their daughters. Charles, too, was still in Noyon and had been in further trouble with the Chapter. In February 1531 he had assaulted the Chapter's mace-bearer when he brought him an order, and followed this up two days later by violence to a *clerc* called Maximilian. The Chapter agreed that he must absolve himself from excommunication; this he promised, but failed, to do. Jean therefore went back to a home where his father and elder brother both seem to have been excommunicate.

His heart was no longer in Noyon; he wanted to get back to his friends in Orléans, but his father's illness kept him, as he wrote to du Chemin:

When I left you, I promised to return soon, and I have been worried that I could not do as I wished. When I was thinking of returning, my father's illness kept me back. The physicians gave us hope of his recovery to complete health; and this only made my longing to see you grow sharper after a few days. But day after day has passed and we have now reached the point where no hope is left; he cannot recover [*certum mortem periculum*]. But whatever the outcome, I will come and see you.[33]

This was on 14 May. Gérard lingered on for another twelve days. When he died, still excommunicate, Charles had to make a special plea for his burial in consecrated ground. Jean was then free to return to Orléans. We may well be offended by the tone of the letter just quoted, where he can talk so unfeelingly and selfishly of the death of his father but call du Chemin *amice mi, mea vita charior*.

He did not remain long in Orléans, however, for on 27 June he was writing to Daniel from Paris, where he had gone to pursue his Greek studies and perhaps to make a start on Hebrew. He intended to stay for some time, for he was looking round for lodgings near the lecture room of Pierre Danès. Danès was one of the Royal Readers in the King's new foundation for teaching the humane languages. A pupil of Budé, he was in his own day ranked by many above his master. Several friends had offered Calvin hospitality, in particular the father of one Coiffart, familiar to the Orléans group, was most pressing. His invitation would have been accepted had his house not been too far from the lectures. We suddenly see that Calvin had a wide circle of friends in Paris and that they were known also to his other friends in Orléans.

The main purpose of the letter of 27 June [34] was to report on the outcome of something the Daniels had asked him to do. Their daughter was to enter a religious house in Paris and to Calvin was entrusted the task of making necessary arrangements with the abbess. Accordingly he went along with his friend Cop, probably Nicolas, on Sunday, 24 June. While the abbess was otherwise engaged, Calvin had a chance to sound the girl out and learn if she understood what she was doing. Time after time she spoke most enthusiastically of taking her vows; the day could not come too soon. Calvin's errand was not to dissuade her. He therefore stressed to her that she must not rely on her own strength but the power of God. The abbess then being free, she arranged with him that he should fix a day, but it would have to be when one 'Pylades' could be present.

The Greek studies under Danès were very soon cut short by a visitation of the plague and Parisians fled for safety to the surrounding countryside. Where Calvin went we do not know, and we hear nothing more of him until mid-January 1532—if the letter indeed belongs to this year.[35] Once again he was involved in Daniel family affairs. Calvin was trying to persuade the brother to remain 'with us', either literally or metaphorically. When he saw that he had failed, he urged him at any rate to go home to Orléans, a suggestion which provoked the brother to warmth. Calvin was innocently waiting dinner for him and a friend one day and at last, worried that they did not come, sent to the inn. He was brought the news that Daniel's brother was away into Italy. The Daniels must not blame Calvin; he has done his best, he says, to prevent the brother from alienating himself from the family.

That he was in Paris on 14 February 1532 is certain. He and his brother Antoine made an affidavit before notaries appointing Charles to act for them in selling some land left by their parents:

We make known that before Simon le Gendre and Pierre le Roy, notaries of our Lord the King at Chastellet in Paris [i.e. the law courts], appeared in their persons Master Jean Cauvin, licentiate-in-laws, and Antoine Cauvin, his brother, clerk, both living in Paris, sons of the late Gérard Cauvin, in his life-time *greffier* [i.e. registrar] to Monsieur the Bishop of Noyon, and of Jeanne le Franc his wife . . .[36]

In April appeared his first book, published in Paris at his own expense, and therefore perhaps with a part of his share of the patrimony. It is very probable that he had started work on it as a student at Bourges, even before 1530, the date suggested by the editors of the English translation. According to Calvin himself, he embarked on it at first without the intention of publication but when he read passages to his friends they (and especially Connan) urged him to publish.

Among the many works edited by Erasmus was the appeal by the younger Seneca to Nero to exercise the clemency 'which all men admired in him'. This *de clementia* was included in Erasmus' edition of the complete works of Seneca published in 1515. As with many of the great humanist's editorial labours the work was imperfectly executed and consequently was severely handled by the critics. He brought out a revised edition in January 1529. It is generally supposed to be a passage in his new preface that inspired Calvin to undertake a commentary on *de clementia*:

I think, however, that I have now brought the work so far that if anyone more learned, more felicitous, and with more time at his disposal, shall improve upon this edition . . . Seneca will, I have every hope, be read with a minimum of trouble and a maximum of pleasure . . . I would like to see this author explained with notes, like little stars, to exclude the temerity of those who would corrupt the text.[37]

Calvin's choice of this particular work as the foundation for his book has given rise to controversy. The older writers understood it as an indirect appeal to the King of France to show clemency to his evangelical subjects. Most modern writers treat it as a purely 'humanist' book, without political or religious intent and therefore constituting a further proof that he could not yet have been converted. Both these views seem to me too stark and doctrinaire, ignoring the realities of Calvin's position. Each also contains something of truth. In writing and publishing his book Calvin could hardly have been unaware of its relevance to the contemporary situation in France. And on the other side, it cannot be gainsaid that the work conforms to one of the significances of the word 'humanist'—that is, devoted to classical literature. But to interpret the commentary on *de clementia* aright we have to try to put ourselves in the situation in which Calvin found himself at the time, forgetting our knowledge of how things actually turned out for him.

He is in his very early twenties. He is trained to civil law. He has not long since begun to move away from the Roman Church. What is he going to do with his life? What can he do but follow the career to which he has been trained? This had formerly been seen as civil law in some ecclesiastical context. But that door has been shut by his conversion. He has, then, to pursue civil law in some capacity outside the Church. Broadly speaking, the alternatives are to practise or to teach. At Orléans he has been treated more like a professor than a bachelor substituting for professors. He cannot fail to be aware of his capacities as a scholar. According to Desmay, he has now begun *régenter*, to regent, to be an official lecturer, at the Collège Fortet—he does not say in which faculty.[38] Is it not therefore highly probable that Calvin plans a career as an academic lawyer? And in those days as in our own the aspirant must show his quality by learned works on his subject. If this is granted, the question why he chose to write on a classical and not a Christian author is already answered. A civil lawyer is hardly likely to further his academic career with a commentary on the Epistle to the Hebrews. But having said this, something remains to be said on the other side. Seneca was not to the sixteenth century the secular writer that he is to us. Did not letters pass between him and St Paul, so that Jerome could call him outright a Christian? These letters were, of course, included in Erasmus' edition of Seneca. Thus it was not a pagan author but a writer with at least Christian sympathies that Calvin chose to interpret.

His method, owing much to Budé on the Pandects, is partly literary, partly philosophical. He shows himself a true child of the new learning, with his use of Greek, his linguistic approach, his attention to the context, his too careful, something brittle style, his heaping up of authorities. The following example is typical enough of the whole:

> Séneca's text runs: '*The face of a peaceful and ordered empire is like a serene and bright sky.*'
> Calvin's commentary:
> '*The face . . . is like.* Why does not the whole empire smile when the sun, the world's eye, beams brightly? The prince's happiness is no private enjoyment; all are glad in his happiness. The simile is therefore apt that a bright sky brightens and renews men's minds.
> *Face.* In Greek either *schema* or πρόσωπον.
> Synesius: ἑαλωκυίας πόλεως σχῆμα.
> Cicero (Ep. 15): Although we have lost πρόσωπον πόλεως. For "face" is referred, not only to human bodies but, as "appearance", to anything at all. Ovid (Trist. 1): This was the "face" of captured Troy. Virgil (Georg. 1): The many "faces" of crimes. See also Gellius and Nonius Marcellus.'[39]

The learning at first sight wears an impressive 'face'. No less than seventy-four Latin and twenty-two Greek authors are quoted or cited. He establishes the Latin text, not hesitating to differ from Erasmus if need be. Some of our respect wanes when we learn that he did not have first-hand acquaintance with all the authors to whom he referred but borrowed freely from compilations—chiefly among the ancients themselves (Aulus Gellius' *Noctes Atticae*, for example), but also from the moderns, like Budé's *Commentarii Linguae Graecae* and *Annotationes* on the *Pandects* and Beroaldus' *Commentarii* on Suetonius, Apuleius, and Cicero. A large part of his learning is therefore derivative; but he is still well read in the classics and, more important, able to handle his borrowed tools with ease.

The linguistic and literary notes, however, serve only to elucidate the sense of the document. On the substance of his philosophical comments there is again disagreement between the critics. Seneca was a Stoic. Is Calvin at this period also a Stoic? For Doumergue, he is here 'not only liberal, he is anti-stoic, philosophically and morally. . . . From the outset Calvin rejects the Stoic view of Providence and opposes to it "illa confessio religionis nostrae"'.[40] For Wendel, on the contrary, he 'takes care . . . to underline resemblances between Stoicism and Christianity. He is sure that Stoics and Christians are at one in affirming the existence of a supernatural providence which excludes chance and over-rules princes'.[41] And here at least Wendel has more of the right, as the particular passage under discussion shows. But again the argument is based on the same misunderstanding that we noted before. To the sixteenth century Seneca was a Stoic with Christian sympathies. It is to be expected, therefore, that certain of his ideas will bear a strong resemblance to corresponding Christian doctrines. Calvin will sometimes point to the resemblance even if the two concepts also contain a serious difference.

He dedicated the book to Claude de Hangest, who had already received the dedication of du Chemin's *Antapologia*. Calvin's little letter is a composition typical of the new learning. It serves both as commendation and as introduction. He apologizes that he has not published anything before. He is aware of the value of his work, in that he has been able to improve on Erasmus' text. His purpose in writing is to give due meed to an excellent author, second only to Cicero, and who had not been prized sufficiently. And he reminds the Abbé of Saint-Eloi how he had been brought up and educated in his family.

And now came a flurry of letters promoting sales. To François Daniel he sent half a dozen copies, one for himself and the other five to be sent on to friends in Bourges. Perhaps Agnetus there will make mention of it in his lectures? And would Daniel ask Landrin to lecture on it in Orléans? [42] To Philip Loré, the bookseller in Orléans, he wrote pressing him to take no less than one hundred copies. He had also, he said, stirred up some professors in Paris to lecture on it.[43]

In spite of all Calvin's efforts his hopes were not satisfied by its reception. Even if it were advertised in the schools of Paris, Bourges, and Orléans, the scholarly world did not acclaim it as a masterpiece, and it must now be said to live only as the first production of a man famous for other things.

5. FUGITIVE FROM INJUSTICE

Calvin did not yet know the unhappy future of his book. And if the world did not trouble itself much about the merits of the work itself, it had to respect the author not merely as a young man of promise, but as one already in process of fulfilling his promise, a man worth keeping an eye on. It was with this reputation that he now prepared to return to Orléans, writing humorously to Daniel that unless du Chemin put him up he would have to freeze under the open sky. The reason for his going to Orléans, where it looks as if he stayed for over a year, is not known. But since he was undoubtedly connected with the university and had already completed the course and taken his licentiate, we are driven to the conclusion that he was teaching.

And here we must mention another aspect of medieval university life. This is the system by which students were grouped according to their nationality or province. These 'nations' were an integral part of the university, yet independent corporations with their own statutes, seals, rights, and duties.[44] At Paris the nations (composed only of arts students) had been four—French, Norman, Picard, and English. Jean Cauvin had, of course, belonged to the Picard, as he did also in Orléans, where there were ten nations. The officers, and especially the *procureur* (proctor, or chief officer), had an important say in university affairs. Elected by the nation, he presided at its meetings, and at Orléans represented the nation at the *collegium doctorum*, the council responsible for the ordinary running of the university.

In May and June 1533 Calvin presided at two meetings of the Picard nation in Orléans in his capacity as 'substitut annuel du procureur'.[45] There seems to be no mention in our authorities of such an office, but it sounds regular and not *ad hoc*. Possibly he was what we should call a vice-chairman, officiating only when the chairman could not be present. The 'annuel' suggests that he was in Orleans for the academic year. We may also infer that he must have been well known to the students who elected him and that therefore his ties with Orléans before his election were close. Nevertheless, Orléans did not hold him beyond this year. After the Long Vacation of 1533, during which we find him at Noyon assisting, as a chaplain of La Gésine, in a Chapter meeting to organize public prayers against the plague, he was back in Paris and writing on the eve of St Simon (that is, 27 October) to 'Monsieur, brother and good friend, Monsieur Daniel, advocate at Orléans'. In this and his next letter he has stirring news to send of religious conflicts in the capital.[46]

Things had been going well for the reforming party lately. The attacks against Lutherans and the persecutions of the fifteen-twenties had died down. International politics had forced Francis into rapprochements with England, recently freed from Rome, and with the German Protestant rulers. Consequently the Reformists were tolerated and, under the protection of Marguerite, ventured out into the open. The Sorbonne reacted sharply and even dared to aim an attack against the King and Queen of Navarre as heretics. This was too much for Francis, who promptly banished Noël Bédier and one or two of his colleagues. The conservatives retaliated through a play put on by the students of the Collège de Navarre on 1 October, satirizing Marguerite and her almoner, Gérard Roussel. The police surrounded Navarre, laid hands on various offenders and put them under house arrest. Meanwhile the theologians had attacked on another front by seizing copies of Marguerite's book *Le miroir de l'âme pecheresse* (1531), in an attempt to proscribe it. Marguerite appealed to her brother, who ordered the university to set up a commission of enquiry. The rector for this academic year was the doctor of medicine Nicolas Cop, whom we have already met as probably going with Calvin to the convent. He was certainly a strong Reformist, perhaps even a 'Lutheran', and he was personally known to Marguerite, who had sent him a copy of *Le miroir* before its publication (his father was known in court circles as one of the royal physicians). It was he, then, who presided at this commission, composed of the Faculties and the nations. Calvin's circumstantial account may be supposed to have come from Cop himself. The outcome of the matter was that the censure of the theologians was overridden and the university prepared a tactful letter to His Majesty thanking him for his fatherly kindness.

But there is one thing worse than defeat, and that is a too successful or an untimely victory. Only six days after Calvin had written so confidently to Daniel, Cop had to deliver his rectorial address—an occasion which in those days did not confine itself to references to university finances and the estimated number of students ten years hence. Taking as his text the Beatitudes (Matt. 5: 2ff.), Cop in effect preached a sermon which owed much to Erasmus' *Paraclesis* (one of the prefaces to his New Testament) and to Luther's *Kirchenpostille*, translated into Latin (1530). A Roman Catholic of our own day would find little in the address to make him uneasy. It is a mark of the extraordinarily provincial and uncatholic quality of Paris theology that they seized on it as heretical. This time the king did not intervene. But when they came to arrest Cop, he had already fled to Basel.

In some way Calvin was implicated in Cop's address. It is more than doubtful that, as used to be held, he himself was the author, although he certainly made a copy of it, for his manuscript still exists. At any rate, he also fell under suspicion. His room in the Collège Fortet was searched and his papers confiscated. He himself had followed Cop's example and left the capital. For the following year he was on the move, in danger, whether actual or, no less disturbing, imaginary. He was a known 'Lutheran', able and vocal. For he was never one of those Nicodemites, the comers to Jesus secretly by night for fear of the Jews, whom he reproved in later years. Nevertheless, he himself confessed in a sermon in Geneva that there had been a time when, from fear of men, he had not spoken out as he should have done. 'I can say that twenty, almost thirty years ago, I was in those distresses [in France], and I could have wished to have been dead that I might see no more of these terrible sights; or at the least, I had wished to have my tongue cut out that I might speak no word (*pour ne point dire le mot*).' [47] He believed that there were perils in the capital, for he relates that it was at the risk of his life that he went there secretly to meet with Michael Servetus, who did not keep the appointment.

After the first alarm in November, when he probably retired to Noyon, he soon returned to Paris; according to Beza, Marguerite pleaded the cause of the Reformists with the King. But in spite of being granted a friendly audience by the Queen of Navarre, he learned that he would be safer elsewhere. He therefore accepted the invitation of a rich young man who, although only now he makes his first appearance, had been his close friend since probably the early student days in Paris. Louis du Tillet was the youngest of four brothers, one of whom was chief clerk to the *Parlement* of Paris, another a royal secretary, the third Bishop of Brieuc and later Bishop of Meaux. Louis himself had so far only reached to be curé of the village of Claix and canon in the local cathedral of Angoulême. This was now to become Calvin's refuge from the blast of the terrible ones.

It has been fairly generally supposed on the word of Florimond de Raemond that it was during his stay here that Calvin began to write the *Institutio*. Colladon and Beza 2 also tell us that he wrote some sermons and 'Christian remonstrances' to be delivered at Mass in various neighbouring villages 'in order to give the people some taste of the true and pure knowledge of his salvation by Jesus Christ'.[48] And certainly we have strong evidence of evangelical activity here in a letter of 1550 to Calvin from Pierre de la Place, a gentleman of that district.[49] But probably too much has been made of this sojourn in Claix or Angoulême where it has been said that in du Tillet's 'splendid library, he had acquired a more extensive and precise knowledge of the fathers'. He could hardly have spent more than four or five months there.

By May 1534 he was back in Noyon, this time to take the definite step that would bring an end to his career as a cleric. An entry in the Chapter Register records that on 4 May he resigned the chaplaincy of La Gésine. It is to be presumed that he resigned the benefice of Pont-L'Evêque about the same time; but for this we have no evidence. The older writers and even, surprisingly enough, some modern, think that Calvin had an eventful month now. They accept Lefranc's misreading of the Register entry for 26 May, according to which 'M. Iean Cauvin [then two words illegible] was put in prison at the gate Corbaut, for an uproar made in church on the eve of Trinity Sunday'.[50] He was released on 3 June but reincarcerated on 5 June. The correct reading, however (which Doumergue gave us as long ago as 1927),[51] runs: 'Un Iean Cauvin, dict Mudit, was put in prison . . .'—'A Jean Cauvin, called Mudit . . .' This namesake was presumably the same who in 1551–2 (when our Jean Cauvin had a water-tight alibi, being in Geneva at the time) was evicted from his canonry for having kept in his house 'une femme de mauvaise gouvernement'.[52]

After May it is impossible to keep up with him. Now he is at Noyon; now at Orléans; now at Poitiers; now perhaps at Claix. That he stays in Paris for any length of time must be doubted. He is writing a treatise (the preface is dated 1534 at Orléans) that is not to be published for several years. At this time the anabaptist groups were vigorous in France and seemed to be winning popularity. Calvin was very well aware of their views and was in touch with some of their leaders. One of their doctrines was that at death the soul went to sleep until awakened by the final resurrection of the dead. To confute this was written the tract later to be called *Psychopannychia*, but now 'The souls of the saints, who die in the faith of Christ, do not sleep, but live in Christ. Assertion'.

The indecisive hiding here and there in France was dramatically ended when in mid-October came the affair of the *Placards*. There were posted in many of the chief towns of France, including Paris, violent attacks on the Mass as a great, horrible, and unendurable abuse in direct contradiction to the Holy Supper of our Lord, sole Mediator and only Saviour, Jesus Christ. The government acted at once. A reward was offered for information. Two hundred arrests were made by the middle of November. Executions, some twenty in all, followed through the next three months. In February was burned Calvin's friend, Étienne de la Forge, a merchant with whom he had lodged in Paris. A royal edict against 'Lutherans' was issued at the end of January. Small wonder that Calvin should decide on flight, or that Louis du Tillet, at least sufficiently compromised, should accompany him. Their escape nearly failed when one of their servants decamped with all their money and one of the horses. Fortunately their other servant had enough money of his own to see them through. They arrived in January 1535 at Basel, a free and friendly city, won to the Reformation by Oecolampadius, Zwingli's friend and Erasmus' collaborator. Here were living Erasmus himself, old and housebound, Wolfgang Capito, Sebastian Münster (with whom he probably continued his Hebrew), Heinrich Bullinger, Guillaume Farel, and Pierre Robert. Cop, too, had fled here after his ill-fated rectorial address. In spite of his exile, therefore, which he never ceased to resent as an humiliating insult, Calvin was not without friends; and although he lacked German in a German-speaking city, the French were sufficiently numerous to make a colony of themselves.

As he settled down in Basel, he was occupied principally with two pieces of writing. The first was as assistant to Pierre Robert on a new French translation of the Bible. Robert had undertaken the work in September 1532 for the Waldensian Christians, and it was published on 4 June 1535 by Pierre de Wingle at Serrières, near Neuchâtel—hence its name of 'the Serrières Bible'. Whether Calvin had any hand in the translating is very doubtful; but he contributed two prefaces. The first in Latin bears the title: 'Jean Calvin to all Emperors, Kings, Princes, and Peoples subject to the rule of Christ'. The second is in French: 'To all lovers of Jesus Christ and his Gospel'. After the publication Robert immediately planned a revision. He himself left Basel, but asked Calvin to read and correct the New Testament section, less satisfactory than the Old Testament in that Robert, a good Hebraist, had translated the latter direct from the original, but had merely revised the New Testament version of Lefèvre, sometimes by the Greek, sometimes by Erasmus' Latin. In September Calvin wrote to their mutual friend Christopher Libertet (or Fabri), now in Thonon, reporting progress:

Our Olivetan wrote to me just after he left saying that he had decided to postpone the publication of his New Testament. I had promised to look it over. It seemed to me that I could put this task off to do at my leisure. Meantime, I gave myself to other studies and forgot about it—or rather, languished in my usual laziness. At any rate, I have not yet started on it . . . But from now on I will take care to set aside an hour a day for this work. My comments—if any emerge—I will entrust to you alone, unless Olivetan should get back before I finish.[53]

But undoubtedly the chief work on which he was now engaged was the statement of faith which he was preparing for the French rulers and for those of his countrymen hungering and thirsting after Christ. The *Christianae Religionis Institutio* was published by the Basel printers Thomas Platter and Balthasar Lasius in March 1536, but it was probably completed before 23 August 1535, the date of the dedication. This suggests that a large part of it may have been written before he came to Basel. It may be that the first three chapters were, if not written before, at least extant as material used in sermons—the expositions of the Lord's Prayer and the Ten Commandments come at once to mind. Nor should we rule out the possibility that the early chapters, or a first draft of them, might have been written to circulate in manuscript a year or so earlier. This is conjecture. What is certainly implied by the opening sentences of the *Letter to King Francis* is that Calvin projected the work before ever he thought of presenting it as an *apologia*.

Chapter 3

Christianae Religionis Institutio

1. ITS CHARACTER AND PURPOSE

Christianae Religionis Institutio is only the head of the title. The whole reads thus:

The Basic Teaching of the Christian Religion comprising almost the whole sum of godliness and whatever it is necessary to know on the doctrine of salvation. A newly published work very well worth reading by all who are studious of godliness. A Preface to the most Christian King of France, offering to him this book as a confession of faith by the author, Jean Calvin of Noyon.

Here we see his two-fold purpose. On the one hand, the work was to serve as an *apologia pro fide sua*, a decisive statement of the doctrinal position of the Evangelicals. The current confusion gave abundant need for such an *apologia*, and the Reformers themselves were aware of their duty to clarify their position. Two at least of their leaders had successfully attempted this. As early as 1521 Philip Melanchthon had published his *Loci communes*, a set of treatises on cardinal doctrines held together by the common theme of salvation by faith in Christ alone. Huldreich Zwingli did something on a rather less ambitious scale for the non-Lutheran Evangelicals in his *Commentarius de vera et falsa religione* of 1525. Guillaume Farel had written a considerably smaller work for French-speaking Evangelicals in his '*Sommaire*, that is, a brief declaration of some matters very necessary for a Christian, to put his trust in God and to help his neighbour' (1534). There was room for a fuller and clearer *apologia* for the French Evangelicals.

Calvin's hand was also forced by the interpretation that the King gave of his persecutions in 1534–5. In a communication of 1 February 1535 to the German Protestant princes the King said that it was quite obvious that the *Placards* had been aimed against the government and were anarchist in intention. That the subsequent repression had been far-reaching was to be explained by the character of Reformism in France, which was quite different from German Lutheranism, being riddled with anabaptism. Was it not the duty of a Christian prince to crush such sects?

Calvin's reply prefaces the *Institutio* as the *Epistle to Francis I*. Marred in only a very few places by the polemical invective that the age demanded as proof of the writer's zeal and sincerity, it is a brilliant and powerful sample of the lawyer's art. Not for nothing had he passed through the Schools of Orléans and Bourges and lectured on Roman law. He pleads, not for mercy or toleration, but for justice: 'Wherefore, invincible King, I demand justly that you take up the whole knowledge of this case, which so far has been treated confusedly and without any legal order, with uncontrolled passion rather than judicial gravity.'[1] The presupposition to Calvin's argument is that the religion of the State was the Christian religion and that the Christian religion was the adherence to the Nicaeno-Constantinopolitan Creed. If the Evangelicals could be shown to stand outside the Christian religion, they were justly to be repressed. All hinges on this point. Calvin's contention was in no way that Evangelicals should be tolerated. Nor did he assert that there could be more than one Church in a State. His claim was nothing less than that the Evangelicals were the legitimate heirs of the Christians of the early centuries and were therefore the one holy, Catholic and apostolic Church, which in France was legally established.

This presupposition, then, is the source of his replies to the objections to evangelical teaching—its novelty, its lack of assured doctrine, its lack of miracles to confirm the doctrine, its inconsistency with the teaching of the fathers and with Church custom, its position outside the church, its engendering of sects. The smartness of wit in his first reply ('I have no doubt our teaching is novel to them. So is that of the Bible and of the Church fathers') too easily distracts us from its historical relevance. The evangelical faith was new in the sixteenth century in the sense that it came as something alien and unrecognizable to a theology that had more and more deserted its origins in the early Church. Calvin in effect was stating, not only that the fashionable theology of the fifteenth and early sixteenth centuries really was a *via moderna*, but also that the whole Church of the Middle Ages, for all its supposed orthodoxy, represented a drastic departure from the spirit that animated Biblical theology and much of patristic theology in the first five centuries.

The heart of the matter was the claim to be the Church. The bare word of the Evangelicals was insufficient, even with the support of Scripture and the partial support of the fathers. The view of the adversaries was that the Church must have a visible form and that that visible form consists in the hierarchy in communion with the Pope. Against this Calvin, arguing from actuality to possibility, insisted that the Church could lack a visible form. It lacked a form in the days of Elijah who, seeing none like-minded in Israel, believed that he alone was left, whereas the Lord knew the invisible seven thousand who had not bowed the knee to Baal. Moreover, the Church is visible, not by the existence of a hierarchy or indeed of an institution, but by its activity corresponding to its being—that is to say, by its proclamation of the Gospel

35

and by its administration of the Sacraments in a way consistent with their nature and purpose.

The book was therefore on the one hand a confession of faith. But it was also *institutio christianae religionis*, instruction in the Christian religion; and that, not as a textbook about an abstract body of truths, but as the teaching of 'godliness', of the Faith that is believed with mind and heart, upon which a man is bold to base the conduct of his life, to which he dares to commit himself in life and in death. Calvin intended it to be elementary. When I this book, he told the King in the opening paragraph,

all I had in mind was to hand on some rudiments by which anyone who was touched with an interest in religion might be formed to true godliness. I laboured at the task for our own Frenchmen in particular, for I saw that many were hungering and thirsting after Christ and yet that only a very few had even the slightest knowledge of him. The book itself betrays that this was my purpose by its simple and primitive form of teaching.[2]

He was writing, then, for the baptized, for those who took their religion seriously, who desired to be good Christians but were disturbed at their lack of success, who above all were distressed that their religion brought them no peace of conscience. By their baptism the guilt of their inherited sin had been forgiven. But they had sinned since their baptism, making shipwreck of their faith and thus of their standing with God. Now they clung desperately to what old St Jerome called the second plank, the sacrament of penance. They were sorry for their sins, or rather, the more they were in earnest the more they realized that they ought to be sorry for their sins and wished that they were more sorry. They knew God to be a stern judge who would exact vengeance for their sins. They made confession, aware of the promise 'whosesoever sins ye loose on earth shall be loosed in heaven'. But where was the peace that should follow? Had they confessed *all* their sins? Had they forgotten any? Only confessed sins are forgiven. They performed the enjoined satisfactions for their sins. They did more; they went on pilgrimages, not for a jolly Chaucerian holiday, but always seeking, always grasping after that which lay just beyond their grasp; they gave alms so far as they could afford; they practised self-denial and mortification. Meanwhile, they attempted to follow their conscience and the Law of God to the best of their ability, trusting in God's grace that he would, of his free mercy, reward them for their efforts with such an inpouring of grace as would turn their will away from sin to love God with all their being. And again, instead of the looked for peace, anxiety: had they really striven to the utmost? They could not tell; it was impossible to know. But if they had not done what they could, God had not rewarded them. The *Institutio* was addressed to men suffering under the pastoral cruelty of the medieval Church.

The form of the book matched its purpose. By adopting the framework of the catechism, Calvin was making use of the old method of teaching the elements of the Faith by an exposition of the three basic authorities for the life of a Christian—the Ten Commandments, the Apostles' Creed, and the Lord's Prayer. To these are devoted the first three chapters: *On the Law*; *On Faith*; *On Prayer*. Chapter Four, *On the Sacraments*, carries the reader into the means by which God gives his grace, and also postulates the following chapter in which the five so-called sacraments are either relativized or rejected. The sixth chapter explains Christian liberty, Church government, and civil government.

2. LAW, FAITH, AND PRAYER

The book begins with a striking sentence into which Calvin concentrates his complete approach to theology: 'The sum of sacred doctrine is contained almost entirely in these two parts: the knowledge of God and of ourselves.' [3] It is not the task of theology to concern itself with God outside his relationship to man, nor with man outside his relationship to God. Under Luther's influence Calvin had turned from the subjectiveness current in theology and based his theology on the belief that the decisions and judgments of God are the ultimate and real truth about man. This is apparent as he at once in his treatment of the nature of man considers man in his standing before God. There meet us at every turn the phrases *coram Deo, apud Deum*—'in the sight of God', 'with God'. He expresses man's origin and destiny in terms of the orthodox doctrine. Adam, man created in God's image, endowed with wisdom, righteousness, and holiness, fell into sin. The divine gifts were lost, the image was blotted out (on this point the Reformers went further than traditional theology had done), and man became a foreigner to God, ignorant, unrighteous, and impotent, faced with death and judgment. This condition of sinfulness Adam transmitted to all his descendants.

No man can plead in self-excuse that he is ignorant of God's standards, for every man's God-given conscience reminds him of his duty towards God, teaches him what is right, what wrong, accuses him of his sin. We need only 'descend into ourselves' to know what God demands. But pride rejects the humiliating exercise of submitting ourselves to inward accusation. God has therefore written down this same Law in the form of the Mosaic Law, the teaching of perfect righteousness. If any man entirely and exactly fulfils all that is commanded, he will be rewarded with eternal life. If any man fails to observe every detail of the Law, he will receive the condemnation of eternal death.

It is precisely at this point of complete hopelessness that the Law, no less, proves itself in God's saving work. It presses its demands and threats to the extremity where man, defenceless, can only admit that God is righteous and true and he himself completely wrong and false. At this depth of humiliation and despair, knowing himself as he is in reality, in the eyes of God, nothing is left but to surrender and beg for mercy. Then the Judge reveals himself as the Father, 'good-natured, merciful, kind, and lenient'.[4] But the Law-giver has not immorally set aside his Law, condoning injustice. The Law has been fulfilled on earth by a man—by the man in whom the Law-giver has himself entered into a union with all men; fulfilled positively in that he has obeyed it perfectly, negatively in that he has suffered the punishment for breaking the Law incurred by all men. The Law-giver will not punish the same sins twice or deny the validity of the union which he has established. Gone, therefore, doubt over whether we have striven to our uttermost to keep the Law and therefore deserve the reward of grace. Christ has kept the Law for us whom he has united with himself in his Incarnation; he has deserved the reward, and this he shares with us. May there not, however, remain anxiety as to the genuineness and extent of our humiliation and repentance, the quantity and quality of our faith? The assurance of salvation is taken off the worthiness of the subject and his acts and placed upon the worthiness of the object and his work. Repentance and faith, being always imperfect, cannot satisfy the perfection of God's demands. The power of faith rests in the ability of its object, Jesus Christ, perfect in obedience, making perfect satisfaction for sin. The weakest trust is entirely justified by its powerful object.

In his exposition of the Ten Commandments, Calvin confines himself almost entirely to their relevance for the believer. The Law thus becomes the positive expression of our fearing and loving God and of the love we owe to our neighbours for God's sake. The whole intention of the Law is 'to teach love'.[5] Each of the commandments (except the second, where he perhaps forgot to put it in) is summarized as a way of fearing and loving God. Certainly it is hard to keep the commandments; but this is no reason for slackness. The believer should pray with Augustine: 'Give what thou commandest and command what thou wilt.' Nor do believers, past sins pardoned, live by the righteousness of the Law, accepted by God for their religious and moral obedience. Always we need forgiveness for our continuing transgressions. For the believer to live by the Law would be to turn again into uncertainty. He could neither be sure that he had entirely kept the whole Law nor guarantee that he would never again offend in any respect. Where then would be Christian confidence? Where faith itself? 'For wavering, varying, being carried up and down, hesitating, living in suspense, losing all hope, these are not faith. Faith is an unshaken, sure, and completely certain determination of the mind; it is having somewhere to rest and take your stand.'[6]

When Calvin calls Chapter Two *De Fide*, it is not clear whether we should translate it by *On Faith* or *On the Faith*. For on the one hand, the Faith is the sum of Christian teaching, of what is known of God in Christ. Hence he follows custom and takes the Apostles' Creed as the statement of the Church's faith. But on the other hand, faith is the recognition and ratification of the relationship which God has established with man in Jesus Christ. It is not only the understanding of the doctrines of the Creed, not only the acceptance of the general truth of those doctrines, but the willing assent to them. It is to believe not only that there is a God but that he is our God; not only that the New Testament record of Christ is true but that 'Christ is Jesus to us, that is, Saviour'.[7]

We know the truths of the 'doctrine of salvation' because we are told them in Holy Scripture; we believe that they apply to ourselves because God has so promised in Scripture. The immediate object of faith is therefore the word or promise of God. In this first edition there is no statement of the doctrine of Scripture, only an insistence that we believe and trust in God's promise or word and that the Bible is this 'word' of God. Therefore faith is the firm conviction both of the certain truth of God in his Word and that what is promised in general is promised to ourselves in particular. More, faith is the sure and certain possession of what is promised, as Hebrews 11: 1 says. The possession of the promise introduces the concept of hope, for we hope for what we do not yet possess (Romans 8: 24–5). Faith is the present possession of what is still hoped for, and thus a having and a not having, 'a seeing of those things which are not seen, a clarity of things which are obscure, a presence of things absent, a showing of things hidden'.[8]

In harmony with his explanation of faith, Calvin expounds the first article in terms of trust: 'Here we profess that we have complete trust fixed in God the Father . . .' [9] The Creator of us and of all things, he upholds and cherishes by his providence. Whatever comes to pass (sin only excepted) whether physical or spiritual, joyful or sad, is from him, from his fatherly kindness. 'Such a Father let us worship with grateful devotion and burning love, giving ourselves completely to his obedience and honouring him in all things.'[10]

The second part confesses that Jesus Christ is the only Son of God by nature, begotten of the Father from all eternity. We hold that he is true God, Creator of heaven and earth, in whom, with the Father, we place all our trust. He is the Redeemer from the tyranny of the devil by his incarnation, when the very majesty of God descended to us, uniting Godhead with manhood, becoming our Emmanuel, genuinely taking manhood and therefore becoming near us, nay contiguous, for he is of our flesh.

The central thought in Calvin's doctrine of the Incarnation is Christ's union with men:

he fashioned to himself a body from our body, flesh from our flesh, bones from our bones, that he might be the same as ourselves. What was proper to us he willed to belong to himself so that what was proper to himself might belong to us, and that he might be both Son of God and Son of Man in common with us.[11]

It cannot be emphasized too strongly that the conception of unity dominates his thinking—the tri-unity of the Godhead, the unity of God and man in Jesus Christ, the unity of Christ and mankind, the unity of the Head and the Body, the unity of mankind. Since Christ's unity with mankind depends upon the unity of God with man in Christ, it is this central doctrine of the Faith that Calvin strives particularly to elucidate here.

On the unity of God and man in Christ depends our salvation. Were Christ not God and man in union, he could not save. But now we believe that he is Jesus, Saviour, and that he is Christ, the one anointed to be king and priest in a twofold office, king ruling over all things in heaven and earth, priest to reconcile the Father to us by the sacrifice of himself on the cross. Now faith is the subjective affirmation or taking up of the union with Christ already objectively established in the Incarnation. Faith is therefore union with Christ. Since by faith we are one with him and share in what is proper to him, we, too, are kings in him, having authority over the devil, sin, death, and hell; we, too, are priests in him, offering to the Father prayers, thanksgivings, ourselves, and all we have. Because the one who from the dead rose again to immortal life was the man united with God and with all mankind, his resurrection is the most certain guarantee of the resurrection of other men. Because in human flesh he ascended into heaven and is enthroned in sovereign authority, he will sanctify, govern, and guide his people until the last day, when he will return to render to all men their recompense.

With the same warmth and relevance, but more briefly, Calvin expounds the confession of faith in the Holy Spirit. Not only is he with the Father and the Son one God, but our God, whom we adore and in whom we place all our trust. He is the one leader and guide to the Father. Dwelling within us, he makes us aware of the immense wealth of blessings that we possess in Christ. He kindles in our hearts a burning love to God and neighbour, burns out the vices of our concupiscence (the repetition of the image is deliberate), and vivifies us to bear the fruit of good works.

The Catholic Church is 'the universal number of the elect, whether angels or men'.[12] But catholicity is a concept not only of breadth (the universal number), but also of unity. The Church is '*one* Church and society, *one* people of God'.[13] The unity consists in the relationship of the universal number to Christ, to whom God has given those whom he chose before the foundation of the world. The Church therefore does not depend on any human intention of social alliance but upon the eternal and unalterable will of God realized in Jesus Christ. The Catholicity of the Church and God's election of his people are inseparable.

It is on Christ and faith in him that Calvin fixes our attention as he treats of election. In Christ alone we learn God's will concerning us. He should therefore be sufficient for us. If, on the contrary, we are not content with Christ, but wish to penetrate more deeply into God's will, we fall into the abyss of his majesty and are overwhelmed by his glory. We know that we are

elect and therefore genuine members of the Church when in faith we are
united with Christ. About the election of others we may not ask, for this
knowledge belongs to God alone. Towards others we must exercise a judgment of love and regard as elect and members of the Church all who profess
the same God and Christ by tongue, by good lives, and by participation in the
Sacraments. All others we should regard as 'not yet' members of the Church,
clearly with the hope that in time they will become one with us.[14]

The effect of the unity of the Church appears in the communion of saints,
which consists in 'a mutual communication and participation of all goods'
(or, 'of all good things').[15] This does not forbid individual possession, a
political constitution necessary as things are. It means that all goods, whether
spiritual or material, so far as is fair, and to the extent demanded, should be
communicated among Christians in the love that they owe to one another.
God communicates to each man severally as he will, certainly, but inasmuch
as his people are collected and compacted into one body, each should share
his possessions with the others. 'This is the catholic Church, the mystical
Body of Christ.'[16]

Let us remind ourselves of Calvin's purpose: he was writing a compendium
of the Christian faith to teach those hungering and thirsting after Christ the
way of salvation. The sum of what he has said so far is that in Christ God
has set before us, who in ourselves are empty and poor, the treasures of his
grace. We must turn to him, begging him to supply our needs. The argument
therefore demands the chapter on prayer.

The first 'law' of prayer consists in humility, the recognition and acknowledgment of our poverty and therefore of our need. This is the subjective moti-
vating force in prayer. To it our 'best of Fathers' has added two objective
impulsions, his command to pray and his promise to grant what is asked.
But how can man, polluted by sin, enter into the pure presence of God? 'God
has given us his Son, Jesus Christ, to be our advocate and mediator with
him.'[17] Led by this unique advocate and patron, we find that God's throne
is a throne not only of majesty but also of grace. Prayer itself is simplified
from the divisions and sub-divisions dear to the exponents of the 'art of
prayer' into asking and thanking:

In asking, we lay before God the desires of our heart, seeking from his goodness,
first, the things which serve his glory alone, and then the things which also minister
to our profit. In giving thanks, we recognize his benefits towards us and acknowledge
them with praise, accrediting to his goodness all good things everywhere.[18]

This doctrine conforms to the pattern of the Lord's Prayer, which Calvin
then goes on to expound.

One or two practical points remain to be made. We are not tied to this
particular form, which only offers a general pattern. Again, although our

minds should be always raised to God, there are certain hours which we should never let pass without prayer—when we rise in the morning; when we begin and end meals; when we go to bed. But also when we or others are closely threatened by trouble we must turn to God for help; when good comes upon us we must turn to him with thanksgiving. Again, we must always leave God his freedom and not tell him what to do. We place our will at his disposal, not his at ours. If we have our minds composed to such a frame of obedience and patience, we shall not grow weary of praying.

3. THE SACRAMENTS

The next chapter sees a change of tone. Not only must believers be taught the value and use of the Sacraments, but long-established, widespread errors must be exposed and corrected. It was on the doctrine of the Eucharist that the sharpest differences in doctrine appeared. These did not originate with the Reformers, for there was already variety of teaching among the Romanists, but undoubtedly the Reformation accentuated the dissensions.

A Sacrament is 'an outward sign by which the Lord represents and testifies his good will towards us'; [19] 'it is a testimony of God's grace, declared to us by an outward symbol'.[20] We are *animales*, creeping on the ground, clinging to the flesh; we think and conceive nothing spiritual. But in the Sacraments God accommodates himself to our grasp, 'leads us down in these same fleshly elements—to himself! And makes us behold in the very flesh—the things of the Spirit!' [21] The sole office of the Sacraments is to turn our eyes to beholding God's promises; that is, they make the Word perceptible to other senses than the ears.

Calvin's theology is, from this first statement of it throughout his life, a theology of the Sacrament. God will not encounter man directly but by means of that which is already a human term of reference, the human means of communication and visible symbols. The communication and the symbols both become encounter with God himself and also genuine encounter of the man in his complete self with God. In allowing only two Sacraments, moreover, Calvin, far from depreciating the sacramental system, is exalting them to the extent that they alone are the point of encounter between God and man, the means by which the believer may be changed into the image of God. As he rebuts the objection that the Sacraments displace the Holy Spirit, whose work it is 'to begin, protect, and consummate faith',[22] Calvin sets out the economy of salvation:

In place of the *one* blessing of God which they preach, we emphasize *three*. First, the Lord teaches us in his Word. Then he confirms it in the Sacraments. And lastly he shines in our minds by the light of his Holy Spirit and opens a way into our hearts for his Word and Sacraments. Else would they merely beat on our ears and meet our sight without at all affecting us inwardly.[23]

Baptism is, first, a symbol of cleansing, that is to say, of forgiveness. In Baptism God forgives once for all and therefore permanently. The grace of Baptism cannot be effaced by subsequent sin nor need supplementation by a second benefit. For in Baptism is conferred the purity of Christ which, far from being overwhelmed by our uncleanness, itself overwhelms and cleanses the stains of sin. And secondly, in Baptism Christ makes us sharers of his death and resurrection. In that we are made one with him, we are made one with him who died to sin and lives to God. Thus this visible Word declares that we, too, have died to sin and live to God. 'We are baptized into the mortification of our flesh. At Baptism it is begun in us. Day by day we practise it. It will be perfected when we pass from this life to the Lord.' [24]

Infants ought to be baptized. We should not be so sure that they have no faith. It is clear from Mark 10: 13ff. that the Lord calls some from among them to be heirs of the kingdom of heaven. Why then can he not give some foretaste of his blessing? Why can they not see him in a glass darkly? It is arrogant to say that they can have no faith. They have a right to Baptism, for they have a common faith with adults.

The two names Calvin uses for the other sacrament express his concept of it: *Coena Domini*, the Lord's Supper, the Lord feeding his people; *Eucharistia*, the Eucharist, the Greek for thanksgiving. The food which the Lord gives is himself. The Lord's Supper is the giving and receiving of the Christ who gave himself on the Cross. The Eucharist is the community's thanksgiving for God's goodness in giving Christ, a sacrifice of grateful worship which is the expression of the community's own self-giving to God and to one another. Christ and his blessings become ours, not by their being taken from him and transferred to us, but by our being united with him. The Lord's Supper has, then, to be understood in terms of union with Christ. Jesus' words of institution (Luke 22: 19–20, I Cor. 11: 23–5) declare this union with himself, for he does not say only 'This is my body . . . this is my blood' but also 'take . . . eat . . . drink'. Indeed, 'the whole force of the sacrament lies in what follows: "which was given for you", "which was shed for you"'. [25]

Here we have the heart and the substance of Calvin's doctrine of the Eucharist. But in the hot debate more had to be said; and in particular the fateful question '*quomodo?*' 'how?' had to be considered. *How* do the bread and wine become the Body and Blood of Christ? It was a question that the Church Fathers had been content to answer imprecisely and even inconsistently. It was the question that the medieval schoolmen had answered definitively by adapting the Aristotelian distinction between *substantia* and *accidentia*. The use of our words 'substance' and 'accidents' is misleading. For 'substance' it is better to say something like 'essential nature', for 'accidents' something like 'sensible appearance'. Using this distinction, the Middle Ages answered the question 'How do the bread and wine become the Body and Blood of the Lord?' in two ways. The one, which became the orthodox teaching of the

Roman Church, asserted that there took place the miracle of the essential nature of the elements being replaced by the essential nature of the Body and Blood of Christ. The other said that the *substantiae* of the Body and Blood of Christ were added to the *substantiae* of the bread and wine and co-existed with them. The former doctrine was called transubstantiation, the latter consubstantiation.

The earlier Reformers, however uneasy about the doctrine, could not transcend this question: *How* do the bread and wine become the Body and Blood of the Lord? And it was largely because they could not, that the damaging strife broke out between them. Luther answered the question positively by recourse to a modified form of consubstantiation. The Zwinglians answered it negatively by a figurative interpretation of the words of institution. But in 1536 Calvin at one stroke renders irrelevant, not merely the contemporary controversy, but the whole laborious scholastic investigation since about the twelfth century. The passage in which he does this is worth quoting in full:

Inquisitive men have wanted to define: How the Body of Christ is present in the bread. Some, to display their subtlety, added to the simplicity of Scripture that he is present really and substantially. Others wanted to go farther, that he is present in the same dimensions as he hung on the Cross. Others invented the unnatural monster of transubstantiation. Some said the bread *was* the Body; some that the Body was within or under the bread; some that the bread was only a sign and figure of the Body. A matter well worth all the words and the quarrels!—or so it is commonly thought. But those who do so think do not realize that the primary question in fact is: How does the Body of Christ, as it was given for us, become ours? How does the Blood, as it was shed for us, become ours? In other words, how do we possess the whole Christ crucified and become partakers of all his blessings? Because this primary question has been omitted as unimportant, in fact neglected and almost forgotten, the conflict has raged over the one obscure and difficult question: How is the Body eaten by us? [26]

Calvin is here doing nothing less than inviting the Church to go back some five, even seven, centuries, before the doctrine had become fixed, and to take up the discussion from there, no longer on the basis of an only pseudo-scriptural question, but of one which, because it was demanded by Scripture itself, was a question which ought to be asked and to which an answer could and should be given. The primary question: 'How is the Body of Christ present in the bread?' is as little determined by Scripture as the primary questions: 'How did the Virgin conceive the God-Man?' or 'How did the Word of God create light?' or 'How did Jesus Christ rise from the dead?' Such questions are bound to lead to unscriptural answers and therefore also to divisive answers, breaking the unity of the Body of Christ. On the other hand, 'How we possess the whole Christ crucified and become partakers of all his blessings' is the theme of the New Testament and the presupposition of the Creeds. The theologian can therefore ask and investigate it as a question with the confidence that it will not lead him away from, but towards, the truth.

Let us see where it led Calvin—noticing that he never tried to answer the other question but only made certain denials about it. First he asks the question: 'How does Christ become ours?' Secondly he gives a twist to the question and makes *quomodo* mean: 'In what way, so far as its effect upon us is concerned, is the Body of Christ in the Sacrament?' With the answer, *vere et efficaciter*, genuinely and effectually. Beyond this he would not go.

We begin with the humanity of Christ. The Son of God took our flesh of the Virgin to be his own; he suffered in our flesh, making with it satisfaction for sins; he received our flesh again at the resurrection and keeps it eternally in heaven. The humanity of the risen and ascended Christ, although glorified, is still humanity; and the quality of a human body is that 'it is contained in a place, has its own dimensions and its own appearance'.[27]

The ascension and session of Christ at the right hand of the Father is an image of his omnipotent reign. But first, his reign is universal, extending to the earth as well as to heaven; and second, it is effectual—that is to say, he acts with sovereign power in every part of his dominion, bringing to realization the redemption which he achieved in his incarnation. 'Christ exerts his power in heaven and earth, wherever it pleases him; he shows himself present in authority and power; he is always present with his own, lives in them, sustains them, strengthens, animates, and keeps them, just as if he were present with them in the body'.[28] By the power of the Spirit that which is true and effective in the presence of God is brought to men and made true and effective in them. To say that the Spirit brings Christ and his blessings to men is to say that Christ gives himself to them. It is a genuine and effectual presence and self-giving of Christ, not in spite of, but because of, its being the work of the Spirit; not in spite of, but because of, the natural Body of Christ being at the right hand of the Father.

The Sacrament is also *eucharistia*. Christ has commanded that it be observed in memory of his death. This is not to be taken as merely remembering a past event but as a backward-directed act of faith, a believing in the crucified Christ. It is therefore also a confession of faith, both to the world that we are Christians, and within the Church and before God that Christ has died for us. Thus this confession of faith is, of its very nature, a giving of thanks to God for the redemption of the Cross, a *eucharistia*.

The Sacrament is thirdly a communion, an inflaming of Christians to love, peace, and concord. Christ communicates to us his body that we may become one with him who in his incarnation has made himself one with us. But it is the multiplicity of believers who are made one body with Christ. The many therefore coalesce into one body. Divisions and dissensions are a negation of unity. The objective reality established by the incarnation and witnessed

45

by the Holy Communion must become a subjective reality in the community. 'We cannot hurt, slander, mock, despise, or in any way offend one of our brethren without at the same time hurting, slandering, mocking, despising Christ in him. We cannot be at variance with our brethren without at the same time being at variance with Christ. We cannot love Christ without loving him in our brethren.' [29]

Thus far Calvin's doctrine of the Lord's Supper. The main polemic in this chapter is aimed against the sacrifice of the Mass. Taking his stand on a strict interpretation of the relevant passages in the Epistle to the Hebrews, he charges the doctrine with destroying salvation, the atonement, and the Sacraments; it is blasphemy against Christ, the eternal High Priest with the function which he executes without assistants. When he insists that Christ's sacrifice of himself was once for all, it is the eternal effectiveness implied in that phrase which he chiefly regards. That which is eternally effective does not need renewal. The Mass is claimed to be the renewal of the once for all sacrifice. The Lord's Supper is the gift and reception of the eternally effective sacrifice of Christ. There is indeed a sacrifice in the Lord's Supper, but it is a *sacrificium εὐχαριστικὸν*, a sacrifice of praise and thanksgiving, a sacrifice of the self-consecration of the community. And this, not to turn away God's wrath but to magnify and exalt him. This is the incense that the Church must burn, this the worship she must offer now and eternally. The Eucharist is therefore an offering of the sacrifice of praise; at it Christ himself is the priest, Christ the altar.

He turns to the practical observance of the Sacrament. And first, the self-examination demanded by the danger of the situation; for the Sacrament is never neutral, it will bestow either life or death. We have to ask ourselves three questions corresponding to its nature: (1) Have I an inward trust in my Saviour who here offers himself to me? (2) Do I confess my faith in Christ? (3) Am I ready to give myself to my brethren and to be one with them? The medieval teaching on confession demanded a puritanical standard impossible of attainment, with worthy reception of the Holy Communion dependent on ethical purity and an adequate contrition and confession. But we come worthily to the Lord's Supper when we offer God our unworthiness that he may forgive us and thus make us worthy by his mercy. We should not even ask about the quality of our repentance, faith, and love. Only their existence is relevant.

There should be a frequent *memoria* of the crucified Christ. No meeting of the Church should be held without the preaching of the Word, prayers, the Lord's Supper, and almsgiving. At the very least the Eucharist should be celebrated once every week. Certainly it is to be celebrated publicly. Private masses destroy the community. And, of course, the Communion is to be administered in both kinds.

In concentrating the sacramental meeting of Christ with his people on Baptism and the Lord's Supper, Calvin was denying that the other five rites (confirmation, penance, extreme unction, orders, and matrimony) were properly Sacraments. His reasons are set out in detail and at length in Chapter Five. None save God alone has the authority to institute a Sacrament, which is like a seal set to the declaration of his will. Only God can bear witness to his intention. The Sacraments instituted by Christ are earthly things chosen and adapted precisely for this purpose. The other five rites are not so established. There is no need for us to follow Calvin through his discussion. It is enough to note that he does not necessarily condemn all these rites or even reject them from the practice of the Church, but that he removes them from a category to which they do not belong. That salvation is the work of God alone means also that God and not man chooses the means of salvation. The Church does not possess the right to choose, for 'the first rule of the minister is that he shall do nothing without command'.[30]

On confirmation, extreme unction, and matrimony he spends little time. The larger part of this long chapter is devoted to penance and orders. In each instance he not only attacks the Roman dogma but also supplies in its place a corresponding evangelical doctrine. Thus for the sacrament of penance he substitutes evangelical repentance and the confession of sin. Repentance is mortification, the putting to death of our flesh and of the old man, that is, of our sinfulness. Again we come to union with Christ. If we are united with Christ in faith, we are united with the one who died to sin. In him, therefore, we have died to sin. That which is true for us in Christ must become true in our experience. Sin must be put to death in our wills and in our actions: 'The way for men to be born again is to participate in Christ, in whose death their perverted desires died, on whose cross their old man was crucified, in whose sepulchre was buried the body of sin . . . The life of a Christian man is therefore a perpetual study and practice of mortifying the flesh.'[31]

At this point Calvin turns to the sacrament of penance, with its *contritio cordis*, *confessio oris*, and *satisfactio operis*. His central objection is that the medieval doctrine is through and through subjectivist. The sinner is exhorted to make sure that he is genuinely contrite; but he is not told how he can be sure. In spite of disclaimers and conditions, the contrition is made the cause of forgiveness; he is forgiven because of the quality of his contrition. 'We teach the sinner to look, not at his compunction, nor at his tears, but to fix his gaze—both eyes!—on the sole mercy of the Lord.'[32] Confession had become a moralistic exercise in casuistry. Sins were distinguished: their qualities, their quantities, the circumstances under which they were committed. When all was done, had all the sins been confessed?

I will say briefly what it all adds up to. In the first place, it is simply an impossibility; and therefore it can only destroy, condemn, confound, cast into ruin and desperation. Secondly, it will divert sinners from a true realization of their sin and make them hypocrites, ignorant of God and of themselves. They will be so busy with the

47

enumeration of their sins in detail that they will forget the hidden bottomless bog of their vices, their hidden iniquities and inward uncleanness.[33]

Certainly there is need for confession of individual sins which burden our consciences. But no longer the categorizing of some actions as virtuous, some as sins, and endeavouring to remember all the sins. And when all is done, there must be the recognition that none can plumb the depths of his own heart.

In sum, the medieval penitential system, starting out from excellent pastoral motives, achieved the opposite of its aims. Far from relieving sinners of guilty consciences and assuring them of forgiveness, it actually increased their feelings of guilt and inadequacy, made them doubtful and despairing. And this was so, not of the Laodicean portion of the population, but precisely of the earnestly religious. Indeed, the sacrament of penance increased doubt and guilt in proportion to the seriousness of the individual. Luther's experiences as a monk may have been extreme, but they were no different in kind from what any seriously religious man would know.

The true *sacramentum poenitentiae* is the Sacrament of Baptism:

They adorn this invented sacrament with the title 'The second plank after shipwreck', because anyone who has by sinning soiled the robe of innocence received in Baptism can restore it by Penance. . . . As if Baptism were wiped out by sin and ought not rather to be recalled to the sinner's mind whenever he thinks of the forgiveness of sins, so as to take heart and courage from it and confirm his faith that the forgiveness of sins promised in Baptism will be realized. And so you will speak most aptly if you call Baptism the sacrament of repentance.[34]

4. LIBERTY

The final chapter contains three topics, Christian liberty, Church government, and civil government. The last two, of which we shall reserve consideration to a later context, arise from the first and are treated in relation to it.

We remind ourselves of Calvin's twofold purpose. Liberty is a dangerous concept in a totalitarian state; doubly dangerous at a time when groups in the name of the Gospel are claiming liberty from civil restraint and even from the accepted morality. He has therefore to dissociate evangelical liberty from any taint of anabaptism. He is also concerned to teach those hungering and thirsting after Christ how they may find him and having found him may live in him. Once again now we hear the constant *coram Deo, apud Deum*. It is with God that we have to do both in our spiritual and in our physical lives. Once again comes the insistence that the Christian should know confidence and joy, that doubt and gloom should be far from him. Christian liberty ought to be taught as a necessary part of the Faith, and that for two reasons. First that we may have a good and clear conscience. And secondly that we may act boldly and confidently, without unnecessary inhibitions. For what hampers action more than doubt? Nor should we be prevented from teaching it by misunderstandings of the doctrine—misunderstandings from the Libertines who use it as an excuse to do what they like, misunderstandings from the reactionaries who conceive that it will overthrow the establishment.

Christian liberty has three aspects:

1. The Christian is free from the Old Testament Law in regard to his standing before God. When we have an uneasy conscience from breaking the Law, the Law can do nothing to help us; it can only continue to repeat its accusation and our guilt. In such a situation only Jesus Christ, given for us, can help us. In judgment before God, we are free from the Law.

2. Freedom from the Law extends also, in a certain sense, to Christian obedience. The Law commands us to love God with all our heart, soul, mind, and strength. But we are far from obeying the command. Along with a sincere love of God there still exist in us the sinful desires that prevent us from loving completely. Again the Law cannot help. It commands, it threatens, it treats us as slaves. And for this very reason to keep the Law is a psychological impossibility. Love is a free movement of the will. To command to love is absurd. But the believer is no longer a slave, commanded to obey under pain of punishment. The teaching of the first three chapters—that the Son of God has become our brother so that we might with him have God for our Father —here bursts forth in a glorious liberation. The Father does not command us with fearful threatenings but 'calls us with fatherly kindness' to follow him, and we may therefore 'cheerfully and very readily respond to his call and follow where he leads'.[35] God will treat us as 'dear little children', overlooking the imperfection of the service we offer to him, forgiving the sinfulness in it.

3. This aspect of Christian liberty concerns practical matters and the *adiaphora*, things indifferent, neither good nor bad in themselves. Once start being sensitive about such matters and you are lost in an endless labyrinth:

If someone begins to doubt whether it is lawful for him to use linen for his sheets or shirts or handkerchiefs or serviettes, he will go on to become uncertain about hessian and at last be doubtful about using even canvas. For he will think to himself, 'Could I not eat my meals without a serviette? Do I really need to carry a handkerchief?' If it should occur to a man that some rather pleasant food was unlawful, he will get to the point of not being able to eat black bread or common dishes without an uneasy conscience before God, for it will occur to him that he could nourish his body on food yet more humble. If he is doubtful about a fairly good wine, he will then not be able to drink some rot-gut with a good conscience, and in the end he will dare touch no water that is sweeter and purer than usual. And at last such a man will think it a sin to step over a straw on the path, as they say.[36]

This sort of puritanism will result in either cowardliness in the face of life or carelessness. Christian liberty will use the gifts of God with joy and thanksgiving.

Liberty, however, is not physical but spiritual. It is liberty before God. It is not necessary to use the liberty we enjoy. We are set free as soon as we understand that we are free to use or not to use something. There is no need, for example, to show newly won freedom from fasting on Fridays by eating meat on that day; it is sufficient to understand that we are free to do so. Those who do not yet understand may be harmed by our action, and the rule of liberty is not a selfish use but love for the brethren. We must not, from lack of love, offend the brother for whom Christ died.

Offences, scandals, may be distinguished very simply as offences given and offences taken. Little can be done about the latter; the hypercritical can interpret any action unfavourably. But we should take care not to give offences to the brethren who have not yet arrived at certainty on the point at issue. 'We should use our liberty if it will build up our neighbour in the faith. If it will not help our neighbour, we should abstain'.[37] This is true, however, only of things indifferent. That which is commanded by God should be done whatever the consequences. But again the care for the brother; this is not a permission to riot and iconoclasm and the like; simply that we should not acquiesce in wrong out of fear of hurting the consciences of weaker brethren.

Thus in 1536 came into existence what we now call 'Calvin's theology'. His stature as one of the major theologians in the history of the Church was not at once recognized; nor, indeed, did the first edition of the *Institutio* give full proof of it. Calvin himself was within three years to deprecate the book's lack of depth and its failure to develop sufficiently the several themes. But the discerning among his contemporaries were not slow to appreciate the virtues of the *Institutio*. Here was a theology treading confidently, yet never brash; a theology in which was nothing common or mean, yet whose sublimity was firmly related to the needs of ordinary Christians; a theology whose horizons were as wide as those in the Fens and whose solid earth was overarched by the high heavens; a theology reaching back into the early centuries of the Church and with a certain air of permanence about it. Calvin had done what it is now clear no other theologian (not even Melanchthon) was capable of doing at that time. He had not only given genuine dogmatic form to the cardinal doctrines of the Reformation: he had moulded those doctrines into one of the classic presentations of the Christian Faith.

Chapter 4

Genevan Trials

1. AN EXILE FROM HOME

After little more than a year in Basel, Calvin set out with du Tillet for Italy. It may merely have been that, an exile from home, he could not settle down anywhere. Or was it that, looking for happier days when he could live in France again, he wished meanwhile to pass his time in a French court where he might have a good position, a place not without influence promising recommendation for a career one day in his own country?

The ducal court at Ferrara housed an incongruous set of people. Hercules II, son of the ill-remembered Lucrezia Borgia, was both a Romanist and a partisan of the Emperor. His duchess, the Princess Renée of France, was the daughter of King Louis XII; her sister, Claude, was married to Francis I. She was also related to Francis and Marguerite of Navarre as second cousin, and for her birth championed the French cause against the Emperor. To the duke, as a Renaissance Maecenas, came some of the great creative artists, like Benvenuto Cellini (who, however, repaid the duke's hospitality by shooting some of his peacocks—'they were the only good things I had seen there' [1]). To her flocked Reformists and Reformers, the fugitives after the affair of the *Placards*—among them the poet Clément Marot. To her came now Jean Calvin, probably under an assumed name. Is it possible that she gave him not only asylum (which he had already in Basel), but also employment, perhaps as one of her secretaries? We must try not to judge these happenings by our knowledge of what came later. He had no intention of being a pastor or of undertaking public office. A life of scholarship now seems to have been his aim. But a scholar must have a regular employment, and to be secretary to a French princess would provide a living and leisure for study.

If he meant to stay at Ferrara for long, however, he was disappointed. On Good Friday, 14 April 1536, one of the duchess's French protégés ostentatiously refused to go to Mass. He was arrested and examined. It turned out that others in Renée's *entourage* were contaminated. Several more arrests were made. The duchess stood up for her friends and besought their pardon, so that poor Pope Paul had to listen with the one ear to the husband demanding justice and with the other to the wife, acting through Marguerite and the French papal nuncio, soliciting their release. Renée got her own way in the end. But before then Calvin had bidden a first and last farewell to Italy and gone back to Basel, and from there to France. For the Edict of Lyon, of 31 May, allowed heretics to live in the kingdom on the condition that they were reconciled to Rome within six months. Only a couple of days later he was at the Law Courts in Paris executing, as 'maistre Iehan Cauvin, licencié ès lois, demourant à Paris',[2] a 'procuration', signed by two notaries, appointing Antoine, resident in Paris but at present in Noyon, his proxy to act for him in winding up their parents' affairs. It is impossible that he should have received in Basel the news of the edict and got to Paris by 2 June. Therefore he must have returned to France before the edict was passed, knowing (or hoping) that he would not be proceeded against. Either, then, he had a personal safe-conduct or advance knowledge of the edict. In either case, this was presumably arranged by Renée.

Antoine put the business through, and so the bit of land, running to eight *septiers*, was sold, ceded, transferred, and promised to messeigneurs the prior and convent of Mont Saint-Lois, commonly called Regnault-by-Noyon, for the price and sum of *sept vingtz quatres livres Tournois*—one hundred and forty-four pounds Tours. Charles would have little enough time to enjoy his share. The end of October twelve-month saw the end of his troubles with the Chapter. He died on a crescendo, for the entry in the *Registres* points fairly clearly to a heresy charge. But if he turned to the evangelical faith, why did he not accompany Jean, Antoine and Marie? When he died he was buried at night beneath the public gallows.[3]

Calvin, concluding that for the foreseeable future France would be shut to him, used less than half of his six months of grace. When he left, he took with him Antoine, their half-sister Marie and, if the partial Lefranc is to be believed, the canon de Collemont and certain other inhabitants of Noyon. This little caravan then set out about the beginning of August for Strasbourg, 'safe from the Storms, and Prelat's rage'. Unfortunately for them, troop movements made the direct route hazardous, and they were forced to make a detour to the south. This brought them through the city of Geneva, where they put up at an inn for the night. Geneva was not unknown by hearsay to Calvin. Pierre Robert had worked there; Louis du Tillet was probably staying there now. He or another friend let Guillaume Farel know of his presence, who straightway sought him out. Farel would act while angels debated, and he was quite capable of bearding a complete stranger to tell him his duty. But the scene that took place becomes more credible if we accept that they were already at least acquaintances. Calvin himself tells the story in the autobiographical fragment in the Preface to the Psalms Commentary:

Wherever else I had gone, I had taken care to conceal that I was the author of [the

Institutio]; and I had resolved to continue in the same privacy and obscurity, until at length Guillaume Farel detained me at Geneva, not so much by counsel and exhortation, as by a dreadful curse, which I felt to be as if God had from heaven laid his mighty hand upon me to arrest me. As the most direct road to Strasbourg, to which I then intended to retire, was shut up by the wars, I had resolved to pass quickly by Geneva, without staying longer than a single night in that city. A little before this, Popery had been driven from it by the exertions of the excellent man whom I have named and Pierre Viret; but matters were not yet brought to a settled state, and the city was divided into ungodly and dangerous factions. Then a person, who has now basely apostatized and returned to the Papists, discovered me and made me known to others. Upon this, Farel, who burned with an extraordinary zeal to advance the gospel, immediately strained every nerve to detain me. And after learning that my heart was set upon devoting myself to private studies, for which I wished to keep myself free from other pursuits, and finding that he gained nothing by entreaties, he proceeded to utter the imprecation that God would curse my retirement and the tranquillity of the studies which I sought, if I should withdraw and refuse to help, when the necessity was so urgent. By this imprecation I was so terror-struck, that I gave up the journey I had undertaken; but sensible of my natural shyness and timidity, I would not tie myself to any particular office.[4]

In this way Calvin was enlisted into the service of Geneva.

2. SIXTEENTH-CENTURY GENEVA

We who know the modern Geneva must not confuse her with the sixteenth-century city. None of us is guilty of such anachronism as we stroll in the *Jardin anglais*, or look enviously in the windows of the smart shops, or sit drinking our coffee while the carillon of Saint-Pierre prettily tells the hours. But how hard not to be deceived in the old city, in streets bearing names mentioned in ancient documents and even in Calvin's sermons, the Bourg du Four, the Molard, the Place Saint Pierre. The names are up at the street corners, but none of the streets presents the appearance it bore four hundred and forty years ago. They say that there is not one private house in the old quarter that was built before the seventeenth century. Of course, Saint Pierre dominated the city then as now—although when Calvin saw it first, a length of wall was lying as it had collapsed in 1441. The same deep-mouthed bell, La Clémence, that we can hear from our souvenir picture postcard-cum-gramophone record, awoke those turbulent citizens to a new day. In the other churches, too, like la Madeleine and Saint Gervais, we are, furnishings apart, back in Calvin's Geneva. The Maison de Ville, soon to acquire its curious ramp, stood at the corner there; but if one went down the street beside it and through the Porte Neuve in the city wall, one did not come to the Promenade des Bastions, the Grand-Théâtre, and the Université, but through fields to the bridge across the Arve.[5]

Imagine, then, a city cramped within strong new defensive walls, the larger part on the southern side of the lake, a smaller area on the north bank. It is a large city for those days, as big as Basel or Zürich, with ten thousand inhabitants in 1537. Danger of attack from enemies compels the building that tries to keep pace with a rising population to be confined within the walls. The city has no suburbs; the walls stand up from the pastures and arable and rough land like cliffs rising sheer from the sea. Geneva is a fortress.

Not that the city was all buildings. They were fond of their gardens in Geneva. The fine big houses in the rue des Chanoines and the Place Saint Pierre and down on les Allemandes and la Rivière looked to have a garden at the back; and even the poorer houses in the jumble of streets and alleys in the Lower City or across the water in Saint Gervais, standing pressed together like books on a shelf, did not reach so far back that no room was left for a vegetable patch. Nevertheless, there was a housing shortage and building land was at a premium.

Socially, too, the Geneva of the early sixteenth century was very different from the city today. No millionaires then and no nobility. In that middle-class community, where high society was represented by the Cathedral canons and the few professional people who lived in the Upper City around the Cathedral, there were some wealthy merchants but no merchant princes. The only banking house in the place was a branch of the Medicis of Florence. The welfare of a middle-class community is based on commerce in the literal sense of the word, on mutual trading with other communities. The Genevan economy, active and prosperous up to the third quarter of the fifteenth century, had thereafter tended to decline very slightly. There was much production, but little of it for export. If we examine the numbers of the workmen admitted to citizenship between 1501 and 1536—the many cobblers, tailors, pastry-cooks, butchers, carpenters, stone-masons, barbers, and apothecaries, and the few goldsmiths and printers—we can see that the city expended most of her industrial vigour on clothing, housing, feeding, and curing her own inhabitants. There was some publishing, but not at all on the scale of later years, and it contributed little at this time to the balance of payments. We must not make too much of the decline in the Genevan economy, however, which was due largely to political and not to geographical causes. No changes in modes of travel, such as affected the condition of many towns in the golden age of the railway, had altered the potentialities in her position on one of the major trade routes in Europe.

On the other hand, it was her geographical situation that was the cause of her precarious political position throughout the century. Once again we must put from our minds the modern Geneva, one of the cities of Switzerland. In 1536 Geneva, this walled fortress, was a republic, squeezed between the Swiss cantons, the Duchy of Savoy, and the Kingdom of France. Lacking suburbs, and with only some four or five tiny and scattered acres in the surrounding countryside to call her own, she was an island, at first in the territory of Savoy and then of her ally Bern. Looking at the matter from another point of view, she was situated on the frontiers of the Swiss cantons, Savoy, and France.

A frontier city is always a desirable possession, whether commercially or politically, and Geneva had long provoked rivalry. In the Middle Ages the struggle for control had lain between the prince-bishops of Geneva and the dukes of Savoy, a struggle resolved when the bishopric fell into the power of the duchy. The house of Savoy had thereafter supplied bishops for most of the fifteenth century. In the following century the struggle became internal, an attempt by forces within Geneva to gain control. The head of the state was the prince-bishop; the two members of the constitution were the Cathedral Chapter of thirty-two canons and the *bourgeoisie*. The latter, among whom the merchants had the strongest voice, favoured friendly relations with the cantons. The Chapter were inconsistent. They sometimes took the side of the citizens against the bishop, but on the whole their ties of family and patronage inclined them towards the bishop and Savoy. Two parties emerged, the so-called *Eyguenots* and *Mamellus* that is, the Eidguenots, the Swiss faction, and possibly the source of the word Huguenot, and the Mammelukes, the slaves of the Pope, the Savoyards.

Thus matters stood when Pierre de la Baume was made bishop in 1522. Although he did not belong to the House of Savoy by birth, he was regarded as a safe man for the Duke—an assessment which was not always to be justified. It is difficult to understand the political logic of this bishop who, failing so ignominiously in Geneva, was not long after to be rewarded with a cardinal's hat and an archbishopric. He followed no consistent purpose but opportunely supported or dropped now the Swiss party, now the Savoy. The citizens took matters into their own hands and, judging that their best chance of independence lay in that direction, formed a triple alliance, a *combourgeoisie*, with Bern and Fribourg. It may well be that their action was illegal, but it had the irrefutable force of a *fait accompli*; and after this *coup* the power of Savoy in the city began to decline, the Swiss relationships to strengthen. As the struggle clarified into a straight opposition between sympathizers of the two policies, so the factions themselves emerged more distinctly into the citizens, led by some of the merchants, supporting the Swiss alliance, and the canons and the Savoyard officials the cause of Savoy. The citizens proved the stronger, and at last they even won control of the Chapter, by now depleted, by their order that only natives of one of the cities of the *combourgeoisie* could hold canonries. Although from without the duchy still had a say in Genevan affairs, the authority of Savoy was broken. Duke Charles kept up a sporadic military harassing, but the Swiss countered with an army to help the republic.

At this point we may explain something of the government, the *Seigneurie*, of this new republic. The head of government was a quadrivirate, the four Syndics who were elected in January of each year by the *commune*, the general

55

assembly of male citizens. The Syndics were the effective and not merely nominal leaders in the *Petit Conseil*, otherwise called *les Messieurs de Genève*, composed of twenty-five members. This was the central administrative body, and in particular dealt with all foreign affairs, reviewed capital sentences and controlled the mint. It met in the *Maison de Ville* at least three times a week. The *Deux Cents*, the Council of Two Hundred, was a lesser administrative assembly with monthly meetings to discuss important legislation. It was also an elective body, for it met annually in February to elect the *Petit Conseil*. Their choice was limited by the law of 1526 which enacted that *les Messieurs* must have been born in Geneva. This was to have important effects over the next thirty years. In practice, moreover, the *Petit Conseil* tended to be self-perpetuating; most of its members sat year after year, some to be removed only by the stronger elective hand of death. The *commune* usually assembled twice a year: in November to determine the price of wine and to elect the president of the civil court, in January, as we have said, to elect the four Syndics. The *Soixante*, or Council of Sixty, plays little part in our story and may be disregarded.

So far we have viewed the struggle of Geneva for independence only politically. But the political situation was first complicated and then clarified by religious controversy. There had been a few Evangelicals in the city in the fifteen-twenties, but it was not until the early thirties that reformers made a serious bid for control of the Church there. Antoine Froment, Farel, Pierre de Wingle, Pierre Viret, and Pierre Robert were all at one time or another active to spread their Gospel. They had the support of Bern, which had declared for the Reformation in January 1528. Fribourg, however, a Romanist city, objected to Bern's support and the triple alliance was threatened. One of the canons, Werly, a Fribourg man, was active in opposition. Riots followed the celebration of the Lord's Supper in a garden on Good Friday, 1533, and Werly was killed. Fribourg now reinstated Bishop de la Baume, who had been in exile. But it was clear that he had no authority; he failed to bring the evangelical leaders to justice for the murder of Werly; in mid-July he left the city for good. In the following May Geneva broke the alliance with Fribourg when it was learned that they were intriguing with the bishop to install a military governor from their own city. The triple alliance had become a simple alliance with Bern.

The *Seigneurie* were not in favour of evangelical reform; but with the external pressure of Bern and the internal pressure of the two leading Reformers, the fiery Guillaume Farel and the more gentle but persuasive Pierre Viret, evangelizing in their midst, it was doubtful how long they could preserve their neutrality. Turbulence increased. In March 1535 Viret was poisoned, but recovered. The servant who administered the poison claimed to be acting for one of the canons. In June a public *disputatio*, lasting for a month, was staged between the two religious parties. The *Seigneurie* still hesitated. After mob violence and iconoclasm they at last suspended the Mass. The canons of Saint Pierre and many of the nuns of the convent of Sainte Claire now left the city. The Dominicans and Franciscans were given the choice of exile or attending the evangelical services. Most of them preferred to conform.

Savoy had still not given up hope and in 1535 Charles besieged Geneva. Both Bern and France (who was now taking an interest in this free city on her frontier) sent an army to help and the republic was saved. The price of victory was a demand for sovereignty from Bern, who, however, accepted with a good enough show of grace a refusal from the freedom loving Genevese. On 25 May 1536 a general assembly of the citizens voted 'to live by the Gospel'. Geneva had become by constitution an evangelical city.

3. CHURCH AUTHORITY

This, then, was how matters stood when, about three months later, Calvin, his brother and sister, and their friends put up in Geneva for the night and when Farel so dramatically pressed him into service. It is possible that in writing to François Daniel on 13 October he may be giving a slightly different version by extending over a few days what he had compressed into a single evening in the Preface to the Psalms Commentary: 'The brethren kept me in Geneva for some days until they had won a promise to return. I then took my relative Artois to Basel, *en route* offending several churches who asked me to stay with them.'[6] Back in Geneva he caught a very bad cold which lingered on through the autumn. He was not kept busy and had time to work on 'the French edition of my little book' (probably the *Institutio*), a copy of which he had hoped to send with the letter.

It is not clear what office Calvin consented to fill. According to Beza and Colladon he was not at first a pastor but a reader in theology. This may mean that he preached without performing any other parochial duties or that he gave expository lectures on the Bible. In 1537 the Bern Council referred to him as 'reader in Holy Scripture', and the Basel printer Oporinus wrote to him in March of that year: 'I hear you are lecturing with great applause and usefulness on St Paul's Epistles.'[7] Before long, however, he was elected pastor. Williston Walker considers that this happened 'nearly or quite a year later', on the grounds that 'as late as 13 August 1537, the Council of Bern distinguished between Farel, "preacher", and Calvin, "reader in Holy Scripture"'.[8] But against this we find a reference in the Geneva registers to 'Farel and Calvin, preachers' on 3 July 1537; and, indeed, Colladon hints that he had been elected pastor by 10 November 1536, when the Confession of Faith was submitted to the Council: 'Being thus declared pastor and doctor in the Church . . . he prepared a short formulary of confession and discipline.'[9]

The lawyer-theologian had now to adapt himself to an entirely new mode of life, to baptizing babies, to officiating at weddings, to conducting church services and preaching, to taking a leading part in church administration. It must be emphasized that Calvin was a full-time pastor, with responsibility for one of the city churches. Too often he is represented as a remote planner organizing the Church life of the city according to a rigid ecclesiastical polity, with Geneva as an area designated for Reformed experiment. Such a doctrinaire figure Calvin was not. He held an ecclesiastical polity and he strove to realize it in Geneva; but the polity concerned the exercise of his pastoral ministry for the glory of God and the upbuilding of the Church.

As we have already mentioned, Chapter Six of the *Institutio* is concerned with Christian liberty, with sections on the power, or authority, of the Church and of the State. Thus Calvin's positive doctrine or authority springs from and is governed by his doctrine of liberty. Not only is it a principle that ecclesiastical power must not infringe Christian freedom,[10] but the authority and the freedom have a common motive force in the Gospel. Just as Jesus Christ is both the Saviour who liberates from sin and the Lord who rules over his people, so the Gospel of which he is the substance or being both liberates the captives ('the truth shall make you free', John 8: 32) and provides the authority by which and under which they live their lives of freedom. This is a single motive force, the same Gospel, not even two aspects of the one Gospel. Thus believers acknowledge one king only, 'their liberator Christ'; they must be ruled by 'the one law of liberty, the holy word of the Gospel'.[11]

Because the Reformers reject the legal system of Rome, the so-called ecclesiastical constitutions, it must not be thought that they deny authority to the Church. The power of the Church, rightly defined, is the ministry of God's Word. This means that power resides, not in the ministers themselves, but in their office; in fact, less in their office than in the Word which they administer. Their only power to command, their only authority to teach, lies in the Word, or to put it another way, lies in their acting in the name of Christ. For Calvin does not here base the authority of the ministry on the inspiration of Scripture—that is, that Scripture as spoken by God is the very Word of God carrying the authority of God. His argument is Christological.[12] Christ is the Wisdom and Revelation of God, who alone has entered into the secrets of the Father. He is the source from whom the Old Testament writers drew their knowledge of God and when he became man he was the final witness to the Father. Hence his is the perfection of teaching. It would be impossible to surpass it, criminal to invent new. Let Christ speak and all be silent! The apostles must teach only and precisely what they have received from Christ; each succeeding generation must receive it, guard it faithfully, and hand it on intact. Hence the Church bears a spiritual weapon, the Word of God, the teaching of Christ. The ministering and dispensing of this *doctrina*, this Word of God, is the true power of the Church:

by it they confidently dare all things, compel all the strength, glory, and sublimity of the world to submit to its majesty and to obey it, rule over all things from the highest to the lowest, build up the house of Christ, overturn the kingdom of Satan, feed the sheep, destroy the wolves, exhort and instruct the teachable, rebuke, reprove, and refute the rebellious and stubborn, loose, bind, and finally, hurl thunderbolts—but doing all things in the Word of God.[13]

Nor has the Church power to legislate for itself, save in things indifferent, for God alone is King, Judge, Legislator, and Saviour. The sort of things Calvin has in mind as indifferent are St Paul's injunctions that women should not preach and should have their heads covered, or the custom of kneeling for prayer or shrouding the dead for burial. Again, he says, a local church has to determine the times of its services, what hymns and chants it is to use, and the manner in which it is to practise excommunication. In all such matters the church should remember, first, the rule of mutual love; second, not to invest its decisions with any eternal significance but to keep the practices free from superstition, and above all to avoid criticism of other churches with different customs; and thirdly, to do everything with the aim of building up the Church. Apart from such matters, the Church has no legislative power of its own; it can only accept and put into practice what is commanded by Christ in his Word.

It is true that God guides the Church by his Spirit, who is the Spirit of revelation, truth, wisdom, and light. But the Spirit does not act independently of the Word. As the Spirit of Christ, he is the Spirit of Christ's Word; as the promise 'he shall guide you into all truth' goes on to say: 'He shall glorify me! for he shall receive of mine, and shall show it unto you' (John 16· 14) Thus the Spirit leads the Church into the knowledge of the will of Christ by leading her into the knowledge of the Word, the expressed will, of Christ. And the expressed will of Christ, which is one with the will of the Father, is, as we have seen, the authority by which and under which the Church lives. From this it follows that the voice of the Church must be obeyed. The Church is Church if and because she proclaims nothing but the Word of Christ. Thus, as the mouthpiece of Christ, the Church has a supreme authority in the *regnum spirituale*. The two aspects have to be held together. It is only as the mouthpiece of Christ, as the minister of the Word of God, that the Church has supreme authority. The authority rests with the Word, the message committed to the ambassador, and even to the Word only because its speaker, Christ, has all authority in heaven and on earth. On the other hand, the Word of Christ which the Church proclaims must be obeyed. The fact that the Word has been declared by men's lips in no way lessens its nature; it is still the Word of Christ, of God.

It must also be asserted that the Church cannot err in things necessary to salvation. The inerrancy, of course, does not lie in the Church as a human institution, but only in the Church as taught by the inerrant Word of Christ through the illumination of the Holy Spirit. Once the Church abandons the Word, she has no truth in her. If she proclaims the Word, her proclamation is the truth—that is, the truth about God, the truth about man, the truth about God's judgment and salvation in Jesus Christ, the truth about God's eternal purpose.

The office of the Church is the ministry of the Word of God. The task of the Church is to proclaim the Word of God. The power of the Church lies in the almighty Word which she proclaims. The authority of the Church lies in the complete authority of the Word which she proclaims. All these statements represent Calvin's concept of the Church's office and task. But as they stand they quite distort it. Another factor must inform the whole. That factor is the human beings, in this instance the Genevese, for whom Christ died and rose again. The task of the Church in Geneva is to proclaim God's Word of judgment and forgiveness to the people. The power of the Church lies, not in destruction but in salvation, for the power of the Word is power unto salvation. The authority of the Church lies in assuring sinners of pardon, of teaching the sure truth of God in regard to doctrine and to personal and social ethics. Or put it another way: The factor that informs the whole is that the Church as the servant of the Word is the servant of those to whom the Word is addressed. The Church is the pastor, not to tyrannize, but to serve the flock.

But what of those who reject the Gospel, those who obstinately refuse to walk in God's ways revealed in Christ through Scripture? What, too, of those genuine believers who fall into sin? The Christian life is the opposite of hypocrisy, play-acting. It is a life of openness and frankness, of confessing sins and not hiding them. What help is to be given to the rejecters and refusers, to the stumblers and those in danger of falling? To preach to the congregation is the prime necessity. But what is proclaimed in general must also be applied in particular. Individuals must be shewn their faults, urged to repentance and to new or renewed faith. This ministry to individuals is also a purifying of the Church of which they are members. We are brought to the question of discipline. The current Roman system was inadmissible for the reasons Calvin had given in the *Institutio*. It remained, therefore, to establish an evangelical doctrine and system of discipline.

The medieval sacrament of penance was grounded upon the power of the keys. Jesus promised Peter: 'I will give unto thee the keys of the kingdom of heaven: and whatsoever thou shalt bind on earth shall be bound in heaven: and whatsoever thou shalt loose on earth shall be loosed in heaven' (Matt. 16: 19). And to the disciples after the resurrection he promised: 'Receive ye the Holy Ghost: whose soever sins ye forgive, they are forgiven unto them; whose soever sins ye retain, they are retained' (John 20: 22–3). On these promises was depended the authority of the priest to hear confession, to assess the penitence of the sinner, and to pronounce absolution. Calvin, like the other Reformers, interprets the promises of the proclamation of the Gospel. The Gospel is the message about Jesus Christ: that God became man, died for men's sin, rose again as God's new creation, reigns effectually over heaven and earth, and will reveal himself in judgment and redemption at the end of time; that by faith in him men's sins are forgiven and they are given new and everlasting life as God's children. This proclamation is both indicative, imperative, and conditional. It declares the achieved and established fact. It exhorts its hearers to repent and believe. It warns that its promises are null and void if they are not taken up. It contains both promise and warning, forgiveness and judgment. The preacher is empowered by the two promises of Jesus to tell his hearers that if they believe the Gospel their sins are forgiven and they are given the kingdom of heaven but that if they reject the Gospel they are excluded from the kingdom, their sins remaining with them. This is a declaration of the very will of God, for the Gospel is not only man's witness to God's work but God's own self-witness.

From this follows the readjustment of the doctrine and practice of excommunication. The authority to forgive and retain sins is preceded by the gift of the Holy Spirit (John 20: 22–3). It must be agreed that this area of activity is the work of the Holy Spirit. But a discrepancy at once becomes apparent if the power to forgive sins in the name of God is placed with the priest. The Spirit knows the heart of the sinner, the genuineness of his contrition, the fulness of his confession. But the priest does not know. Therefore sometimes at least errors will be made; the hypocrite will be absolved, the penitent not absolved, even excommunicated. Clearly in such cases the judgment in heaven and on earth will not coincide unless God forswears his righteousness. But if Christ's promise is true in general, the Romanists must dare to stand by it in particulars. The promise is clear and unambiguous: 'Whatever you bind on earth shall be bound in heaven; whatever you loose on earth shall be loosed in heaven.' Apply this to a human error of judgment by the priest and either one must insist that God is committed to an injustice or admit that an error of justice has occurred. The former is impossible. Therefore (unless one adopts the impossible position that no error ever has been made) a discrepancy exists between the promise and the actuality. But Christ's promise must be universally true. Therefore it cannot apply to the Roman sacrament of penance. But if it is referred to the proclamation of the Gospel, it remains universally true.

There existed clear mandates from Christ himself for the purifying of his Church, not only in the sayings about loosing and binding which we have already quoted, but also in the quite specific method of excommunication: 'If thy brother shall trespass against thee, go and tell him his fault between thee and him alone: if he shall hear thee, thou hast gained thy brother. But if he will not hear thee, then take with thee one or two more, that in the mouth or two or three witnesses every word may be established. And if he shall neglect to hear them, tell it unto the church: but if he neglect to hear the church, let him be unto thee as a heathen man and a publican' (Matt. 18: 15–17). Discipline, then, was essential to the life of the Church. Where there was no discipline there could continue no Church. But the complication of the concept of the Christian State is evident in the attempts to establish discipline in the various evangelical Churches. Zwingli's acceptance of the Christian state and opposition to a separated Church led him to a discipline that was the ecclesiastical aspect of civil law and that was enforced by the government. Indeed, his 1530 Ordinances at Zürich were more concerned with public morality than with loosing and binding by the Church. In Basel, on the other hand, Oecolampadius attempted, almost successfully, to establish a discipline depending on the authority of the Church—or rather, depending for its operation on that authority. Ultimately it depended on the government for its adoption. Oecolampadius' system was adopted. A consistory of twelve was set up to administer discipline. It consisted of four ministers, four magistrates, and four representatives of Church laymen. Their *modus operandi* was simply to follow Christ's command. First one member was to go alone to admonish an offender. If he failed, two or three were to go. If still unrepentant, the offender was to be called before the twelve. Finally, he was to be excommunicated. He could release himself from excommunication only by performing penance. This attempt failed through lack of support from other churches, and a modified scheme, depending more on the cooperation of the government, was adopted.

4. ORGANIZATION IN THEORY AND PRACTICE

On 16 January 1537 Farel and Calvin laid before the Council their *Articles on the Organization of the Church and its Worship at Geneva,* probably largely composed by Calvin. The recommendations they make are modest at first appearance, far-reaching in their implications.

Following the *Institutio,* it is urged that the Lord's Supper ought to be celebrated at least every Sunday, in fact as often as the Church assembles.[14] But because under the Papacy the people had communicated at most two or three times a year, so revolutionary a change might be undesirable. Therefore, at first let there be a monthly celebration. It could be held in each of the three main churches in turn, but for the use of all the citizens and not of the one parish only. The ministers will organize the administration—a necessary undertaking, if we reflect that it was intended that on each occasion a large part of the adult population would communicate and they unused to an evangelical service of the Lord's Supper. What must above all be attended to is that the Lord's Supper be not polluted by the participation of those who show 'that they do not at all belong to Jesus'.[15] The discipline of excommunication was set up by the Saviour himself to preserve the purity of his holy Supper, to bring the fallen to repentance, and to serve as a deterrent to others. As such, it was 'one of the most profitable and salutary things' that he gave to his Church, so that 'a Church cannot retain its true condition without observing this ordinance'.[16]

But excommunication must be 'reduced' to necessary causes and no longer employed as an economic, political or social sanction. The best method of excommunication will be by appointing overseers in the various quarters of the city who shall report serious faults to the ministers, so that the offender may be urged to repentance and amendment. Should he prove obstinate, he is to be reported to the whole Church. If he persists in his hardness of heart, he is to be excommunicated; that is, he is to be expelled from the society of Christians and from the Eucharist and given over to the power of the devil. Calvin explains this phrase, used in 1 Cor. 5: 5 and 1 Tim. 1: 20, as meaning excommunication: 'As, then, we are received into the communion of the Church and remain in it on the condition that we are under the protection and guardianship of Christ, so he who is cast out of the Church is in a way delivered over to the power of Satan, for he becomes an alien and is cast out of Christ's kingdom'.[17] He is, however, to continue to attend sermons, so that God's Word may have a chance of reaching his heart. If he gives evidence that he is penitent, he is to be restored.

Since the evangelical faith had only recently been preached in the city, and there were still many Romanists, the ministers also urged excommunication on the grounds of failure to confess the faith. *The Confession of faith, which all the citizens and inhabitants of Geneva . . . must promise to keep and to hold* had been presented to the Council on 10 November 1536. Let the members of the Council be the first to subscribe and then the citizens, 'in order to recognize those in harmony with the Gospel and those loving rather to be of the kingdom of the pope than of the kingdom of Jesus Christ'.[18] Those who would not subscribe were to be excommunicated.

Secondly, worship should include the congregational singing of psalms, so as to give fervour and ardour to the prayers which otherwise are apt to be dead and cold. Since, however, neither tunes nor words are known to the congregation, many of whom are probably illiterate, there shall be a children's choir which shall sing clearly. The people for their part shall listen 'with all attention' and gradually pick up the words and music.

The *Articles* refer explicitly to catechizing as an ancient form, no innovation. The *Confession of faith* was made once for all in Geneva. Thereafter the faith would be handed down in unbroken succession from generation to generation. What is necessary for any age is, however, doubly necessary now, when the Word of God has been neglected so long and parents have not taught their children properly. Therefore a 'brief and simple summary of the Christian faith' is to be prepared. It will be taught to the children and they will be examined periodically by the ministers.

Finally, there is need for a revision in the marriage laws. This is such a complicated and delicate matter that it would be better to proceed by way of practice and precedent. Let a commission of councillors and ministers be appointed, who will both judge cases on their merits and also draw up ordinances based on the most frequent causes of trouble. These ordinances would then be presented to the Council and if approved would pass into law.

The *Little Council* studied the *Articles* on 16 January 1537. They drew up certain regulations on marriage to be debated by the *Two Hundred* and passed the rest of the articles with one exception. This was the request for frequent celebrations of the Eucharist. The modest compromise of once a month was cut down to once a quarter. Discipline, however, had been accepted, and therefore would no doubt be put into effect. At one point, however, we see that Calvin was not immune from the disease of ambiguity which attacks all lawyers attempting to draft legislation. The offender who had been reproved, said the *Articles*, might still treat excommunication lightly and not mind living and dying as a rejected person. In that case, the Council was told, 'it will be your duty to consider if you must for long tolerate and leave unpunished such contempt and mockery of God and his Gospel'.[19] Thus it was not expressly said by whom the sinner was to be excommunicated. The civil authority was certainly involved in that it had the duty of punishing the sinner, and that, not for a strictly civil crime but for despising God and the Gospel. Whatever passed in discussion, the document as accepted contained this ambiguity. When the *Two Hundred* met the same day they approved the decisions of the *Little Council* and further showed their zeal for the house of God by enacting that on Sundays during sermon time 'neither butchers, nor tripe sellers, nor others, nor second hand dealers shall stay open beyond the last stroke of the great bell; that those who have idols at home break them up forthwith; that there is to be no singing of idle songs and no playing of games of chance; nor are the pastry cooks to cry their wares during the time of sermon'.[20]

Zeal for subscribing to the *Confession of faith*, however, was less evident. The Councils had to be reminded in March that they had passed the *Articles*, and it was not until 17 April that the machinery for securing the citizens' subscriptions was devised. The ministers needed to remind the *Two Hundred* again on 29 July. They then decided that the citizens should subscribe district by district in Saint Pierre. The matter dragged on into November. Some subscribed; some refused or delayed. None came forward from the rue des Allemands, inhabited by some of the strongest opponents of the new Church order.

The meeting on 26 November opened stormily. Either Farel or Calvin, it is not clear which, was accused of saying to some councillors that he would rather drink a glass of their blood than drink with them. The bloodthirsty Reformer explained that what had actually happened was that he first remonstrated mildly with them and then, in response to their 'You wish us nothing but ill', replied, 'I wish you so much ill that I would shed my blood for you'. A councillor reported that some of them had been called perjured for swearing to a mere written confession. The Reformers replied that this was the wrong way to look at it. What was asked was a solemn oath to keep to the faith of God and to follow his commandments, as had been done in Nehemiah and Jeremiah—in other words, a solemn renewing of the covenant. The Council said that the Bernese commissioners called it perjury. The upshot of the matter was that another committee was appointed to look into it, and Farel and Calvin went to Bern with explanations. But the *Confession* had only a limited subscription.[21]

During this year some of the less thoughtful Genevese conceived (or had suggested to them) the suspicion that was to be used against Calvin for the next twenty years. Certainly Farel and Calvin were ministers and said that their work was the preaching of the Word and the administration of the Sacraments. But they were both Frenchmen, and France had begun to take an interest in Geneva. If John Wesley in the eighteenth century could be suspected of being a Jacobite, these two could with more colour be taken for agents of the French government. When in February 1538 a French agent actually did pay a secret visit to the city and later make overtures for a French alliance through two of the leading supporters of the Reformers, suspicion seemed confirmed. Mobs demonstrated outside their houses at night, firing off guns and threatening to chuck them into the river. Thus, to oppose Calvin became an act of patriotism.

In 1537 Calvin's reputation suffered also in another respect. Pierre Caroli, since the days when he had been one of Briçonnet's preachers at Meaux, had vacillated between Rome and the Evangelicals. He turned up as a Romanist in Geneva in 1534 and after a disputation professed himself again converted to the reformed faith. He was made minister first at Neuchâtel and then at Lausanne. Reported by Viret to the *Consistoire* of Bern for advocating prayers for the dead, he retorted by accusing Farel and Calvin of Arianism, a charge which they asked to be debated at a special synod. There he challenged them to subscribe to the three Creeds. 'To this Calvin replied that we had subscribed to belief in one God and not to Athanasius, whose Creed no genuine Church had ever approved.'[22] He also refused Caroli's right to demand subscription. But harm had been done, and even their friends became anxious lest they should be falling from orthodoxy. In the event the Bern Council cleared them of the charge of Arianism, at the same time deposing Caroli, who now returned to the bosom of France and the old Church.

About the same time another ecclesiastical-political quarrel began to develop. Bern had been Geneva's ally these dozen years. She had fostered the struggling evangelical Church. What was more natural, then, than that she should expect to have a say in Genevan Church affairs? While the Syndics had been well-disposed towards the Reformers, and while the chief minister at Bern had been Calvin's friend Megander, any differences could be discussed in an accommodating spirit on all sides. But after the February elections of 1538 the four new Syndics were willing for Bern's influence in the city to increase and were at the same time opposed to the Church policy of the ministers. About now, too, Megander moved to Zürich and was replaced by Peter Kuntz, or Konzen, who never let an opportunity pass of attacking the Reformers' work in Geneva.

Bern had convened a synod of the Swiss evangelical Churches to discuss the so-called 'Bernese ceremonies', in the hope of introducing uniformity in a few external rites. These were: (1) that Baptism should be administered at the font; (2) that the bread at the Lord's Supper should be unleavened; (3) that the four great festivals of Christmas, Easter, Ascension, and Whitsun should be observed. These are hardly issues to make a great fuss about. Calvin himself had already spoken of leavened or unleavened bread, red or white wine, as things indifferent, and he introduced the festivals into a Geneva which knew nothing of such things. But now the ministers were unwilling to follow Bern's lead. They preferred to wait, they said, until the forthcoming Synod at Zürich had given a final verdict. Relations between the ministers and the Council became very strained. Calvin was censured for calling them in a sermon 'a council of the devil'. His colleague, the blind Frenchman, Courauld, preferred to keep to the verifiable, and was put in prison for referring to them as 'a council of drunkards'. When on Good Friday the Council asked them to use unleavened bread at the Easter Communion, they temporized. On the following day, ordered to obey on pain of being forbidden to preach, they still gave no reply. On Easter Day they preached as usual but did not celebrate the Eucharist. The mob took the occasion to indulge in further riots and threats. The next day the *Two Hundred* ordered that they should leave Geneva as soon as substitutes had been found, but on the Tuesday said they need not wait for the substitutes and were to go within three days.

From Geneva Farel and Calvin went straight off to Bern, representing the situation in such strong terms that the Council there, afraid that Geneva might lapse into Romanism, took up their cause, but in vain. The two ejected ministers next carried their case to the Synod now sitting at Zürich, where Calvin presented fourteen articles on Church polity. He accepted the Bernese ceremonies, with some safeguards for tender consciences. But Bern for its part was to admit that the Genevan ceremonies in previous use were not contrary to Scripture. For the rest, the articles repeated the Geneva *Articles*. The Synod, although they considered that a large part of the blame lay with Calvin for 'misplaced vigour' and a lack of tender-heartedness towards 'so undisciplined a people', asked Bern to mediate and to get the ministers restored. In May a delegation was sent to Geneva, but failed in its purpose; and at the beginning of June, Calvin and Farel, now without homes, most of their possessions, and work, decided to go to Basel, which they reached after a rough and wet journey.

Chapter 5

The French Minister in Strasbourg

1. MATTERS DOMESTIC AND PASTORAL

There followed, if not halcyon days after the storm, at least a time of comparative calm, of reflection, of constructive pastoral work, of writing of the highest quality. There were the frustrations, the sorrows, and the straitened purse. But the abnormal strains of the past eighteen months now eased in the pleasing sensation of being appreciated and seeing his work fruitful. As for Geneva, the struggle was at first too close for him to do more than try to come to terms with it personally. They must humble themselves, he wrote to Farel, and wait upon God, who has it all in his hands.[1] Had he made a mistake in staying in Geneva in the first place, he wondered. But no; that was assuredly God's calling. Now that he had been released from an insupportable burden, it would be tempting God to engage in anything of the sort again.[2] 'After that calamity, when my ministry seemed to me to be disastrous and unsuccessful, I made up my mind never again to enter on any ecclesiastical charge whatever unless the Lord should call me to it by a clear and manifest call.'[3]

He would settle in Basel for the present until he understood what God wanted him to do. Other Swiss and German Reformers believed that he had been too severe with the Genevese, and were firmly of the opinion that Farel and he should not work together again. By now Farel had been called away from Basel to take charge of the Church in Neuchâtel. Bucer and Capito wanted Calvin for Strasbourg, as minister of the French Church there and to lecture in theology. He went to see them, hesitated, returned to Basel, and refused the invitation because it did not include Farel. Bucer then took a leaf out of Farel's book and accused him of rejecting God's call like another Jonah. Never would his studies prosper. By September Calvin had taken up his new position in the city that he expected to be his permanent home, and in a few months applied for and was granted citizenship, something for which he never asked in Geneva.

Strasbourg, not at this time belonging to France, but close to its eastern borders, a city that had early declared for the Reformation and yet showed remarkable toleration towards the varied shades of evangelical opinion and towards Rome, had become one of the chief cities of refuge for the persecuted in France. There were some four or five hundred members of the French Church of which Calvin now became minister. A happy situation for him; a Frenchman among Frenchmen, a refugee among refugees, a poor man among generally poor men. He was hard worked, but not overstrained: 'I have my own share of contests and wrestlings where I am, and most arduous they are. But they do not overwhelm me; they merely keep me in training.'[4] He preached or lectured every day, with two sermons on Sunday, and he cultivated what was denied him in Geneva, a pastoral ministry with individuals.

The anabaptist Hermann of Liège, who had disputed against the ministers at Geneva and now lived in Strasbourg, was one who returned to Church membership through him. We see how Calvin's theology of the Church needed no adaptation to become evangelistic. Calvin took his ground on St Cyprian's dictum *extra ecclesiam nulla salus*, 'there is no salvation outside the Church'. This granted, he went on to prove that the evangelical Church was the true Church. Hermann thereupon (no doubt after reflection) saw and confessed that he had sinned in separating from the Church, and begged forgiveness and restoration. On various doctrines, and these central, he was open to teaching. On predestination he was doubtful about the distinction between foreknowledge and providence. Calvin accepted him purely on the basis of an alignment with the Church, with the repentance and good intention that this implied.

The Lord's Supper was celebrated monthly, after careful preparation. On the Sunday before, Calvin would announce that those who wished to communicate must inform him. He was careful to explain why he insisted on this discipline. First, it was for instruction, to explain the faith more carefully; secondly, to admonish those in need of correction; and thirdly, to comfort any who were troubled in mind. He found it necessary to explain to his congregation that he was not re-introducing Romanist confession. Certainly, he goes so far as to say, he would prefer that system to remain in force rather than to have no discipline at all. But he disapproves of it and assures his congregation that he is only enjoining what Christ himself appointed, and that obedience to Christ is Christian freedom. The charge of Papacy seems to have been common. A certain scholar who ran a gambling den on the side and was rumoured to be an adulterer, announced that he intended to communicate. Calvin forbade him. 'He made sport of it . . . saying that he left confession to the Papists. I replied that there was a kind of Christian confession, for all that.'[5] Rather than have a celebration for which the Church had not been prepared, he would prefer to have no celebration at all.

The congregational singing that had been one of the four points in his policy for Church reform in Geneva was introduced here also. The first of the metrical Psalters was published at Strasbourg in 1539 for the French Church to use in its worship. A French-speaking refugee from the Low Countries wrote of how it affected him:

Everyone sings, men and women, and it is a lovely sight. Each has a music book in his hand . . . For five or six days at the beginning as I looked on this little company of exiles, I wept, not for sadness but for joy to hear them all singing so heartily, and as they sang giving thanks to God that he had led them to a place where his name is glorified. No one could imagine what joy there is in singing the praises and wonders of the Lord in the mother tongue as they are sung here.[6]

The public lectures that Calvin was now delivering were expositions of St John's Gospel and 1 Corinthians. It would seem that he also taught in private, as the *magister* of *pensionnaires* whom he lodged in his house, a move taken partly to ease his financial situation, of which we now hear a good deal: 'I can't call a single penny my own. It is astonishing how money slips away in extraordinary expenses.'[7] He hoped to be given a prebend's stall in the Cathedral, but this fell through. As the numbers of the students increased, his state grew a little easier.

One curious episode now shows us Calvin in quite a different rôle, even if one for which he had been trained. On 20 November 1539 he wrote to Farel telling him about the difficulties of a certain Count Guillaume. This was Guillaume de Furstenberg, formerly a commander in the army of the German Protestant princes and then in that of Francis I. He was now embroiled in a quarrel whose immediate object was a subordinate officer but which was part of more serious trouble with no less than the Constable of France. Calvin had been dining with him at his Strasbourg residence. More, he had been forced to spend two whole days 'writing letters for him'.[8] On the following 10 January, the Count kept him for the whole day—'although he could have completed in an hour all he wanted with me, and you can guess how much I enjoyed it when I tell you I had to sit among the soldiers with whom his house is filled'[9] But according to Herminjard and to Rodolphe Peter, this was all a part of Calvin's writing for him a defence, which appeared as *Declaration made by Monsieur Guillaume, Count of Furstenberg, on the quarrel he has with Sebastian Vogelsperger*. The opponent replied with what he claimed was the truth, to which Furstenberg through his advocate, Calvin, wrote *Second declaration made by Monsieur Guillaume, Count of Furstenberg, against the reply, published by a wicked and worthless man called Sebastian Vogelsperger*. Calvin, it seems, was still willing to augment his salary with some lawyer's business. Was this the only case, or were there others of which we do not know?

The time at Strasbourg started sadly. Farel's nephew died of the plague, Calvin helping to look after him in his illness. Then Courauld, his blind colleague in Geneva, who had become pastor at Orbe, died in October 1538.

Calvin's grief knew no bounds. He could think of nothing else all day and, awake with his customary insomnia, 'I am utterly exhausted by these melancholy thoughts all night long'.[10] At the news of Pierre Robert's death at Ferrara in 1538, his sorrow was more restrained, but he found it hard to write Farel a coherent letter. Olivetan, that shadowy Reformer, seems to have been closer to Calvin than the absence of letters between them suggests. He left behind him a wonderful library, amassed when he was translating the Serrières Bible. Herminjard calls it 'richer in theological works than any other in the *Suisse romande*'.[11] Many of the books were left to Calvin, and in Herminjard we may read about those that Calvin chose to keep.[12]

There came a separation more painful than death. Louis du Tillet, who had sheltered him at Claix, who had fled with him from France, who had shared life at Geneva with him, now suddenly and without warning returned to France and the Roman Church. Calvin had not heard from him for some time and wondered what was the matter. Had he offended du Tillet perhaps by too great freedom of speech? Then a certain Jehan (perhaps du Tillet's brother, secretary in the *Parlement* of Paris) called on Calvin to tell him what had happened. A week later he received letters from du Tillet himself. Once again it was a question of the true Church. Calvin replied that if du Tillet acknowledged that the Evangelicals were the Church, he could not join again the Romanists without separating from the Church and therefore from God. If he judged the Evangelicals to be schismatics, he should ask whether this was also the judgment of Christ.

In September 1538 du Tillet wrote again, suggesting, no doubt sincerely, that the banishment was a sign of God's displeasure. Here was a subtle temptation, all the more insidious in that it must already have occurred to Calvin himself. His ministry in Geneva had ended in disaster for the Church and ignominy for himself. How if this were a sign that God's blessing had not been with him? Was it a warning and reproof for leaving the Church, a call to return? Calvin accepted the rebukes and explained the attitude he consistently maintained. Against the opposition in Geneva and those who sat in judgment on him he asserted his innocence, at the same time acknowledging that what happened had been a chastisement for his errors and ignorance. He could not, however, doubt that it had been God who had called him to work in Geneva. And ready as he was to bear his friend's blows, he would not refrain from asking him to apply to himself what he had said. Was it really fair for him in his safe study to condemn the Evangelicals who preached the Gospel openly, while he would not allow *them* the right 'to condemn the manifest enemies of God and his majesty?'[13] Du Tillet, perhaps sincerely, had asked to be allowed to contribute to Calvin's finances. Calvin regarded it as a bribe. Here he politely declined, but to Farel he wrote: 'Louis sold his bounty at too high a price, for he almost urged me to recant.'[14] To du Tillet he ended:

One of my companions [Courauld] now stands before God to render account for what was our common cause. When we also come there, it will become known which side is guilty of rashness and desertion. It is to God that I appeal from the judgments of all worldly wise men who imagine their word carries enough weight to condemn us. There the angels of God will bear witness who are the schismatics.[15]

The erratic Caroli reappeared. Within two years of being publicly accused of Arianism by him, Farel, ignorant of Burke's knowledge that it is criminal to trust those whom you know to be untrustworthy, was welcoming him back among the Evangelicals. In October 1539 he repaired to Strasbourg to put himself right with Bucer and Sturm. Calvin narrated what happened in a letter to Farel, on whom he blamed everything. Caroli had explained to the ministers that he had only seceded to Rome because Farel and Calvin had refused to subscribe to the Creeds. The brethren accepted his version, but censured his action. Calvin was now called into the room to give his account. Aware of the delicacy of his situation, he found it difficult to make a satisfactory defence. The ministers thereupon told Calvin, and through him, Farel, that they disapproved of their conduct in the matter. They asked Calvin to recite Caroli's faults. He refused, knowing from experience his plausible tongue. A set of articles were then drawn up and were sent to Calvin late that evening, Caroli having first, it seems, corrected them. Calvin met the ministers again next day:

There I sinned grievously through not keeping my temper. For my mind was so filled with bile that I poured out bitterness on all sides . . . I stated my resolution to die rather than subscribe [to these articles]. Then there was so much on both sides that I could not have been ruder to Caroli himself had he been present. At last I forced myself out of the dining room; but Bucer followed me and calmed me with fair words and took me back again. I said that I wanted to consider the matter more fully before giving a final answer. When I got home, I was seized with an extraordinary paroxysm and could find no relief but in tears and sighs. And what made it worse was that it was your fault . . . If I could have spoken to you face to face, I would have turned on you the whole of the fury I poured out on others.[16]

It is hard to see why the ministers acted as they did. Did Bucer suppose that Calvin had a like devious character to his own? The incident is, on any showing, an illuminating example of the distrust among the evangelical leaders.

After he had been at Strasbourg a while, Calvin's friends began to urge him to marry. His health was poor; he was not perhaps a good manager of his own affairs; his impatience and irritability might be softened by marriage. Calvin was willing, and sent Farel a list of the attributes he sought in a wife. He was not concerned with physical beauty, so long as she was chaste, sensible, economical, patient, and would take care of his health. They have a girl in mind. If Farel thinks she will do, 'set out at once, in case someone else forestalls you'.[17] This possibility failed, and next was proposed 'a certain damsel of noble rank'. Calvin was not happy about it, for she spoke no French and might also perhaps give herself airs. Her brother and his wife were very keen that the match should go through. Calvin agreed on condition that she would promise to learn French. Antoine was despatched to escort her to Strasbourg and the wedding was fixed for not later than 10 March 1540. But on 29 March they were still not married and Calvin was saying that he would never think of marrying her 'unless the Lord had entirely bereft me of my wits'. [18] June found him yet a bachelor, the latest candidate proving not to have an unblemished past, apparently. But then in August he was married to Idelette de Bure, the widow of a one-time anabaptist, with two children, a boy and a girl. There were de Bures in Noyon, and Lefranc believed that she and Calvin might have been acquainted in youth. But de Bure occurs as a name in other districts of France.

2. THE NEW INSTITUTIO

The first edition of the *Institutio* had served its purpose. The whole edition was sold out within the year. Either a reprint or a new edition was demanded. Calvin, already dissatisfied with it, had conceived a broader scheme for which the catechism form was not suitable. He would have made the revision much earlier had not his work at Geneva prevented him. When he was free he took it up in earnest and had it finished by the end of July 1539. The new edition was published as *Institutio Christianae Religionis, now at last truly corresponding to its title. The author Jean Calvin of Noyon. With a full index. Hab. 1, 'How long, O Lord?' Strasb., by Wendelin Rihel in the month of August in the year 1539.* Some copies were printed with the author's name given as Alcuin, no doubt for circulation in Roman Catholic countries, where the name Calvin was by now too well known.

The quaint 'now at last truly corresponding to its title' indicates that not the whole of the Christian religion had been treated in 1536. Here in the preface, *Jean Calvin to the Reader*, he says: 'I have aimed at embracing a summary of religion in all its parts'.[19] The scope, then, is vastly widened; but it represents a broadening, not beyond and outside Scripture, but of his understanding of the Scriptural material itself. The *Institutio* is now formally orientated towards the Bible: 'my object in this work has been so to prepare and train students in theology for the study of the divine Word that they might have an easy access into it and keep on in it without stumbling'.[20] It is not possible to describe the *Institutio* at this point without also taking in Calvin's Biblical work.

The *Institutio* is based upon the exposition of Scripture; and the exposition of Scripture is based on exegesis, that is, the understanding of the actual text of the Bible.[21] As we shall see, Calvin already intended to write commentaries on at least the New Testament. These commentaries would attempt to interpret the mind of the New Testament writers. They would therefore not stop at a linguistic, grammatical, or historical investigation of the texts, but would aim at a theological understanding. But this would demand that the main topics or doctrines taught in a New Testament book would be considered in their inter-relations; and for this to be done they would have to be arranged in an orderly manner. This view of the commentator's task was not peculiar to Calvin, but had been imported into Biblical work by Melanchthon from secular sources, and in fact went back to Aristotle by way of Cicero. Melanchthon, however, almost confined his commentaries to a set of essays on the doctrines in the book, omitting the exegetical basis. Martin Bucer went to the other extreme, and published commentaries which included a translation of the text, a paraphrase of it, exegesis and exposition and also the *loci communes*, the systematic treatment of the main doctrines. The result was vast volumes, unsuitable for busy men, as Calvin pointed out, holding that 'the chief virtue of an interpreter lies in clear brevity'.²² He himself solved the problem of having two books in one by quite simply separating them into two books. The one was the commentary itself, the other the *Institutio*, with, of course, the difference that the *Institutio* represented the *loci communes* not of any individual book of the Bible but of the whole of Scripture.

The new edition of 1539 was both an amplification and a reconstruction. The earlier form, with its chapters on the Law, Faith, Prayer, the Sacraments, the five so-called sacraments, and Christian liberty, is largely kept; but new chapters are added and the whole becomes some three times the length of the 1536 edition. Of the seventeen chapters, six are quite new, five are existing sections expanded into chapters, while the remaining six are carried over with degrees of alteration. With a stroke of brilliance he takes his first sentence, 'Well-nigh the sum of sacred doctrine consists in these two parts, the knowledge of God and the knowledge of ourselves' and makes of it the first two chapters, *On the Knowledge of God* and *On the Knowledge of Man*. The chapters on Law and Faith follow, greatly augmented, but then an expansion of the section on penitence becomes a chapter in its own right. Three new chapters come next, *On Justification by Faith and on the Merits of Works*, *On the Likeness and Difference between the Old and New Testaments*, and *On God's Predestination and Providence*. Chapter 9, *On Prayer*, is an amplification of the earlier Chapter 3; and what had been Chapter 4, *On the Sacraments*, is split into its constituent parts and enlarged to make Chapters 10–12, *On the Sacraments*, *On Baptism*, and *On the Lord's Supper*. Again, Chapters 13–15 are the three parts of the old Chapter 6, this time with little increase: *On Christian Liberty*, *On the Power of the Church*, and *On Political Administration*. There follows a misplaced chapter later to be restored to its proper place as Chapter 13, and the work ends with a new chapter *On the Life of the Christian Man*.

It is a larger book, but it contains nothing new, nothing that was not in the first edition at least in embryo. Calvin has not changed his mind, and indeed he was never to retract any doctrine in the *Institutio*. But his lecturing on Romans, St John, and 1 Corinthians and his expository preaching, his close association with Bucer, a man of wide learning and mental penetration, his own further reading in theology and Church history, have all contributed to clarify and enlarge his thinking. It must also be said that Calvin now understands his own age better than he had done before. The first edition would, *mutatis mutandis*, have fitted the Church scene at any time within the preceding one hundred and fifty years. The new one belongs to its precise age and speaks to the men of its age.

3. THE COMMENTARY ON ROMANS

I think I have so embraced the sum of religion in all its parts and arranged it systematically that if anyone grasps it aright he will have no difficulty in deciding what he ought principally to seek in Scripture and to what end he should refer everything in it. Thus I have, as it were, paved the way. And if I shall hereafter publish any commentaries on Scripture, I shall always condense them and keep them short, for I shall not need to undertake lengthy discussions on doctrines or digress into *loci communes*. By this method the godly reader will be spared great trouble and boredom, provided he approaches [the commentaries] fore-armed with a knowledge of the present work as a necessary weapon. But because the commentary on the Epistle to the Romans will furnish an example of this intention, I prefer to let the thing appear in practice rather than forecast it by words.[23]

These words were written on 1 August 1539. As the dedication to *Romans* was written on 18 October, it is likely that he had been working on both books since he had settled in Basel in June 1538. *Romans* had been in his mind for two years or more before this, and preparation for the commentary was no doubt provided by his lectures in Geneva in 1536–7. It was published by his friend Wendelin Rihel at Strasbourg in March 1540. The second title page of some copies carries the same pseudonym as some copies of the *Institutio—The Commentaries of Alcuin on Paul's Epistle to the Romans*.

The basis and justification of the reshaping of theology carried out by the Reformers was a changed understanding of the Bible. The Middle Ages, no less than the Reformation, was the age of the Bible. The theological training provided by the universities revolved around the two set texts, the Bible and Peter Lombard's *Four Books of Sentences*. These and these alone the lecturers had to expound in the same way that the older law lecturers had expounded the *Corpus Iuris Civilis*. There was, then, ample opportunity for the clergy to be well acquainted with the Bible. The Reformers were dissatisfied, not with the quantity but the quality of Bible study that was taking place. And this on the grounds of the theological principles that

74

governed the interpretation of Scripture. The sovereign authority of Scripture over the Church had been relativized by an unclear conception of the authority of tradition. The effect was that Scripture was no longer regarded as self-authenticating and therefore as self-explanatory. The sovereign authority of God cannot be authenticated by any save God himself. But that which is true of God must, if Trinitarian theology means anything, also be true of God's Word. First, then, the Reformers (beginning when Luther admitted that Scripture stood above the authority of councils and popes) asserted the sovereign authority of Scripture as the Word of God and therefore also established the principle of self-authentication and self-explanation by which they would interpret Scripture. If Scripture is taken alone, as Luther insisted against Erasmus, its central message is clear and unambiguous. Another opponent, Latomus, objected that Scripture was a 'wax nose' which can be twisted in any direction. In fact Scripture will only yield different results to different readers when its authority is relativized and therefore when it is interpreted by other than its own criteria. Scripture interpreted by Scripture will yield a clear and unambiguous central message. This is the burden of Calvin's dedicatory letter to Edward VI in the *Catholic Epistles*, January 1551. And he goes on to say that it is the duty of evangelical theologians so to expound Scripture that its genuine meaning may be revealed, free of inconsistent accretions. 'I, at any rate, have destined the rest of my life, if leisure and freedom are granted me, chiefly to this task.'[24] From about 1536 he intended to provide, alongside the *Institutio*, commentaries on at least the epistles in the New Testament.

The form of *Romans* set the pattern for those that were to follow. After the initial *Argumentum* or Theme, which in *Romans* confines itself to a doctrinal analysis of the epistle, but which in later commentaries referred where necessary to questions of authorship and date, came the commentary proper. He divides the epistle into convenient paragraphs (it will be remembered that the New Testament was at this time, although divided into chapters, without verses) which he places at the head of each section in his own literal Latin translation from the Greek. For him the Greek is the definitive text and not the Vulgate, the Latin translation made by St Jerome in the fourth century and the authoritative version for the Middle Ages and the Council of Trent. There were already several Greek New Testaments in print which he could use.[25] The chief were Erasmus' fourth edition of 1527, the large Complutensian Polyglot published in 1522, and the edition printed in Paris by Simon de Colines in 1534. Calvin certainly knew and used Erasmus in more than one edition and later he seems also to have used the Complutensian. But it is probable that his basic Greek text was that of de Colines. This, as the historians of the printed Greek New Testament tell us, was a most interesting text. Based on Erasmus and the Complutensian, many of its readings nevertheless came from manuscripts and did not appear in any other sixteenth-century printed Greek Testament. It was therefore to a limited degree independent of the dominant Protestant text which Erasmus formed and handed on to Robert Estienne and Beza and which became the *Textus receptus*, the authority of which was not to be broken until the nineteenth century. Many of the readings in de Colines would now be accepted without question as genuine. By using this text, then, Calvin's commentaries are also based upon a rather sounder text than any other contemporary Greek Testament would have provided.

The text and translation established, there follow the exegesis and the exposition. Without standing in the forefront of current Biblical scholarship, Calvin was a competent linguist and historian. He goes for his information to the most reliable sources at his disposal: Budé's *Annotations on the Pandects*, crammed with interesting linguistic information, and his *Commentary on the Greek Language*; Erasmus' *Annotations on the New Testament*; the Greek patristic commentators and especially Chrysostom, the early Church historians, the Jewish historian Josephus, and classical writers like Pliny.

His greatest quality as a commentator was his self-disciplined subordination to the text. The technical studies were merely a means to this end. Yet to say that he let the text speak to him would be trite and misleading. Rather, he conducted a continual enquiry between the detail and the wider context. The attention to the context saved his lexicography from becoming static, from imposing what we may call an invariable dictionary meaning on to words. But he did not simply listen to the voice of the Bible. As he listened to the context he questioned the immediate text; as he listened to the immediate text he questioned the context. It was by this continual process of hearing and of asking on the basis of what he had heard that Calvin was able to arrive in the remarkable way that he did at the 'mind' of the author.

Calvin did not, however, write commentaries in order that he might inform the sixteenth century about religion among the ancient Semites or in the first century A.D. The Bible is God's Word to man. This means, not simply that the writers transmit a message which they have received from God, but that in it God himself speaks as really as if he were speaking with his own mouth. Calvin's doctrine of the Scriptures contains some puzzling features; to attempt to harmonize them would be to distort. The main points in it, however, are these: (1) Scripture is the record of God's self-revelation to men; (2) it is also the interpretation of that self-revelation; (3) the record itself is made at the instigation of God; (4) the interpretation is God's own interpretation of the recorded events; (5) the language of the record is given to the writer by God. In this sense the Bible is God's Word to men, in which he reveals the relationship with them which he has determined and established in Jesus Christ, the relationship of Creator-creature, of Redeemer-redeemed.

God's Word to men is the Bible. God does not address men in a direct encounter of Divinity with humanity, but by means of creatures, creaturely events, creaturely communication. The Bible is a collection of documents recording the history of God's relation with men, and therefore is such a creaturely communication. In that they are documents, they are to be studied and understood only by the methods in which any documents are studied and understood. The creatureliness of the Bible is no hindrance to hearing God's Word but rather the completely necessary condition. Thus the Scriptures are at one and the same time both God's speech to men in the thoroughgoing sense given above and also a collection of human writings which therefore betray idiosyncracies of literary style, even some inaccuracies and imprecisions. Calvin saw no inconsistency between saying that 'the apostles were the amanuenses of the Holy Spirit' and finding in the apostles' writings literary weaknesses or geographical or historical errors. For, according to Calvin's concept of accommodation, God genuinely speaks to man in such a a way that he is comprehensible to him. Within the Divine Trinity, the intercommunication is in the Spiritual language of Divinity. Man does not understand that language, but speaks Hebrew, Greek, Aramaic. And thus God in his kindness, says Calvin, speaks to man in the language that he understands, like a mother using baby talk to her infant.

It was for this reason that Calvin bestowed such pains on the technical means of understanding; for this reason, too, that he interpreted Scripture according to what is called the plain, genuine, literal, or native sense. The 'spiritual' interpretation had regarded the literal sense as only the wrapping within which is contained the true meaning intended by the Holy Spirit. Although Calvin sometimes speaks as if all he were opposing was a spiritual interpretation imposed on the text ('wild allegorizing' as one would say), his real view was that the literal meaning itself is the record and interpretation of God's self-revelation in Christ, and that therefore it is unnecessary to seek another meaning. The commentator's task is to make clear this meaning and so to bring to light the knowledge which God gives of himself in Scripture and the knowledge which he gives of man and of man's world.

4. GENEVA CHANGES ITS MIND

By the time *Romans* was published an alarming possibility was being canvassed. Geneva, that unsteady city, was changing its mind again. Some now would like to have Calvin back. For a year after the expulsion of the ministers, the city had kept on a moderately even keel politically, but the Church life had declined seriously. The Genevese had got the sort of ministers they thought they wanted, without moral or intellectual weight, unable to exert authority. The followers of Calvin and Farel misguidedly tried to remain loyal to their exiled leaders and thus were forming parties within the Church. Calvin, aware of what was going on, did his best to put the evils right. In a pastoral letter to the Church he wrote: '[God] not only commands us to render a willing obedience with fear and trembling to the Word when it is preached to us, but also commands that the ministers of the Word are to be treated with honour and reverence, for they are clothed with authority as his ambassadors, and he wishes them to be acknowledged as his own angels and envoys.' [26] Saunier, the principal of the Collège, went so far as to raise doubts on the lawfulness of receiving the Sacraments from the new ministers. Calvin and Capito, whom he consulted, laid down the principles: Christians should hate schism and do everything they can to avoid it. If they see that God's Word is being preached and the Sacraments administered, they should recognize the existence of a Church there, whatever the ministers are like and even if the doctrine taught is not so pure as it should be. What is of primary importance is that unity should be established and preserved: 'I cannot hear without great and intense horror that any schism should settle within the Church.' [27]

In March 1539 Bern wished to negotiate a new treaty of alliance, particularly in reference to some land south of Geneva to which they had laid claim but over which, meeting with opposition, they had accepted certain rights. Delegates were sent to Bern with strict instructions for their mission. These they disobeyed, and the Bernese got all they wanted. The Genevan Council refused to ratify the agreement; there was a great quarrel; the delegates fled the city and were, *in absentia*, condemned to death. They were, moreover, replaced by *Guillermins*—slang for the followers of Monsieur Guillaume [Farel]. This was, as events turned out, not merely a set-back but the beginning of the end for the *Artichauds*, or Bernese party, who had been instrumental in banishing the Reformers. About now Calvin's return was first mooted, but he refused to consider it. For one thing, he would not go without Farel. For another, 'the thought that chiefly alarms me is what I see when I consider the great gulf into which I should have to enter and which would swallow me up completely'.[28]

Yet he still felt a responsibility to help; and an opportunity was soon given him. Some high authorities in the Roman Church judged from the ejection of the ministers that Geneva might be open to persuasion to return to the fold. They were mistaken, for the *Artichauds* were in no way orientated towards the Romanist states of France and Savoy but towards the evangelical Bern. Even had there been any hope, they had left their attempt too late; for it was not until March 1539 that Cardinal Jacopo Sadoleto, Archbishop of Carpentras, addressed a letter to the Council calling Geneva back to the faith of its fathers. Sadoleto was a good choice as spokesman, an upright man, a scholar and Biblical commentator, a critic of abuses in the Church. The Council was sufficiently worried to look round for someone with authority to answer him. After Viret had refused, Calvin was asked and wrote off an answer in September. 'It will be a week's work,' he wrote confidently to Farel.[29] Week's work or more, this is one of that brilliant set of writings which emerged from

Portrait of the young Calvin

Painted apparently in the 1540s, this is thought to depict Calvin at about the age of thirty-five, before his troubles in Geneva and his weak health had aged him prematurely.

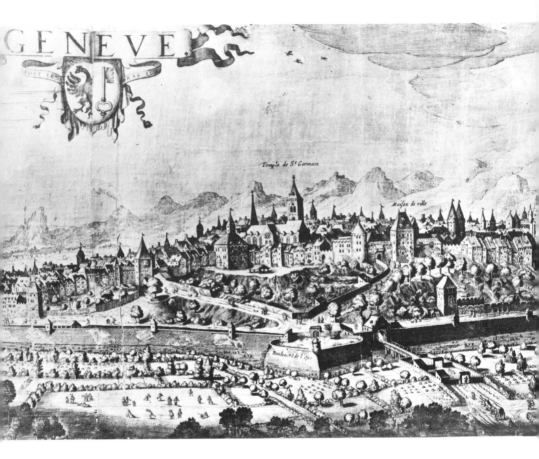

GENEVE.

Temple de St Germain

Maison de ville

Boulevert de l'Oye

Calvin's Geneva

'Imagine, then, a city cramped within strong new defensive walls . . . Geneva is a fortress' (see Ch. 4:2).

Le Collège de Genève

Little changed today from when it was built in 1559 to house the new Academy and College (see Ch. 8:3).

Letter from Calvin to M. de Falais

Calvin's court hand, as evidenced by his letter to Queen Elizabeth of England, is quite elegant. His regular correspondents, however, had to accept letters written in a hurry. This letter is dated *De Genefve ce .5. d'aoust* [1545] and signed *Vostre serviteur, humble frere, et entier amy à iamais Iehan Calvin* (see Ch. 9:2).

IN OMNES PAVLI A-
postoli Epistolas, atque etiam in Epistolam ad Hebræos, item in Canonicas Petri, Iohannis, Iacobi, & Iudæ, quæ etiam Catholicæ vocantur,

IOH. CALVINI COMMENTARII.

Hanc Commentariorum postremam esse recognitionem, ex lectione atque collatione cum prioribus, deprehendet lector.

Oliua Roberti Stephani.

M. D. LVI.

Title-page of the 'Commentaries on the Epistles', 1556

According to the inscriptions, this copy belonged to David Fergusson, a leading Scottish Reformer; it later passed into the possession of the family of his son-in-law, John Row, who was famous minister of Carnock and historian of the Scottish Reformation.

Sermon on Isaiah 30:1–8

The first page of a sermon preached by Calvin on 4 August 1557, taken down in shorthand by Denis Raguenier and written out in full by an unknown scribe (see Ch. 6:3).

A student's sketch

This was apparently dashed off while Calvin was lecturing on the old testament in the Auditoire very near the end of his life. It was done on the end-paper of a book which once belonged to Pierre Viret and more recently to Herminjard. The student is said to have been Jacques Bourgoing.

Calvin in his study

This Dutch engraving of the seventeenth century is, of course, an imaginative reconstruction of the room. Calvin is holding the *Institutio*. Others of his works are on the two tables and the bookshelf.

INSTITVTIO CHRI-

ſtianæ religionis, in libros qua-

tuor nunc primùm digeſta, certíſque diſtinĉta capitibus, ad aptiſſimam
methodum : auĉta etiam tam magna acceſſione vt propemodum opus
nouum haberi poſſit.

IOHANNE CALVINO AVTHORE,

Oliua Roberti Stephani.

GENEVAE.
M. D. LIX.

Title-page of the 'Institutio Christianae religionis', 1559

Many of Calvin's books bore the famous printer's device of the olive tree of Robert Stephanus,
former royal printer in Paris, who fled to Geneva in 1550.

his stay in Strasbourg and which, purely as literature, he never surpassed—in Latin the 1539 *Institutio*, the 1540 *Commentary on Romans*, and this letter to Sadoleto; in French the 1541 *Institutes*, one of the major influences in the evolution of the language from medieval to modern French, and the *Petit traicté de la Cène* of 1541. The reply to Sadoleto is a masterpiece of the lawyer's art, a defence which is an indictment of the prosecution. With high seriousness and passionate conviction (how ever could Carew Hunt call its language 'unemotional and austere'?) he clears the Evangelicals of the charges of heresy and schism and in his turn recalls the Cardinal-archbishop to the faith of the fathers and apostles of the Church.

In the February elections of 1540, two of the Syndics were *Artichauds*, two *Guillermins*. The two former were Claude Richardet and Jean Philippe, one of the foremost architects of Geneva's political freedom. At a festival in the following June, these two started or became involved in a brawl, in which Jean Philippe killed a young man. He was executed within a day. Richardet sought to escape by climbing from a window, slipped and was killed. The wider significance of this startling event is that the Syndics responsible for the expulsion of the ministers, Jean Philippe, Claude Richardet, Jean Lullin, and Ami de Chapeaurouge, were all gone. The first two had died in disgrace, the others had been two of those disobedient delegates on whom the death penalty had been pronounced. Not long after this, one of the ministers, Morand, could not put up with Geneva any longer and left, to be followed in September by his colleague Marcourt.

Geneva was now quite humbled. It was realized that the policy of 1538 had been a disaster politically and ecclesiastically. It was believed that there was only one man who could put things to right, and that man Jean Calvin. The problem, of course, was how to get him. On 21 September 1540 the Council instructed one of its members, Ami Perrin, to devise some method of recalling him. Two embassies were sent to wait on him. At Strasbourg they found he had gone to the colloquy between Romanists and Evangelicals at Worms, whither they had to follow him. They had no success, for the Strasbourg authorities had urged him to promise nothing definite. All that happened was that Calvin got very upset: 'Tears flowed faster than words. Twice they so interrupted what I was saying that I had to withdraw for a time.' [30] Yet it seems that, if Strasbourg would release him, he was ready to go. In theory this had always been so. The previous September he had written to Sadoleto: 'Although I am for the present relieved of the charge of the Church of Geneva, this circumstance ought not to prevent me from embracing it with paternal affection. For God, when he charged me with it, bound me to be faithful to it for ever.' [31]

Yet he could not restrain his horror at the thought of again subjecting himself to the indignities, insults and even danger that had been his lot: 'Rather would I submit to death a hundred times than to that cross on which I had to perish daily a thousand times over.' [32] In another letter to Farel he wrote more fully:

Whenever I call to mind the wretchedness of my life there, how can it not be but that my very soul must shudder at any proposal for my return? I will not mention the anxiety by which we were continually tossed up and down and driven to and fro from the time I was appointed your colleague . . . When I remember by what torture my conscience was racked at that time, and with how much anxiety it was continually boiling over, forgive me if I dread the place as having about it something of a fatality in my case. You yourself, with God, are my best witness that no lesser tie could have held me there so long, save that I dared not throw off the yoke of my calling, which I was convinced had been laid on me by the Lord. Therefore, so long as I was bound hand and foot, I preferred to suffer to that extreme rather than for a moment to listen to the thoughts that were apt to come into my mind of moving elsewhere, thoughts which often stole in upon me unawares. But now that by the favour of God I am delivered, who will not excuse me if I am unwilling to plunge again into the gulf and whirlpool which I know to be so dangerous and destructive? [33]

In the light of such strong feelings, it is remarkable that he can also write: 'I am utterly unable to arrive at any settled determination, save that I am prepared to follow entirely the Lord's calling as soon as he shall have made it plain to me.' [34] But the most he will consent to do is to visit Geneva with Bucer after the Colloquy is over. Let the Council, he suggests, ask Bern to permit Monsieur Pierre Viret, who is well known to them, to take charge for a time. When he himself comes with Bucer, something more permanent can be arranged.[35] This plan was approved, and Viret was seconded to Geneva for six months.

The negotiations went on, Geneva pressing for his speedy return, his friends urging him with degrees of insistence, Strasbourg pulling in the other direction, Calvin willing, uncertain, apprehensive, distrusting his own judgment. One thing he was determined on. He did not want any more misunderstandings. Geneva had genuinely to want him, to understand that to have him would be to have what he stood for, a Church governed by the Word of God and the system of discipline that he had tried to enforce before. If they did not want that, then he did not want to return. Nevertheless, in a courteous and friendly letter to the Council, he went out of his way to save their face.

By the summer of 1541 the idea of merely paying a visit with Bucer had been dropped. Instead it was agreed that Strasbourg should lend Calvin to Geneva for six months. On these terms he returned. His style of entry into the city was very different from that of five years before as a refugee. Now an escort was sent to accompany him, and a waggon despatched to Strasbourg for his family. One of the better houses in the rue des Chanoines was allowed to him furnished, and he was to be given an adequate stipend of five hundred florins plus twelve strikes of corn and two casks of wine. On Tuesday, 13 September 1541 he entered Geneva. In the *Registres* we read:

M. Iehan Calvin, minister of the Gospel. The same has arrived from Strasbourg, and has delivered letters from Strasbourg and from the pastors there, as well as from Basel; these have been read. Afterwards he made, at some length, his excuses for his delay in coming. That done, he asked that the Church be set in order, and a memorandum was drawn up to this effect, and that councillors should be elected to consider this. And as for him, he offered himself to be always the servant of Geneva.[36]

Chapter 6

The Genevan Church Settlement

1. THE ORDONNANCES

In response to Calvin's statement that 'the Church could not hold together unless a settled government were agreed on, such as is prescribed to us in the Word of God and as was in use in the early Church',[1] the Genevan Council agreed at once that ordinances 'for the ordering of the Christian religion' should be drafted. The work of the committee of councillors and ministers was finished in about a fortnight; but then followed the more lengthy process of examination and revision, first by the *Little Council*, then by the *Two Hundred*, and finally by the *General Council*. At last on 20 November the *Ordonnances ecclesiastiques* passed into law. In essence the original draft had been accepted, but the alterations made were of some significance for the future.

The *Ordonnances*, intended to legislate for the whole of Church life, were composed principally in terms of ministerial function. A well-ordered Church lives under the supervision of the four orders of pastors, doctors, elders, and deacons. The task of the Church is to preach the Gospel and administer the Sacraments, to teach believers the faith, to train them in obedience, and to care for the afflicted. Broadly, each of these tasks belongs to each of the offices, although there will be some overlapping. A pastor may also be qualified to teach; he will certainly be involved in the exercise of discipline and in the care of the afflicted. But his essential task is to preach the Word of God, to administer the Sacraments, and to assist in the exercise of discipline. A pastor is instituted to his office by the election of the company of pastors and its confirmation by the Council. It is the Council which accepts him and gives him his certificate to execute his office. He swears an oath that he will faithfully serve God, that he will defend and be loyal to the Ecclesiastical Ordinances, that he will uphold the honour of the *Seigneurie* and the city, and that he will obey the duly constituted laws of Geneva, with the proviso 'so long as I be not at all hindered from rendering to God the service which in my vocation I owe him'.[2] Pastors are to meet weekly for study of the Scriptures, and quarterly for mutual criticism of faults. For more serious faults (of which a representative list follows) the delinquent is to be examined by his colleagues and if found guilty reported to the Council who, if the case is proved, shall depose him. In its passage through the Councils this part of the *Ordonnances* was revised to make it clear that ministers are subject to civil law and that 'the final sentence of punishment is to be reserved to the *Seigneurie*'.[3]

The practical details of the Church services are settled. On Sundays there are to be sermons in each of the three parish churches, Saint Pierre, la Madeleine, and Saint Gervais, at dawn and at nine o'clock, with another at three o'clock in Saint Pierre and Saint Gervais. The children's catechism class is at midday in each of the three churches. On Mondays, Wednesdays, and Fridays there are to be sermons in the three parishes—the Council making an alteration to the effect that they were to be consecutive, no doubt so that, if there were a shortage of clergy, the same minister could take more than one service. It was thought that the work in Geneva demanded five ministers with three assistants. As far as possible, parish boundaries should be respected, Saint Gervais and la Madeleine having their existing boundaries and Saint Pierre, a new parish, embracing what had formerly been Saint Germain, Saint Cross, Nôtre Dame-la-Neuve, and Saint Legier.

The task of the doctors of the Church is to instruct believers in true doctrine and to expel errors. So far as theology proper goes, there are to be two professors, one to expound the Old and one the New Testament. But theology depends on the ancillary disciplines, 'the languages and humanities'. For the teaching of these a school-master and his assistants must be appointed in the boys' school and the separate girls' school.

The elders, who are laymen, are responsible for the machinery of discipline. They are to be twelve in number, all chosen from the Councils, two from the *Little Council*, four from the *Sixty*, and six from the *Two Hundred*; some shall come from each quarter of the city. They are to be nominated by the *Little Council* in conference with the ministers and presented for acceptance to the *Two Hundred*. If in office they prove unsuitable, they may be changed at the end of the year; otherwise it is better if they continue longer and use the experience they have gained. The elders and the ministers form the *Consistoire*, the Consistory court, responsible for discipline. It will be seen that there was a majority of laymen over the ministers. The President was the elected Syndic, who, moreover, carried his official bâton of office until 1560. Nevertheless, the *Consistoire* was a Church and not a civil court.

The *Consistoire* is to meet every Thursday. Having no authority to summon persons before them, those whom the *Seigneurie* wish to be admonished are to be summoned by an officer of the Council. Offenders who 'listen to reason' are to be dismissed. The stubborn are to be admonished several times—that is, on several occasions. If they remain unrepentant, they are to be forbidden access to the Lord's Supper and reported to the Council. Non-attendance at Church for obviously inadequate reasons and contempt of Church order merit admonition. Obstinacy after three admonitions is to be met by excommunication and a report to the Council. But it is emphasized that all this should be done with moderation, for the corrections 'are only medicines for bringing back sinners to our Lord'.[4]

At this point the Councils added an article to the effect that the ministers had no civil jurisdiction and that the *Consistoire* was not to usurp the authority of the *Seigneurie*. It ended: 'Even where there will be need to impose punishment or to constrain parties, the ministers with the *Consistoire* having heard the parties and used such remonstrances and admonitions as are good, are to report the whole matter to the Council, which in its turn will advise sentence and judgment according to the needs of the case.'[5] If this clause referred to excommunication, it is hard to see why it was not used later to settle the controversy. The judgments of 18 September 1553 and 22–4 January 1555 seem to make clear that the punishment imposed was for the breach of civil law and was not excommunication.

As for the fourth order, Calvin understood the New Testament diaconate purely in reference to the care of the poor and needy. The *Ordonnances* provide for two classes of deacons, an administrative and an executive. The former are to act as guardians and, so to say, charity commissioners, the latter actually dispensing relief to the poor and tending the sick in hospital.

Once again the desire to have the Lord's Supper celebrated monthly is set aside by the Council in favour of four times a year; Easter, Whitsun, the first Sunday in September, and Christmas. Notice of the celebration is to be given on the previous Sunday, but it is not expressly enjoined that those who intend to communicate shall notify the minister.

This, then, was the Genevan settlement of religion. The story of Calvin's work in Geneva is the relation of how he performed his part in it, under what conditions, against what opposition, and, if that can be measured, with what success. But we must take care not to commit the common error of treating the practice and enforcement of discipline as his chief or almost only work. Discipline was but one part of the settlement. Nor, strictly speaking, did it exist in its own right; it was designed to make practically and personally effective the preaching of the Gospel and administering of the Sacraments of the Gospel.

2. THE CHURCH AT WORSHIP

Over one person Calvin now determined that he would exercise control. This was himself. He had been blamed for being too severe, too unaccommodating. He acknowledged the reproof and set himself to correct the fault. So well did he think that he had learnt, that for the same fault he could even in his turn reprove Farel, who had got on the wrong side of his congregation in Neuchâtel.[6] To Oswald Myconius at Basel he was able to report that his gentleness was winning him friends:

They all know by experience the pleasant and human character of Viret. I am in no way more harsh, at any rate in this matter. Perhaps you will hardly believe this, but it is true all the same. I value the public peace and hearty concord among ourselves so highly that I restrain myself. Even our opponents have to give me this credit. And this feeling prevails to such an extent that day by day those who were once open enemies have become friends. Others I conciliate by courtesy, and I feel that I have been successful in some measure—although not everywhere and always.[7]

His chief trouble came not from opponents but from colleagues. He begged Bern that Viret be allowed to stay permanently, but gained for him only a poor six months' extension of his leave of absence. Farel, also invited, considered he should stay in Neuchâtel. 'Our other colleagues,' Calvin wrote to Myconius, 'are a hindrance rather than a help to me. They are rude and self-conceited, with no zeal and less learning. Worst of all, I cannot trust them, much as I wish to, for they show their alienation from us in many ways and give hardly any signs of a sincere and trustworthy disposition.'[8] But a little later he acknowledged that they are passable, although one of them 'has a confused manner of delivery, and even were he to pay more attention to correct and distinct utterance, his meaning would still be obscure'.[9] The list of intolerable and tolerable faults in a minister given in the *Ordonnances* shows that Calvin was far from extreme in his demands. Some of his early colleagues were grossly unsuitable in their morals; few of them put their office before themselves. During the bad plagues of 1542 and 1543 none but Pierre Blanchet would agree to minister in the isolation hospital. Only slowly and as the number of evangelical refugees from France increased did Calvin manage to build up a faithful pastorate.

There were difficulties, too, with the regent of the Collège. On its reopening, Mathurin Cordier had been invited to return and take the post. He, perhaps from fear to experience again the smarts of Geneva to which he had urged Calvin to submit, pleaded his duty in Lausanne. One of Calvin's *pensionnaires* from Strasbourg was therefore appointed, Sebastian Castellio, an able scholar and a good school-master. Some trouble arising about the salary, he resigned, but was soon again appointed. He quarrelled about his French translation of the New Testament with Calvin, who criticized certain renderings. Would Calvin go through it thoroughly with Castellio? No, he was too busy to make special appointments, but he would look through it on his own as his time permitted. Castellio did not like this and began to grumble against Calvin behind his back. A while after, he applied to be admitted to the pastorate, but was rejected on two grounds; the first his rejection of the figurative interpretation of the clause in the Creed, 'he descended into hell'; the second his opinion of the Song of Songs as a lascivious and obscene poem.[10] On this rebuff he again resigned from the Collège, and went to Lausanne with a friendly letter of recommendation from Calvin.[11] But the Bernese authorities had no work for him and he returned to Geneva. He could not let well alone. At the *Congrégation* on 29 May 1544 he joined in the discussion by launching an incredible attack on his former colleagues. They looked only to their own interests, they were impatient, drunken, whore-mongers, persecutors, et cetera. Calvin complained to the Syndics and Castellio had to leave Geneva.

In 1542 was published the Geneva service book, *La Manyere de faire prieres*—'The manner of praying in the French Churches, both before the preaching and after, together with French Psalms and Canticles sung in the said Churches; followed by the order and form of administering the Sacraments of Baptism and the Holy Supper of our Lord Jesus Christ, of Espousal and confirming the marriage before the congregation of the faithful, with the services both of Baptism and of the Supper. The whole according to the Word of our Lord'. The subtitle ran: 'The Form of Ecclesiastical Prayers and Hymns, with the Manner of Administering the Sacraments and Celebrating marriage, according to the custom of the ancient Church'. And on the title page, three texts: 'Teach and admonish one another in psalms, in praises, and in spiritual songs with grace. Singing to the Lord in your heart'; 'Sing to the Lord a new song, and let his praise be heard in the congregation of the *debonnaires*'; 'Let all who have breath praise the Lord'. We have given the title page at length because it reflects the spirit of the Genevan liturgy—the desire to reproduce in sixteenth-century form the worship of Scripture and the early Church, the emphasis on preaching and praise, its cheerfulness and positive quality. The prefatory *Epistle to the Reader* expresses the unity of the Church in worship and the participation of the whole congregation. It therefore dwells chiefly on three elements: that the service be conducted in the language of the people, that the Sacraments, 'the visible words', need to be explained, and that there should be congregational singing.

Before we take up this last point, we may see the order of an ordinary Sunday morning service. The minister began with a set confession of sin in the name of the congregation, adding some verses of Scripture as he thought good, and then pronouncing the absolution in the form: 'To all those who in this way repent and seek Jesus Christ for their salvation, I pronounce absolution in the name of the Father, and of the Son, and of the Holy Spirit. Amen.' Hereupon the congregation sang the first four commandments and the minister prayed that these laws might be 'written in our hearts so that we may seek only to serve and obey thee'. The rest of the commandments were sung as the minister entered the pulpit. He prefaced his sermon with the set prayer leading into the Lord's Prayer. Before the sermon began, however, the congregation sang a psalm and the minister prayed an extemporary prayer. After the sermon an extemporary bidding prayer (which for Calvin began: 'Now let us fall down before the majesty of our good God, praying him that he will give his grace not only to us but also to all peoples and nations of the earth . . .') led into the long prayer beginning 'Almighty God, heavenly

Father, thou hast promised to hear our requests that we make to thee in the name of thy Son Jesus Christ, the well-beloved, our Lord', and praying for rulers, for pastors and the Church, for the salvation of all men, for those in affliction and especially for the persecuted under the Papacy, and for the salvation and sanctification of our own souls. The minister then gave a short explanation of the Lord's Prayer, and, after the singing of another psalm, dismissed the congregation with the Aaronic blessing. Apart from the singing and the sermon, the service was short, occupying less than a quarter of an hour.

Nothing is more characteristic of Reformation theology and few parts of Reformation Church activity have been so neglected as the congregational singing. It was far from being a pleasant element introduced rather inconsistently into a service otherwise ruled by a sombre view of life. We have already seen that in 1537 one of the four foundations for the reform of the Church was congregational singing. We have seen that in Strasbourg Calvin introduced singing into the French Church. We have seen that it was demanded by the *Ordonnances*. We have seen in effect that Calvin placed singing at the heart of his theology of the Church. The reason is not far to seek. To put it with the utmost simplicity: The Church is the place where the Gospel is preached; Gospel is good news; good news makes people happy; happy people sing. But then, too, unhappy people may sing to cheer themselves up—'Art thou weary? music will charm thee'. In the remarkable second half of the *Epistle to the Reader* Calvin justifies his introduction of congregational singing.

He can easily justify it from early Church practice, but this is not enough. He takes his stand on the influence of music in general which practically everyone feels: 'Among other things which recreate man and give him pleasure [*volupté*!], music is either the first or at least one of the principal; and we should reckon it a gift of God intended for this use.' [12] 'There is, as Plato has wisely considered, hardly anything in the world which can turn or move men's ways in this or that direction. And in fact we experience that it has a great secret and almost incredible virtue to move hearts in one way or another.' [13] (No one, we may note as a side-light on Calvin's character, could have written this who had not himself felt it.) This God-given force he wishes to restore to its true end in the worship of God, rescuing it from its perversion to the service of aimlessness and uncleanness. The old Church fathers had often attacked the men of their day for their unchaste and immodest songs which, not without cause, they reckoned a deadly and satanic poison to corrupt the world. As now we remember Calvin's determined stand against the prevalent dissolute songs in Geneva we see that it is not only a matter of public morality, that chaste ears be not offended; far more is it a liberation of the God-given art from the service of God's enemy to whom it does not belong. In Church worship, Christians stand in the presence of God and his angels, and, as

Chrysostom said, singing is like associating with the angels. But how dead and cold worship can be! Singing is 'like a spur to incite us to pray to and to praise God, to meditate on his works, that we may love, fear, honour, and glorify him'.[14] And the best songs are the psalms, for the Holy Spirit himself has composed them. 'When we sing them, we are certain that God is putting words in our mouth and they are singing in us to exalt his glory.'[15] Singing, moreover, is not only a matter of sound but also of understanding. Here is the difference, as Augustine says, between birds and men. A linnet, a nightingale, a popinjay, will sing well, but without understanding, but 'the gift of man is to sing knowing what he says'.[16] As for the music, it should not be light and flighty like secular music but should have *pois et maiesté*, weight and majesty, agreeable to its subject and fit for singing in church. Hence, let us sing 'these divine and heavenly canticles with good King David'.[17]

The psalms used at Strasbourg were published in 1539: *Aulcuns pseaulmes et cantiques mys en chant*—'Some psalms and canticles arranged for singing'. This contained nineteen psalms, the *Nunc dimittis*, the Ten Commandments, and the *Credo*. Twelve of the psalms were adaptations from an unpublished collection by Clément Marot. The rest of the psalter seems to have been the work of Calvin himself. The origin of the tunes, printed only as the melody line, has not been traced, but it is thought that Mathias Greiter of Strasbourg at least compiled and arranged them. From the end of 1542 Clément Marot was a refugee in Geneva. It was not the place for him and he did not stay long; but he wrote another nineteen metrical psalms, some of which Calvin substituted in the 1543 Psalter for his own inferior versions. Of equal value with Marot was another refugee, Louis Bourgeois, who lived and taught music in Geneva for sixteen years from 1541. How derivative his hymn tunes are it is very hard to say, but certainly as they came from him they admirably fulfilled Calvin's demand for weight and majesty. Some have taken their place in modern hymn-books, and very fine they are, even in their edited harmonies in *Hymns Ancient and Modern*; is not the Old Hundredth unsurpassed among hymn tunes? Later came friction between the composer and Calvin, who disliked harmony in congregational singing, no doubt as detracting from simplicity: 'All that is needed in the praise of God is a pure and simple modulation of the voice.' Bourgeois' harmonized Psalter had therefore to be printed in Lyon instead of Geneva.

Besides the regular and the occasional church services (of which Calvin took his share—in the decade 1550-9, for example, he celebrated about two hundred and seventy weddings and about fifty baptisms), the ministers were to visit the sick and the prisoners. The *Ordonnances* ruled that 'no one is to be totally confined to bed for three days without informing the minister'.[18] No other regular visiting was demanded, but doubtless the ministers visited those in trouble of one sort and another. Saturday after dinner was set aside for the visiting of the prisoners. On Thursdays the *Consistoire* met for the administration of discipline, and on Fridays the ministers for what came to be called the *Congrégation*, a Bible study at which a passage of Scripture was expounded by a minister and then discussed by the assembly. The Venerable Company of Pastors also met quarterly for mutual frank and loving self-criticism. In the Church, as Calvin conceived it, every man helped every other man. If in Christ Jesus all believers are united, then a private believer is a contradiction in terms. Not only are the blessings and the virtues given for the common good, but the faults and the weaknesses concern the other members of the Body. There was to be no hypocrisy of pretending to be other than a sinner, no dissembling or cloaking of sins; but, just as God is completely honest with men, and men must be honest with God, so also believer with believer courageously honest and open. The quarterly meeting was a little day of judgment when, flattery and convention laid aside, each man saw himself through the eyes of his fellows and, if he were wise, harboured no resentment but knew the uniquely joyful release of voluntary humiliation.

3. CALVIN THE PREACHER

The first part of the office of the pastor, say the *Ordonnances*, is 'to proclaim the Word of God, to instruct, admonish, exhort and censure, both in public and in private'.[19] The reason for the great weight that the Reformers laid on preaching was not educational or social but theological. It was not that preaching, with pamphleteering, was the current medium for propaganda, although at times no doubt it was used for that purpose. Nor was it merely that preaching was the most effective means for educating a community into new ideas. The force that drives the machinery of preaching is theological. The real reason is to be found in the Biblical concept of the Word of God.

'The Word of God' so easily becomes a catch-phrase of weak and uncertain meaning that we have to remind ourselves that for the Reformers it had enormous significance, fresh, living, explosive. 'The Word of God' meant 'the Word that God himself speaks'. It was the Word of God that created the universe; that is, God spoke and what he said called into being that which had not been. It was by his Word that God in his free majesty encountered man. 'The Word' was a synonym for the Son of God who became man and who lived among men as the living declaration of God's eternal will to man. 'The Word' was also the creative utterance of the Word made flesh; his words brought Lazarus again from the dead; his words give life to the world; his words are cleansing; his words will judge men at the last day. But then, as the Reformers read the Acts of the Apostles and the Epistles, they perceived that the preaching of the apostles and evangelists was also called 'the Word of God' or 'the Word of the Lord'. So that it was necessary to regard the terms 'Gospel', 'preaching', and 'Word of God' as synonymous.

But what made the word of the New Testament preachers into the Word of God? The answer is not quite simple. On the one hand, their word was the Word of God in that it was the faithful interpretation of the being and activity of the Word of God, Jesus Christ. More than that, however, as that faithful interpretation it was a continuation of the activity of the Word of God, Jesus Christ; but a continuation in the sense that he himself, Jesus Christ, the Word of God, continued to work. The virtue lay, not in the apostles, but in the Word of God. Hence it was not with the apostles alone that the preaching of the Gospel was the Word of God: the Gospel would be the Word of God whoever proclaimed it. The necessary condition always is that the preaching shall be the faithful interpretation of the being and activity of the Word made flesh. It is necessary that preachers shall not 'put forward their own dreams and fancies, but hand on faithfully what they themselves have received'.[20] In the Holy Scriptures and in the proclamation that faithfully interprets the Holy Scriptures, God himself speaks, declaring his existence, his purpose, his will, redemptively revealing man to himself as the creature of God, as the sinner, as the redeemed. And what is more, God does not speak to man apart from the message of the Scriptures. This being so, how could the Reformers fail to place preaching at the forefront of their pastoral work?

Calvin will very frequently use the most definite language to assert that the preaching of the Gospel is the Word of God. It is as if the congregation 'heard the very words pronounced by God himself'.[21] A man 'preaches so that God may speak to us by the mouth of a man'.[22] 'And what is the mouth of God? It is a declaration that he makes to us of his will, when he speaks to us by his ministers'.[23] If we have a zeal to serve and honour God, and would desire peaceably that our Lord should have his royal throne in the midst of us, if we would be his people and dwell under his protection, if we desire to be builded up in him, and joined to him, and persevere in him to the end, if (in brief) we desire salvation, we must learn to be humble disciples to receive the doctrine of the Gospel and to hear the pastors whom he has sent to us, as if Jesus Christ himself spoke to us in person.[24] He was careful to make the necessary distinction between the preacher and the Word of God. The preacher is not God, but an envoy sent by God. In himself he is nothing. All his authority and all the justification for his preaching lies in his ambassadorship, that is to say, in the two facts that God has called him to preach and that he preaches only what God in Holy Scripture commands him to preach. When, however, these two conditions are fulfilled, the preacher cannot retreat from the claim that the Gospel which he preaches is the Word of God and as such demands the complete obedience of himself and his congregation.

Preaching is also bound formally to Scripture, and that so closely that it must always be exposition of Scripture. This can be achieved by preaching on isolated passages like the Epistles and Gospels for the Church year. Following the practice of many of the Church fathers, but even more extensively, Calvin preached through whole books of the Bible Sunday after Sunday or day after day. Indeed, to such a length did he carry this that as he wrote in a letter soon after his return to Geneva in 1541, on his first Sunday in Saint Pierre he continued from the place where he had stopped on Easter Day 1538, 'by which I indicated that I had interrupted my office of preaching for a time rather than that I had given it up entirely'.[25]

At first he preached, we must assume, twice on Sundays and once on every Monday, Wednesday, and Friday. But in the autumn of 1542 some who appreciated his preaching urged him to preach more frequently, 'which I have already commenced and shall endeavour to do until the others have become more acceptable to the people'.[26] But this proved too heavy a burden and after two months the Council released him from preaching more than once a Sunday.[27] In October 1549, however, sermons were ordered for every day and from now he usually preached on every day of alternate weeks as well as twice on Sundays.

His custom was to expound the Old Testament on weekdays, the New on Sundays, although sometimes he gave up Sunday afternoons to psalms. We have little evidence as to what books he expounded or even what individual sermons he preached before 1549. Certainly he was preaching through Hebrews until August 1549, and it would therefore seem that he began that book in 1548. At some time probably between 1546 and 1548 he was expounding on Sunday afternoons the metricized psalms in the service book. Since he did not preach on Romans, St John's Gospel, Philippians, Colossians, and the Catholic Epistles after 1549, we may conjecture that he preached on them earlier. More than one secretary tried to take down his sermons, but none of them was competent to do more than note the main headings.

The significance of the year 1549, which continually crops up in this connection, is that this was the year in which the *Compagnie des étrangers*, the society of refugees, who generally prized his ministry in a way that many of the Genevese did not, undertook to support a professional scribe whose whole work would be the taking down and transcribing of his sermons (or at least, seeing that they were transcribed), and delivering them to the charge of the deacons. Few preachers have been so handsomely complimented. The *Compagnie* was fortunate in finding a Frenchman called Denis Raguenier, who had learnt or evolved a remarkable system of shorthand which enabled him to write down these sermons of about six thousand words each, with a quill pen and ink, in an unheated church winter and summer, and what is more for the better part of an hour at a time. Calvin himself did not revise the sermons or have any hand in them after they were preached. From the time that Raguenier began his work, all the sermons were recorded, transcribed and bound in sets.[28]

And so we can trace him preaching on Sundays with one hundred and eighty-nine sermons on the Acts between 1549 and 1554, a shorter series on some of the Pauline letters between 1554 and 1558, and the sixty-five on the Harmony of the Gospels between 1559 and 1564. During this time the week-days saw series on Jeremiah and Lamentations (up to 1550), on the Minor Prophets and Daniel (1550–2), the one hundred and seventy-four on Ezekiel (1552–4), the one hundred and fifty-nine on Job (1554–5), the two hundred on Deuteronomy (1555–6), the three hundred and forty-two on Isaiah (1556–9), one hundred and twenty-three on Genesis (1559–61), a short set on Judges (1561), one hundred and seven on I Samuel and eighty-seven on II Samuel (1561–3) and a set on I Kings (1563–4). Before he smiles at such unusual activity of the pulpit, the reader would do well to ask himself whether he would prefer to listen to the second-hand views on a religion of social ethics, or the ill-digested piety, delivered in slipshod English, that he will hear today in most churches of whatever denomination he may enter, or three hundred and forty-two sermons on the Book of the Prophet Isaiah, sermons born of an infinite passion of faith and a burning sincerity, sermons luminous with theological sense, lively with wit and imagery, showing depths of compassion and the unquenchable joyousness of hope. Those in Geneva who listened Sunday after Sunday, day after day, and did not shut their ears, but were 'instructed, admonished, exhorted, and censured', received a training in Christianity such as had been given to few congregations in Europe since the days of the fathers.

Calvin preached without notes and, it would seem, direct from his Hebrew Old and Greek New Testament. He had little time for immediate preparation, but his close knowledge of the Bible and his wide reading stood always at the command of his memory. Moreover, he had, after all, written commentaries on many of the books he was expounding. Perhaps all his preparation was to refresh his mind and give thought to the application of the passage to the congregation and the situation:

If I should enter the pulpit without deigning to glance at a book, and should frivolously think to myself, 'Oh well, when I preach, God will give me enough to say', and come here without troubling to read or thinking what I ought to declare, and do not carefully consider how I must apply Holy Scripture to the edification of the people, then I should be an arrogant upstart.[29]

The form of his sermons is determined by the exposition. In theory it follows the pattern of explanation of a clause or sentence and its application to the people, sometimes in the context of an immediate situation. In practice, the form is flexible, even loose. It is saved from being rambling by his capacity for keeping to the point and breaking the material up into short sections, usually with some such formula as 'So much for that point', or 'So you see what the prophet [or apostle] meant to say'.

His manner of delivery was lively, passionate, intimate, direct, and clear. This is as much as to say that it is the whole of Calvin. Like many reserved persons, he could forget himself in the pulpit and speak from the heart as easily as in print. He could be furiously and coarsely angry and he could be gentle and compassionate. Now like a judge of the old cast, now like a father or mother. Thus:

And here we see that those who want the Law to be rejected today and spoken of no more, are like dogs and swine. They are like certain vile blackguards who not long ago spewed out their 'Consummatum est' in all their taverns, so that I was forced to resist them very vehemently in my sermons.[30]

And thus:

We see many who have no other reward for following the Gospel than being persecuted, hunted, despoiled of their goods. Some have lost all their possessions, others are kept fast in prisons, and yet others are put cruelly to the flames. Although (I say) many poor believers have had no other recompense for receiving the Gospel, yet the joy spoken of here is more than excellent, and we must learn to repose in the love that our Lord Jesus Christ bears to us, seeing that he wishes to be to us like a father, a saviour, and to have us for his children. All this, then, must sweeten the sadnesses that we have, and we must take courage in the grace and goodness of our Lord Jesus Christ.[31]

His language was clear and easy. He spoke in a way that the Genevese could understand, even, it would seem, to the point of using some of their idiosyncracies of French, some of which may still be encountered today. To clarity of sense and diction he paid great attention, carefully explaining unusual or technical words in the Biblical text. There is a remarkable little passage where he is afraid that the people will confuse two words with similar sounds and so lose his meaning: 'Let us note that the Gospel is like *un van* [a winnowing fan] in two ways. (I do not mean *le vent* which blows, but *un van* to winnow, or a sieve—which many of you will understand better).'[32]

He is also given to enacting racy scenes between himself and an opponent:

'Ho! you can't tell me what to do.'
'My friend, what you are really saying is that you do not want God to reign over you, and you want to abolish the law.'

Or again:

We can see many who are enraged when we correct or threaten them.
'What! Is this the way you teach? We want to be won over by kindness.'
'Do you? Then go to God and learn how he teaches you.'
See how these sensitive souls cannot bear a single reproof to be offered to them. And why?

'Ho! We want to be taught differently from this.'

'Well then, go to the devil's school; he will flatter you well enough to your perdition.' [33]

It would be as impossible to convey the whole of the teaching of the sermons in a short space as it would be to give the teaching of the many books of the Bible which they expound. But it is perhaps necessary in the first place to correct what many people would imagine his preaching to be. The sermons are not severely logical lectures on the sovereignty of God, predestination, providence and Church discipline. Nor are they nothing but attacks on the *Seigneurie* for halfheartedness in supporting the ministry, on the populace for flagrant sin or unveiled contempt of the ministry, on the Papacy for ecclesiastical abuses, or on theological opponents for their stupidity. All these elements will be found in the sermons, but these are not strictly their theme.

Their theme is the theme of Holy Scripture. Thus it is easier to declare what an individual sermon is about than the whole body of sermons. If his text is a passage from Job he will expound and apply that passage. If from Ephesians, then he will expound and apply that passage. He will never commit the contempt of Scripture that prevails today of reading a verse from the Bible and preaching about something quite different. We have already seen that in his commentaries he subjects himself in a remarkable manner to the text of his document, endeavouring and intending to explain the author's meaning. He does the same in his preaching. Although the unity of Scripture is everywhere presupposed, he will let the individual passage speak its own message. His sermons, then, have as many themes as Scripture. But he has himself provided a guideline to the interpretation of the sermons:

As often as we come to the sermon we are taught of the free promises of God, to show us that it is in his pure goodness and mercy that we must entirely repose, that we must not be grounded on our own merits or anything that we can bring on our side, but that God must hold out his hand to us, to commence and accomplish all. And this (as Scripture shows us) is applied to us by our Lord Jesus Christ; and that in such a way that we must seek him entirely . . . and that Jesus Christ alone must be our advocate. That, I say, is shewn us every day. It is also declared to us that God's service does not consist in imagining foolish devotions . . . and that we must serve God in obedience. After, we are shewn that we must sacrifice our hearts and our affections in the first place, and that hypocrisy is detestable to him. All that is daily declared. After, we are shewn how it is we must call upon God. We are shewn to what signs we have been baptized and what is the fruit of our Baptism all the days of our life and even to our death; and why it is that the Supper is administered. All that, then, is declared to us.[34]

In sum, then, the redemption of God in Christ and the believer's life of obedience are the themes that are daily preached in Saint Pierre. All that is negative in the sermons is but the converse of this positive preaching; it does not exist in its own right. Not the threats of perdition, but the promises of eternal life; not the wrath of God, but his goodness and mercy; not the denial of man's merits, but the assertion of Christ's merits; not the attacks on current superstitions, but the urging of obedient service and self-sacrifice; not the rejection of the sacrament of penance, but the preaching of the two glorious Sacraments of the Gospel. This is what Calvin preached throughout his ministry in Geneva.

It was preaching which, for all its liveliness, passion and clarity, made heavy demands on the congregation. In no way were they a passive audience; they were gathered into participation. On the lowest level they had to take the trouble to understand—an effort, we may note in passing, to which may not improbably be attributed much of the intellectual quality among common people that was to characterize 'Calvinist' countries. As Karl Holl wrote:

People today turn up their noses at the many sermons in Geneva and the 'intellectualist' instruction. But we should realize that on this intellectualism depends a good deal of the penetrating power of Calvinism. The Calvinist knows *what* he believes and *why* he believes it.[35]

More than that, there was demanded the participation of faith. The grace that was preached became fruitful when it was believed and accepted. Otherwise it became death-dealing (2 Cor. 2: 16). Certainly, this participation was created by the Holy Spirit. The Gospel preached was a human and physical activity, a man's voice uttering words that were heard and understood by other men. But God in his graciousness gives his Spirit in the preaching of the Word, opens the ears and enlightens the mind to understand what is preached as his own Word, coming from him to loving personal and creative encounter with the hearer. And the first to be obedient, said Calvin, must be the preacher himself: 'It would be better for him to break his neck going up into the pulpit, if he does not take pains to be the first to follow God.'[36] 'I so speak to the congregation that the teaching must first be addressed to myself.'[37] The way in which he treats himself as a member of the congregation is shown by his customary use of 'we' and not 'you'.

In the sermon the congregation was gathered into the participation of worship in the sermon. For the sermon is as much an act of worship as the Eucharist and as central to the Church's service. God speaks; man believes— and rejoices with thanksgiving. The sermon, we might say, is the audible Eucharist, the Lord's Supper the visible Eucharist. Calvin was fond of saying that in the pulpit Christ must preside. The verb is significant, reminding us of the 'president' of the Eucharist in the early Church. Thus Christ, the substance of the Gospel, offers in it his broken body and shed blood. And he leads his people, like the precentor in the choir, says Calvin, in praise and thanksgiving. We should also remember that, if the ideal expressed in the 1537 *Articles* had been put into practice, every daily service in Geneva, with its sermon, would have been a celebration of the Eucharist.

We have given far more space to Calvin's preaching than is customary in lives about him. This is not merely because a large part of his time and energy was devoted to preaching, so that he is not fully seen unless he is seen in the pulpit, but also because it is impossible to do justice to his work in Geneva unless preaching be given the main place. To describe only his struggles over the discipline is to give quite a distorted picture. We may firmly say that none should write on Calvin's discipline who has not studied his preaching and read many of his sermons.

Chapter 7

Opposition to a Godly Society

1. THE OPPOSITION MUSTERS

In Geneva Calvin encountered bitter and prolonged opposition to his work. But it would be wrong to write about his career there predominantly with reference to the opposition. From that it is but a step to presenting him as one of that most unhappy and unpleasant breed, the cantankerous minister who has got across his people, or, no less repulsive, as the tyrant of Geneva. Moreover, the opposition's struggle against Calvin was by no means the most important part of his life. It is of more significance historically and theologically that he wrote his books and preached his sermons than that he had to listen to an uncontrollable woman screaming abuse at him because she could not get her own way. The interest for us in the opposition lies precisely in the fact that it was opposition, that it demonstrates the reaction provoked by his Church polity. It is in this way, as we seek to understand Calvin's theology and practical Church work, that we are brought to consider the activities of the opposition.

The troubles were caused by two factors. The one the undisciplined wilfulness and fear of a strong section of the community. The other that blend of determination, excitability and intelligence that constituted Calvin's character. If God's Word plainly enjoined some principle, it had to be obeyed. The possible evil that might result would either turn out not to be an evil or would be averted. The evil would certainly come if God were disobeyed. What happened to Calvin himself was of no consequence so long as God's will was obeyed. The emblem he used for a signet, of a hand offering a heart, with the motto *Prompte et sincere*, was a true symbol. But to his belief that God had called him to be his ambassador in Geneva add his intellectual pre-eminence above colleagues, councillors, and commoners. Then we have all the stuff of a monarchy—not an absolute monarchy, for he always obeyed the *Seigneurie* and I do not suppose he ever broke a Genevan law in his life—but a concentration of moral and intellectual authority, and the immeasurable power which depends on it, in one man.

The adversaries, concerned for their personal pleasures and liberties, both disliked and feared this authority as a threat against their existence. We know

—we can prove from his writings easily enough—that Calvin was no Malvolio. But to them he was precisely and literally Malvolio, and they foresaw a Geneva where, because he was virtuous, there should be no more cakes and ale. The troubles were not a straightforward conflict between Church and State. Even when they degenerated into something like that, there were always complicating factors involved. Nor was it a direct national struggle between patriots and aliens. This was one of the persistent battle slogans; but it was the patriots who sought foreign domination or at least influence, the alien who ensured the independence of Geneva, even if the Geneva of an intermixed race. Nor was it an attempt by the Church to gain freedom of speech or freedom of worship. Sometimes the Council or an individual had to be warned against infringing the freedom, but the freedom itself was already sufficiently guaranteed.

In 1543, the question of the right of excommunication had been raised between the Council and the *Consistoire*. The Syndic who presided claimed it for the Council. Calvin objected in his excitable manner that they would have to kill or banish him first. Before the Syndics he fully explained his position, and 'without any difficulty I have got what I asked for'.[1] But his hint to Viret that there had been an intrigue of the disaffected behind this bears the stamp of truth. It is inconceivable that if Calvin, the most lucid writer in Europe, candidly explained his concept of discipline the Syndics would fail to understand him. It would therefore seem that the *Seigneurie* accepted that Calvin's view of the *Ordonnances* was the correct one and that this was the law of Geneva.

About 1545 or 1546 the uncoordinated opposition began to coalesce into a party. The name of Libertine which became attached to them describes them well. They could not endure the yoke of a discipline that was exercised consistently and without favour to riches or rank. Their motive was not political in the sense that they were opposing to one form of Church government a responsible alternative. It was, however, political in that they were attempting to overturn Genevan law relating to Church order. It would be far from the truth to regard them as lofty-minded citizens concerned with creating a viable relationship between Church and State.

The nucleus of the party consisted of some few inter-related families; the Favres, the Bertheliers, the Vandels, the Septs. Many of them were members of one or the other Council; some served their time as Syndics. The wealthy merchant François Favre, now a man in his sixties, his son Gaspard, and his daughter Françoise (to Calvin, Penthesilea, queen of the Amazons) were for a time the centre of annoyance. When peace had been made with them, the two Bertheliers, Philibert and François-Daniel, took their place. These were nephews of Pierre Vandel, an attorney and a Syndic in 1548 and 1552. They were the centre of a dissolute group ready for any mischief who called themselves *les enfants de Genève*, true blue sons of the republic. The sort of fellow that Philibert Berthelier was will be seen from the answer he gave Calvin after they had tried to interrupt his preaching by exaggerated fits of coughing. When Calvin remonstrated to the Council, Berthelier coarsely replied that if he stopped them coughing, 'nous peterons et roterons'.[2] The Sept brothers, Balthasar and Michel the younger, were related to the Favres by marriage, as was also the foremost member of the group, Ami Perrin. Perrin it was who had sheltered the preachers from the mob in the early days of the reform. Perrin it was who had been sent to escort Calvin back to Geneva. Perrin was one of the committee responsible for drawing up the *Ordonnances*. He was not only several times Syndic but also Captain-General, that is, commander of the Civic Guard. And Perrin was not only related to the Septs but had married Françoise Favre. These family connections drew him away from Calvin; his great ambition ('our comic Caesar' in Calvin's phrase) and his undoubted abilities put him at the head of the opposition. But he was a man too big for his size and in the end he showed that he lacked, not only political sense, but also the decision that might have brought him success.

The Ameaux affair in 1546 reveals how the opposition was strong enough in the Councils to attack Calvin obliquely but not strong enough to withstand his counter-attack. Ameaux, who had been in trouble with the *Consistoire*, vented his feelings by calling Calvin a bad man, a mere Picard, who preached false doctrine. He was arrested, tried by the *Little Council*, and sentenced to pay a fine of sixty crowns and to make public acknowledgment of his fault. But when the case went to the *Two Hundred* for ratification, they reduced the sentence to Ameaux' making an apology to Calvin before them. Calvin would have none of this; until Ameaux had made suitable reparation for his insult against the name of God (for he had said that the Word of God was false doctrine), Calvin would not enter the pulpit again. Near riot was excited. The *Two Hundred* gave way and Ameaux was sentenced to make expiation by parading through the city in his shirt and carrying a torch, kneeling at certain places and begging God for pardon.

A few months later Perrin moved into open opposition. In April 1546 his wife was cited before the *Consistoire* on a charge of having danced, a breach of Genevan law. This was at a party attended by many of the notables of Geneva. It turned out also that, among others, Ami Perrin had offended, as had the current president of the *Consistoire*, Amblard Corne. They were all imprisoned. Corne accepted the punishment meekly and was restored. Perrin, however, pretended that the story was untrue and would not even attend the *Consistoire* when summoned. Calvin wrote him a letter which left him in no doubt of his intentions. He was, he said, sorry that Perrin had not come to the *Consistoire*, for it would have afforded an opportunity of thrashing the whole matter out with him and Corne. If impartiality is a principle of law, partiality certainly cannot be tolerated in the Church. Perrin should know Calvin's aims and character by now: 'I am one who has the law of my heavenly

Master so much at heart that I will not be moved from asserting it with a good conscience for the sake of any man living.' He was not unmindful of Perrin's good name and his position; it was precisely that good name and authority that he was striving to maintain. People were saying, indeed it was a saying that had originated from Perrin's own wife, that these things ran in a seven-year cycle and this was the seventh year (more or less!) since he and Farel had been banished. Such talk held no terrors for one who 'did not return to Geneva for the sake of leisure or gain and who would not mind having to leave'. Perrin should therefore understand that Calvin was going to do what he had said he would do. He wished above all to make him realize that he ought to devote himself to 'the primary virtue of obeying God and maintaining good order in the community and the polity of the Church'.[3] Perrin seems not to have been unmoved by this letter, for he behaved quietly and humbly before the *Consistoire* in May.

This year saw also three affairs of interest to the social historian. The first concerned the taverns. It would seem that the law was not only levelled against the evil of drunkenness but was also positive in character, an attempt to penetrate with a Christian spirit this area too of Genevan life. It might be termed, therefore, the sanctification of the tavern. The many taverns, to give a polite name to these wineshops, were closed and in their place were opened five *abbayes*. (The curious name possibly means a club.) They were to be run not merely as respectable but as religious public houses. They were to be non-profit making. Everyone was to say grace before and after eating and drinking. There was to be a French Bible on the premises. Swearing, slandering, and dancing were forbidden. Psalms might be sung and anyone so moved might address the rest of the company for their edification. The *abbayes* did not last long and the taverns were soon back in force. But the (to our modern view) ingenuousness of this experiment should not make us forget the similar sanctification of fellowship in some Puritan regiments in seventeenth-century England, and the good company and good lessons given to Christian and later to Christiana and her little band in the House of the Interpreter.

The second concerned the drama. After a passion play had been successfully presented soon after Easter, a group of players asked permission to perform 'les actes des appostres pour leddiffication du peuple'. The Council asked Calvin to pronounce on the soundness of the piece. He declared it sound and godly but said that the ministers thought it should not be performed just now, although they would not oppose it. It was, however, licensed, and the minister Abel Poupin was entrusted with the organization. The Council at the same time forbade (without, it seems, consulting the ministers) a performance of 'la bataille des puissances de harcules et aultres anticques',[4] thus no doubt disappointing some local Bottom who 'could play Ercles rarely, or a part to tear a cat in, to make all split'. However, when 'les actes des appostres' was put on, it drew fierce pulpit invective from the minister

Michel Cop. This caused one of the frequent Genevan riots, which Calvin and Poupin had to quiet. They also managed to calm the players. Calvin was angry with Cop, not only for that he had spoken at the wrong time but also because 'I could not at all approve of what he had said'. The end of it all was that the acting continued for the present, with Viret come to watch and 'to restore our furious friend to his right mind'.[5] A week later, however, the ministers requested and the Council ordained that such 'ystoires' be suspended until a more propitious time.

The third matter was that the ministers attempted to regulate the giving of Christian names. There were, they said, too many foolish names, too many blasphemous, too many meaningless. The Council ordered Calvin to compose a list of prohibited names. The list included the divine names—Dieu-le-Fils, for example, or Jésus; names of idols; religious words like Dimanche, Pâques, or Croix; diminutives instead of the original name; and even words ugly to the ear. It should be noted that there was no list of permitted names, nor did the ministers desire such extravagances as became common in seventeenth century Puritan circles.

The year 1548 brought some lull in the storm. Certainly Philibert Berthelier began to be more active, and the Favres continued to figure in the registers. Perrin was restored as Captain-General. In September Calvin was in trouble with the Council about a letter he had written to Viret in 1545 criticizing them. He apologized and in October the Council pardoned him and told him to do his duty better in the future. Farel, who was present, could not stomach this and broke out into a fierce expostulation. What right had they to tell Monsieur Calvin to do his duty better, a man who had never failed to do his duty, who had always had the best interests of Geneva at heart, a man who was pre-eminent in the world of learning, who had even, when necessity demanded it, reproved great persons like Luther and Melanchthon?[6] Then they all went off and had dinner together.

2. CALVIN AT HOME

After a few years, Calvin's house was needed by its owner, and he moved into the house on the site that now bears a commemorative plaque. Although now famous throughout Europe for his writings and as an ecclesiastical statesman, Calvin lived in a most unpretentious manner. Both his house and the furniture belonged to the Council. He was therefore incensed that rumours were spread of his thousands when he did not possess 'one foot of land' and had not enough money 'to buy an acre' except when his quarterly salary came in. 'I am still using someone else's furniture. Neither the table at which we eat, nor the bed on which we sleep, is my own.'[7] He had a big house, large enough for his wife and himself and her daughter, for Antoine, his wife and their young children, for the servants; and still there was room for guests.

Of Calvin's married life we know next to nothing. They had only one child, a boy who was born prematurely and lived for only a short time. This was in 1542. Idelette, the pale figure who lives in history only beside her husband, suffered much ill health afterwards. Nor did she escape from the slanders of the Libertines. Françoise Favre spread it abroad that she was no better than she should be, since she and her first husband had, in the manner of many anabaptists, never contracted a civil marriage. She was ill for months in the autumn and winter of 1545, again in 1547, and so seriously in 1548 that Calvin feared for her life. She died at the end of March 1549, worrying at the last about her two children, while Calvin promised that he would treat them as his own. 'Truly mine is no common grief. I have been bereaved of the best friend of my life, of one who, if it had been so ordained, would willingly have shared not only my poverty but also my death. During her life she was the faithful helper of my ministry. From her I never experienced the slightest hindrance.' [8] He never married again. In a surprisingly unreserved passage in a sermon on I Timothy he told his congregation why:

As for me, I do not want anyone to think me very virtuous because I am not married. It would rather be a fault in me if I could serve God better in marriage than remaining as I am ... But I know my infirmity, that perhaps a woman might not be happy with me. However that may be, I abstain from marriage in order that I may be more free to serve God. But this is not because I think that I am more virtuous than my brethren. Fie to me if I had that false opinion! [9]

What is 'my infirmity'? His bad health? Or perhaps his irritability?

Antoine Calvin was less fortunate in his marriage. In the autumn of 1548 his wife was accused of adultery, but acquitted. They continued to live together. But in 1557 she was taken in adultery with Calvin's servant, Pierre Daguet, a hunchback. Antoine obtained a divorce and his wife was banished. It was then discovered that Daguet had been quietly helping himself to odds and ends of his master's belongings. But it was a far greater blow to Calvin when a little later his step-daughter Judith was also convicted of adultery. For a few days he was too ashamed even to leave his house.

In this quarter of the Upper City around the Cathedral lived also some of the friends from earlier years. Nicolas Cop, the living reminder of All Saints' Day 1533, lived next door in the rue des Chanoines. François Budé, son of the great Guillaume, had left Paris and settled with his mother, his two brothers and two sisters in Geneva. He lived round the corner in the Puits Saint Pierre. Laurent de Normandie, formerly a lawyer and mayor of Calvin's own Noyon, but now the largest publisher in Geneva, had a house in the Place Saint Pierre. Other former friends or associates lived elsewhere in the city. Robert Estienne, Stephanus, the most famous scholar printer in France in the first half of the century, removed at the end of 1550 to Geneva with his entire business and became Geneva's foremost printer. His famous device, the *Oliva Roberti Stephani,* graced the title-pages of many of Calvin's commentaries and of the 1559 *Institutio.*

An old friend came to Geneva in 1547. This was one of the de Montmor sons with whom Calvin had been brought up, but whose Christian name we do not know. At the time of his coming Calvin was looking out for a husband for a certain Mlle de Wilergy. His friend seemed suitable, fairly young at thirty-four, good-natured, very gentle and docile. Although he had 'drunk deep of youthful follies in earlier life',[10] he had not, so far as Calvin could discover from discreet enquiries, contracted any venereal disease, unlike the Sieur de Pare, an earlier aspirant for the girl's hand.

Calvin was a good and faithful friend. Like most men, he had his affective casualties; but they were few in comparison with his life-long attachments— de Montmor, Laurent de Normandie, Mathurin Cordier, from his boyhood; Beza, Wolmar, Cop, from his youth; Farel, Melanchthon, Bullinger, from his early manhood. There were always the flatterers and the hero-worshippers, like Jean de l'Espine who would write to say that he wished he could hear Calvin's 'most sweet voice' and gaze upon his 'most happy face'.[11] But he distrusted praise and preferred to learn his faults. It was perhaps this openness and honesty that kept him his friends as much as his evidences of love. And for his part, as he said in a time of distress, he could not live without friendship.

Calvin's home in the rue des Chanoines was as much a centre of Church activity as a haven from the world. Nicolas Colladon well knew the unceasing busyness:

I do not believe there can be found his like. For who could recount his ordinary and extraordinary labours? I doubt if any man in our time has had more to listen to, to reply to, to write, or things of greater importance. The multitude and quality alone of his writings is enough to astonish everyone who looks at them, and even more those who read them . . . He never ceased working, day and night, in the service of the Lord, and heard most unwillingly the prayers and exhortations that his friends addressed to him every day to give himself some rest.[12]

Wolfgang Musculus rightly called him a bow always strung. The letters and the other writings had to be written or dictated in between sermons, lectures, meetings and visitors calling on a dozen items of business. And all the time his health was breaking up. He wrote to de Falais in despair in March 1546:

The difficulty arises from the annoyances and interruptions of the train of thought which intervene to break off a letter in the midst twenty times over, or even more, beyond all bounds. As regards health, I was much more feeble when I wrote to you a little ago than I am now. But although I am pretty well physically, I am unceasingly tormented with a heaviness which will not let me do a thing. Apart from the sermons and lectures, there is a month gone by in which I have scarce done anything, in such wise that I am almost ashamed to live thus useless.[13]

Colladon has left us also an account of his daily life:

As to his ordinary life, everyone will bear witness that he was very abstemious, without any excess or meanness, but a praiseworthy moderation. It is true that for his stomach's sake he abstained from some common foods that he was fond of, but this was without being fastidious or troublesome in company. One fault he had was that in his abstinence he took little regard to his health, mostly being content for many years with a single meal a day and never taking anything between two meals . . . His reasons were the weakness of his stomach and his migraine, which he said he had proved by experiment could be remedied only by a continual diet. Sometimes I have known him go without any food into the second day.

How far Calvin's abstemiousness was intended to serve his health and how far it was a voluntary fasting it is not possible to say. If we consult his writings we have to balance *Institutio* III. ix, whose title we may translate *On the present practice of the future life*, with *Institutio* III. x, *On the use of the present life*. If in the one he urges believers to cultivate a contempt for their earthly life and to look forward with joy to the day of death and the final resurrection, yet in the other he calls inhuman that philosophy which deprives man of his senses, robbing him of enjoyment and delight in food and clothing, flowers and trees, gold and ivory. The primary rule is: the freedom of enjoyment without the servitude of self-indulgence. If his own practice was a fasting, then we may be sure that it was undertaken as an athlete's training and not for its own sake.

3. THE INSTITUTIO AGAIN AND NEW TESTAMENT COMMENTARIES

Colladon goes on to describe Calvin's manner of working:

Being so frail he also slept very little; but for all the lassitude that ensued from this he never failed to be ready for his work and the exercises of his office. When it was not his turn to preach, he had books brought to him in bed at five or six o'clock, so that he might compose, having someone to write for him. If it was his week, he was always ready at the hour to go into the pulpit; then afterwards at home he lay down on the bed fully clothed and pursued his labours on some book . . . This is how in the mornings he dictated the most of his books, when he could give his genius full flow.[14]

While the dictating was going on, someone would be sure to call and perhaps stay for half an hour or even an hour. But then usually 'he remembered the connection where he had stopped and went on with what he had been saying without being reminded'.[15]

His major works in these years were new editions of the *Institutio* and commentaries on nearly all the books of the New Testament. Throughout his life Calvin was searching for the form that would best express his theology. In 1536 the framework of the catechism had been used. When the catechism had been abandoned in 1539, the new form of seventeen chapters had been held together only by the common theme, by the unity of the outlook, and by an unfolding and inter-relating of the one theme. In spite of its freshness and brilliance, in spite of the clarity and certainty of its French translation, this edition only narrowly escaped being a set of unrelated *loci communes*. This form, however, was to be kept for the next twenty years.[16] The two major revisions were mainly of enlargements. Thus the edition which Rihel published at Strasbourg in March 1543 contained twenty-one chapters. Two new chapters had been added, the one on Vows, placed between those on the Law and on Faith, and the one on Human traditions directly before Christian Liberty. The chapter expounding the Apostles' Creed had been divided into four and the Chapter 14 in 1539 on the Power of the Church put into the section of the Creed on the Church. This amplification of the exposition of the Creed was the most significant change made, for it shows that Calvin's mind was already moving in the direction of the final form. As the edition was finished by January 1542, we conjecture that the revising occupied Calvin during his first autumn and winter back in Geneva. The next edition in 1545 was only a tidying up of 1543; but the French translation, which also was published in 1545, preceded the Latin by a month and was in fact a translation of 1543. This was not printed by Rihel but by Jean Gérard, or Girard, of Geneva.

On 15 February 1549 Valeran Poullain, a great admirer of Calvin's writings and an indefatigable urger to further efforts, wrote from Strasbourg: 'I understand that you are thinking of a new edition of your *Institutio*. I have read it carefully, have corrected some printer's errors, and have also made notes in the margin. I have also compiled an index of all the Scriptural places, whether cited or expounded, for the use of students, so that they may have a direct way to apply Scripture.'[17] It is no doubt Poullain's index which is advertised on the title page as one of the innovations in the new edition. But the printer, again Gérard, seems for some reason to have delayed publication: I do not know whether it is Gérard's laziness, wrote Calvin to Farel, whose book *Le Glaive de la Parolle veritable* was also being held up, or because his domestic affairs are in confusion, or because he has given other books the priority, but I have certainly spoken to him often about it. 'The *Institutio*, which ought to have been completed a month ago, is not finished yet.'[18] It came out at last in 1550, a further enlargement of the 1543–5 edition. It had the same number of chapters and in the same order, but, for greater convenience in finding the place, the chapters were also divided into sections. Gérard published the French translation of this edition, but Stephanus was responsible for the first reprint of the Latin. One of the most striking improvements in the editions since 1543 has been the vastly increased reference to the Church fathers, and to a lesser extent to the Schoolmen. Ambrose, Cyprian, Theodoret, Jerome, Leo, Gregory I, and Bernard of Clairvaux all figure largely, but with Augustine far and away taking the leading place. Calvin's theology more and more found its formal place within the main tradition of Catholic theology.

His intention had been to write commentaries on all of St Paul's letters and even on the whole of the New Testament letters. *Romans* had appeared in 1540; but after that for some years silence. *I Corinthians* did not follow. Farel wrote to ask what had happened to it. Calvin replied: 'As to your exhorting me to write, I only wish I had more time and better health.'[19] Poullain also begged for the commentary. Calvin is not being very wise, he says; he is letting the devil divert him to other tasks when he should be writing commentaries:

I want Calvin to determine once for all just this—that he will never rest until he has written commentaries on all the letters of Paul, then on the prophets, then on the rest of the sacred books. Gracious God! how they would help the Church! How much they would do for the glory of Christ! What inextinguishable immortality they would win![20]

We may think that it is hardly consistent in the other Reformers to coerce Calvin morally into a parochial ministry and yet insist that he should write more books than someone who had nothing else to do. But Poullain had not long to wait; *I Corinthians* was out by the end of February or the beginning of March 1546, published by Wendelin Rihel in Strasbourg.

When the manuscript of *II Corinthians* was sent to Rihel, however, it got lost on the way. Calvin had no second copy and was frantic with worry. He told Viret that if it did not turn up he had decided to give up working on St Paul.[21] It reached its destination in the end and Calvin vowed that he would never again send a manuscript without having a second copy—a precaution that one would have thought a trained lawyer would have taken in the first place. After this scare, Calvin gave up publishing through Rihel, with whom he had continued only from feelings of gratitude for kindness shewn in Strasbourg days. He turned instead to Gérard, who published the first editions of all the commentaries up to 1551. And certainly, he kept him busy. The French version of *II Corinthians* in 1547, *Galatians, Ephesians, Philippians, Colossians* as one set in 1548, *I and II Timothy* the same year, *Titus and Hebrews* in 1549. Omitting *Romans* and the six years gap, therefore, he had published commentaries on the whole Pauline corpus within four years. These were now gathered into one volume as *The Most Excellent Commen-*

taries of Jean Calvin on all St Paul's Epistles and also on the Epistle to the Hebrews. From the latest revision by the author . . . Geneva, Jean Gérard. M.D.LI.* The revision was probably made in the first six months of 1550. *I and II Thessalonians* and *Philemon* seem to have appeared for the first time in this collected edition. The revision was not extensive, except for *Romans*, written so many years previously. The aged humanist Ambrose Moiban of Bratislava, a former pupil of Reuchlin, proposed, so to say, the vote of thanks from the world of New Testament scholarship:

I congratulate you on the remarkable gift of God, by which, ἐν ἐνεργίᾳ of the Spirit, you interpret the Holy Scriptures so felicitously. I have never met you, but I have always loved your writings. I have read and re-read your works, and am never tired of them. And especially am I happy that this year you have adorned the whole of Paul with your most holy thoughts.[22]

From St Paul, Calvin turned at once to the Catholic Epistles. *James* had already appeared in a French translation in 1550; but the whole set was published the same month as the collected *St Paul*. He did not, however, include II and III John. In 1556 a complete edition of the commentaries on all the New Testament epistles was published by Stephanus. This time the revision was extremely thorough, so thorough as to extend to minutiae of spelling (e.g. *quum* for *cum*, *numquid* for *nunquid*) and to a complete and most careful revision of his Latin version of the Greek text. He indicated also where he had changed his mind on the meaning of a verse or a word.

As early as 1550 he made a start on the historical books of the New Testament, beginning with the Acts, on which he was also preaching on Sundays. But his commentary swelled to such proportions that he had to divide it into two volumes. The first was published in 1552. Before the second could make its appearance in 1554, *St John's Gospel* had come out in 1553. *Acts* and *St John* were swiftly followed by the very large volume of the *Harmony of the Gospels*, published by Stephanus in July 1555. This consisted of the first three Gospels arranged to make a single narrative. With it Calvin's New Testament commentaries were complete, for there is none on the Revelation of St John.

As if this were not enough for one man to have done in a lifetime (and he had done it, in effect, in a decade), and while he was still occupied with St Paul, he brought out the first of his Old Testament commentaries, that on Isaiah (1551) dedicated to the young King Edward VI of England, to whom also had been dedicated the *Catholic Epistles*.

4. THE OPPOSITION GROWS

The opposition to Calvin, forming a majority among the Syndics elected in 1547, increased in courage with strength. The Favres continued their vexations, but, after being imprisoned, left the city for their country home. A more startling event now occurred. On 27 June a threatening letter couched in the childish abuse of blood and thunder was found in the pulpit of Saint-Pierre:

Big pot-belly, you and your fellows would do better to shut up. If you drive us too far, you will find yourselves in a situation where you will curse the day you skipped your monastery. We've had enough of blaming people. Why the devil have these —— renegade priests come here to ruin us? Those who have had enough take their revenge. Beware that you don't get what happened to Monsieur Werly of Fribourg. We don't want all these masters. Beware of what I say.[23]

The document was unsigned.

Calvin took it seriously: 'A paper has been found in the pulpit threatening us with death unless we keep quiet.' [24] One of the Favre group, Jacques Gruet, was arrested. When his house was searched, several incriminating writings were found, letters critical of Calvin and some anti-religious passages copied from books. Most revealing was a letter to the *Seigneurie* expressing as well as anything the feeling behind the opposition:

Do not be ruled by the voice or the will of one man. For you see that men have many and divers opinions in them. Each individual would wish to be ruled as he liked. A drunkard would wish to go around with drunkards, idlers likewise. Wise men want everyone to be like themselves. But this is not possible and often the opinion of one single man will cause much evil . . . If there is a personage who is saturnine by nature, he desires, if he has power, that everyone be saturnine like himself and he will hate everything contrary to his nature. And if he has this pre-eminence and authority, he wants what is natural to him to be put into effect. On the contrary, one who is joyful will ask for pleasure and fun . . . Therefore it seems to me that a *seigneurie* should establish a state in which there is no discord of making a people subject to something against their nature. There is no king or government of a republic that allows a man to do what he does not wish to be done to himself. For example, one man murders another. He deserves punishment if the murder was deliberate . . . In short, everyone who maliciously and voluntarily hurts another deserves to be punished. But suppose I am a man who wants to eat his meals as he pleases, what affair is that of others? Or if I want to dance, or have a good time, what is that to do with the law? Nothing.[25]

If we did not know what Gruet meant by 'joyful', 'pleasure and fun', and 'a good time', we might feel sympathy with the common people in their exasperation against discipline and the strict enforcement of the civil laws.

Under prolonged torture Gruet confessed to the following crimes: That he had declared the Mosaic Law to possess only a human and relative and not a divine authority; That he had declared that all laws were made at man's whim; That he had been in contact with a foreign power; That he had endeavoured to subvert Church order; That he had written a certain supplication to the *Seigneurie* tending to the subversion of 'the edicts, statutes and ordinances of our *Seigneurs* and *superieurs*'; That he had written in a counterfeit hand the letter found in the pulpit, menacing God and his ambassadors; That he had committed lèse-majesté in not informing the *Seigneurie* of letters that he had received menacing another; That he had written letters persuading others to lewdness.

Some at least of these charges were capital. The Court condemned him to death and he was beheaded on 26 July. A discovery made a few years later confirmed the enormity of his views. In 1550 the workmen doing some jobs in the house where he had lived found under a floor a notebook in his handwriting. Its pathological ravings on religion horrified all who were allowed to see it. The Virgin Mary was a lecherous wench. Christ he called a liar and a fool, wicked, a mere rustic, whose miracles were sorceries and who got the death he deserved. The Council ordered the book to the flames. It was now not only Calvin who was shocked. Pierre Vandel, the *procureur-general*, himself a Libertine, called the book abominable, horrible, infamous, detestable, blasphemous. To the consensus of opinion justice had been done.

Francis I of France died on 31 March 1547, and was succeeded by Henri II. The *Seigneurie* deputed Perrin to convey the respect of the republic to the new monarch in Paris. When in September he returned, it was to face two pieces of trouble. In the first place, he brought back his wife and her father into the city—a rash action. Even the Captain-General could not protect lawbreakers against their punishment. They were both arrested and made to apologize to the *Consistoire* for their conduct in 1546. Favre was also deprived of his rights of citizenship. Perrin took the sentences as an insult to his position and stormed at the Council. He was promptly arrested and put in prison. Meanwhile, the *Consistoire* had dealt gently with Favre, Calvin reasoning with him so kindly as quite to win him over and to say that 'if Monsieur Calvin had always spoken so *doucement*, all this need never have happened'. There was truth in what he said. They shook hands all round.

But something else was coming out about Perrin's stay in Paris. He was accused of having held conversations, not divulged to the Council, with a leading member of the French government about an alliance. A part of the deal was that the Captain-General was also to command a French troop of light horse in Geneva. This had come to light through Laurent Meigret, Meigret-le-Magnifique, a former member, little significant, of the court of Francis I who had fled to Geneva during the troubles of 1534, but who acted as a French agent with the connivance of the Genevan Council. Perrin when accused brought counter-accusations against Meigret, and in this was supported both by a deputation from Bern and by representations from Savoy. As with all secret political intrigues, it is impossible to get to the bottom of it. Perrin, after being kept in prison for several weeks, was released but stripped of his honours. The dangerous office of Captain-General was abolished. This caused another riot, which Calvin has described in a letter to Viret:

The Two Hundred had been summoned. I had already told my colleagues that I would go to the council chamber. We got there rather early. As a lot of people were still walking about outside we went out by the gate beside the council chamber. Much confused shouting was heard from that quarter. This got so loud that there was surely a riot. I at once run up to the place. Everything looks terrible. I throw myself into the thickest of the crowds, to the amazement of everyone. The whole mob makes a rush towards me; they seize me and drag me hither and thither—no doubt lest I should be injured! I called God and men to witness that I had come to present my body to their swords. I bade them, if they wanted to shed blood, to start with me. Even the worthless, but especially the more respectable, at once cooled down. I was at length dragged through the midst of them to the Council. There new fights started, and I threw myself between them . . . I succeeded in getting everyone to sit down quietly, and then delivered a long and vehement speech, which they say moved all of them.[26]

He now felt that he had had enough of Geneva: 'I have not yet decided what I am going to do, except that I can no longer tolerate the ways of this people, even though they may bear with mine.'[27] But things quietened down. Meigret was at last released from prison; Perrin was restored to the Council; and there took place another reconciliation and shaking of hands.

5. THE BATTLE OVER DISCIPLINE

The decisive battle over discipline was now beginning, concentrated upon the right to excommunicate, but fought on several fronts, ecclesiastical, theological, civil. The aim of the Libertines was to curb Calvin's authority, not to break it completely. There was really no possibility of dismissing and banishing him again. For many years the majority had no such wish, and when the opposition gained power they found it was not absolute but conditional upon a great respect for authority that had grown up in the last dozen years, upon the reverence that a large part of the population (and not only the refugees) had for Calvin himself, and upon what we should call world opinion. It was one thing for Bucer to be forced to leave Strasbourg for refusing to subscribe to the *Interim* of the Emperor Charles V. It was quite another for Calvin to be banished from Geneva because Ami Perrin and Philibert Berthelier found his Church polity irksome. It would be better for the Philistines if Samson remained in Gaza, his locks shorn.

The Libertines kept up their opposition in one way and another, stirring up trouble, insulting the ministers, defying the authority of the *Consistoire*. The startling scandal of Roux Monet set them back for a while. This young secretary in the justice department was a particular friend of Perrin, who nevertheless could not, and did not try to, protect him when he was arrested on a charge of possessing obscene pictures, 'his Gospels', as he called them. The court minutes are lost, but there seems to have been more to the case than the ostensible charge. The prosecuting lawyer, Vandel, himself a Libertine, would not let him speak in his own defence. Contemporary sources relate that Monet boasted to have lain with the wives of four of the honourable councillors, among them Françoise Perrin and Madame Vandel. Whatever his crimes, he was condemned and executed.

The case of Philippe de Ecclesia is a revealing example of the little power that the ministers, and Calvin in particular, actually possessed even in such a matter as Church appointments.[28] De Ecclesia, minister in the village of Vandoeuvres, was summoned before his fellow ministers in February 1549 and reproved for uttering absurdities at the *Congrégations*. He apologized and it was decided to keep the matter strictly private. But the next month he was before them again, now accused of slandering all his colleagues severally and the doctrine they preached, and furthermore of continuing in his own erroneous teaching. His defence was unsatisfactory and the case was referred to the Council. They asked the ministers to forgive and restore him. At a full meeting of the Venerable Company it was decided that he should not be allowed to continue, and the Council was informed. The first Syndic, at this time Perrin, conveyed their opinion that, although he had behaved badly in the past, he must turn over a new leaf. They would give him a final warning. The ministers replied that they quite disapproved but must accept a situation they could not alter. Three years later, when the parish of Jussy, a village some three miles beyond Vandoeuvres, became vacant, the ministers decided that de Ecclesia should go there and that Jean Fabri should take his place at Vandoeuvres. De Ecclesia would not obey and complained to the Council, who upheld him, ordering a new election. The ministers stood by their decision. Whereupon the Council said that they themselves would choose a minister and ordered François Bourgoin to Jussy. Bourgoin asked his brethren to allow him to resign his ministry. This they would not permit and pressed him to go to Jussy, at least for a time. Calvin and Fabri appeared before the Syndics in an attempt to persuade them, but unsuccessfully. At this point, however, de Ecclesia was accused of usury, a criminal offence. In December 1552 he was brought before the ministers on several charges, including heresy and ill-treating his wife. Again he complained to the Council. The case still dragged on until the end of the next January when '*Messieurs* resolved that de Ecclesia should be deposed'.[29]

On the other hand, the Council upheld Calvin in the affair of Jerome Bolsec. Maistre Jerome had been a monk and a doctor of theology at Paris. When he had fled the country for his evangelical opinion, he adopted the practice of medicine. Thus, settling in Geneva, he became physician to de

111

Falais. At the *Congrégation* of Friday, 16 October 1551, Saint-André expounded John 8: 47: 'He that is of God heareth God's words'. We do not know what he said, but if he interpreted the verse as a direct reference to predestination he was going beyond Calvin, who does not so interpret it either in *St John* or in the *Institutio*. Farel was there and added some comments. After him Bolsec took up the theme on which he had already argued with Calvin, the doctrine of double predestination. Election and reprobation, he is recorded to have said, are not eternal decrees of God but are dependent on faith. 'He affirmed, moreover, that those who posit an eternal decree in God by which he has ordained some to life and the rest to death make of him a Tyrant, and in fact an idol, as the pagans made of Jupiter.' [30] It was incorrect, he said, to father this doctrine on Augustine. Many verses of Scripture, too, had been twisted or even mistranslated to support the doctrine. Calvin had come in late and unobserved. When Bolsec had finished, he spoke for an hour in a powerful extemporary refutation. At the end of the meeting an assistant in the justice department arrested Bolsec, on the charge, be it noted, not that he had denied predestination, but that he had said that 'we were making an idol of God'.[31]

Calvin's doctrine of predestination first appeared in its developed form in the 1539 *Institutio*, although it had been present as a constant presupposition in the first edition. It was not original and J. B. Mozley can even say: 'I see no substantial difference between the Augustinian and Thomist, and the Calvinist doctrines of predestination . . . Those who suppose that S. Augustine differs from Calvin in his doctrine of predestination, do not really know the doctrine which S. Augustine held on the subject'.[32] Mozley is right in general; and Calvin himself supposed his doctrine to differ from Augustine's not at all.

Calvin begins at the same practical point as Augustine. Why, when the Gospel is preached, do some believe and some reject it? The answer that some will to believe and some will to reject cannot be final; it is merely explaining faith and unbelief. How can one who has hitherto willed to reject now will to believe? Man is a sinner, that is, a being who wills to reject God. It is clear from the New Testament that faith is the gift of God, that man's will is changed from a rejecting to a believing will by the creative act of the Holy Spirit. So, then, those who believe the Gospel do so because their rejecting will is changed into a believing will. This is, of course, Catholic doctrine. To say that men change their own wills would be the grossest Pelagianism. But it must be asked whether this act of the Holy Spirit was a snap decision by God, or whether it was premeditated. When did God determine to perform the work of grace in the man's heart? The question is answered both by explicit statements of Scripture and also by the general Scriptural concept of God. For the former the *locus classicus* is Eph. 1: 4: 'he [God] hath chosen us in him [Jesus Christ] before the foundation of the world', in other words, eternally. And for the latter, God is seen always in Scripture as the one who is faithful to his choice, who, when he loves, loves to the end, not as one who is now for and now against. God's decision is therefore as eternal as God himself. Thus eternal election is proved. And what of those who reject the Gospel? This is answered by recourse to the numerous passages of Scripture that speak of God hardening this or that person or people, or of his passing over those whom he does not choose. Hence, the man who rejects the Gospel does so because God has not chosen him. The not choosing has to be interpreted not merely passively as an omission but actively as a rejection. And if the *when* of the rejection is asked, it is answered by the Augustinian doctrine as eternal. Hence Calvin's definition of predestination runs:

We call predestination God's eternal decree, by which he determined with himself what he willed to become of each man. For all are not created in equal condition; rather, eternal life is foreordained for some, eternal damnation for others. Therefore, as any man has been created to one or the other of these ends, we speak of him as predestined to life or death.[33]

Predestination to life is usually called election; to death, reprobation or rejection. The order of salvation therefore is: first, election in eternity; second, calling in time, and in the calling, repentance and faith in Jesus Christ; third, glorification in the kingdom of God. The calling through the Gospel, and the consequent faith is the fulfilling of election. Calvin follows Augustine here also in relying on a strand of thought in St John's Gospel according to which the Father gives to the Son those who already belong to him: 'thine they were, and thou gavest them to me' (17: 6), 'all that the Father gives me will come to me' (6: 37).

This doctrine is open to many objections, and these objections have been made often enough; we shall shortly hear Bolsec making some of them. But these objections are elementary, such as would occur to any serious-minded person, and we must not imagine that a subtle and thorough theologian like Calvin would be unaware of them. He makes certain safeguards which he obviously regards as sufficient. Whether they are sufficient is another matter; but we should not think that we can dent Calvin's armour with reeds. Bolsec at any rate was a poor theologian technically, and, it would seem, particularly weak on the history of doctrines; he even thought that Calvin's doctrine originated with Valla in the fifteenth century. He had a few sound criticisms of Calvin, but he was making them from the wrong point of view and so nullifying their force. He asks Calvin whether there is in God any will other than that revealed to us in Scripture. He is willing to say that God has elected from among men whom he has pleased and that this election is in Jesus Christ, apart from whom none is acceptable to God. But against such unexceptionable statements he will make election dependent on faith, reprobation on the rejection of the Gospel. And so he enters the venerable objections to the doctrine: it is making God the author of evil; it is making God a tyrant; it is making man a puppet; it is making two ways of salvation, one by election the other by Christ. The truth of the matter is that Bolsec was one of those people who can feel that there is something wrong with this doctrine in its classic formulation and are forced to deny it for the wrong reasons. Augustine's and Calvin's doctrine, we may well think, was not good. But Bolsec's denial of it was far worse. It would have led to a Pelagianized Church; and of all Churches the Pelagian is religiously and morally the weakest.

Bolsec had committed an offence against Genevan law and he was tried by the civil court. But the ministers, and especially Calvin, had to supply the questions to be put to the prisoner, for the judges themselves were even more ignorant of the doctrine than Bolsec. The trial was therefore a theological examination before the magistrates. In this peculiar situation, the ministers wrote to three of the Swiss Churches for their opinion, no doubt in the hope that their judgment would be confirmed. Unfortunately, the replies were less than helpful. Basel sent back a declaimer of Bolsec; but the statement of their own position fell far short of what was hoped for. They would prefer to be simple, they said, and 'we ask the Lord to keep us in this simplicity right to the end'.[34] But they are always ready to be taught. As for Bolsec, they wish to have nothing to do with him; he is a sophist and something of a heretic. Zürich was less accommodating. They too fell short in their statement, but worse, they exhorted the Genevan ministers to try to arrive at a peaceful understanding with Bolsec. He may have been intemperate, 'but, our brethren, we look for moderation in you also, for you seem in your letter which has been given to us to be extremely severe'.[35] Only Neuchâtel, led by the loyal Farel, came down on the side of Calvin. 'Who has explained all these things in a purer, truer, more godly manner than our brother Calvin in his superb *Institutio*? . . . Let Jerome and any other mortal man bite and gnaw; they will not be able to overthrow any point of a truth so sure and settled.' [36] Bolsec is no better versed in holy things than the filthiest pig. He is a villainous wretch and a treacherous subverter of Scripture.

The court accepted these replies as condemning Bolsec and banished him from Geneva. This did not at all please M. de Falais, who had twice petitioned the *Seigneurie* for his release, basing his request on the plea that Bolsec understood how to treat his ailments better than anyone else. De Falais blamed Calvin for Bolsec's downfall. Calvin blamed de Falais for his fickleness. Their friendship terminated abruptly. Bolsec himself later returned to the Roman Church and in 1577 sought revenge by writing his virulent misrepresentation that he called a life of Calvin.

During 1552 the Libertines had been gaining power. Perrin's brother-in-law Pierre Tissot, who had held office three times as Syndic, had also been Treasurer, and had been on the Council for many years, was now appointed Lieutenant, that is, the judge in the civil court. Philibert Berthelier became an

Auditor, or assistant judge. In the February elections the Libertines won a majority in the Syndics, with Perrin as First Syndic. Soon after, the post of Captain-General was revived and given to him. They elected four new members to the *Little Council*, three of whom are already known to us— Balthasar Sept, Gaspard Favre, and Vandel. Three of the Councillors were the troublemakers in 1552. Philibert Bonna had been censured by the minister Raymond Chauvet about 'certain attachments to the wife of Domeny'.[37] He, Berthelier and Sept followed Chauvet as he was walking to Saint Pierre, shouting insults at him. After three months of legal wrangling they were imprisoned and also excommunicated. One of the reconciliations that the Council was so fond of engineering took place between the parties. The offenders then thought that they would be free to communicate. They were told that they must first show signs of repentance. Balthasar in particular asked that his child should be baptized. The *Consistoire* decided that as he was excommunicate his child could not be baptized. So matters remained into 1553. Calvin had to excuse himself going to Fabri's wedding. Things were so bad that he had not been outside the city walls for a month: 'they have never shewn a more unbridled licence . . . The entire republic is now in disorder and they are striving to uproot the established order'.[38] Soon he had to make a journey, however, for he heard that Farel was dying. Calvin found it even so and performed the last offices of a friend. He was filled with grief and on his return told everyone the bad news. By the end of March the robust Farel was well on the way to recovery and Calvin was writing to apologize for burying him prematurely; 'may the Lord grant that the Church may see you survive me . . . But now let us so live for Christ that we may daily be prepared to die for him'.[39]

With their control of the *Little Council* the Libertines waxed bold. In March, with the Easter Communion in sight, the Syndics demanded from the *Consistoire* a list of all excommunicate persons together with the reasons for their ban. The ministers went in a body to them and said they would rather hand in their resignations. By the middle of the year things had grown unendurable. Ministers, even if they were citizens, were forbidden seats on the *General Council* open to all citizens. The Council on its own authority moved Bourgoin from Jussy to Geneva and sent des Gallars to take his place. The ministers' protest went unheeded.

The opposition seemed to take a delight in rousing Calvin's temper; and it is no wonder that he became even more irritable, answering insult with insult. He bewailed it in a letter:

It is very difficult for me not to boil over when someone gets impassioned. Yet so far no one has ever heard me shouting. But I lack the chief thing of all, and that is being trained by these scourges of the Lord in true humility. And therefore it is all the more necessary that I should be tamed by the free rebukes of my brethren.

Do not spare me, he goes on; I am ashamed to think that you have dealt over-kindly with me out of fear.[40]

The persistent persecution at last succeeded in its aim. On Monday, 24 July Calvin admitted that he was beaten and asked to be allowed to resign: 'M. Calvin has remonstrated and asked that the Council will not be displeased if, since he sees that some wish him ill, and many grumble and turn away from the Word, he goes into retirement and serves no longer.' [41] Request refused. The Libertines want a Calvin subservient, not a Calvin martyred by banishment and opposing them from Basel or Zürich.

Chapter 8

Defeat into Security

1. THE TRIAL AND DEATH OF SERVETUS

It was at this point, when Calvin's authority in Geneva was at its lowest, when he was in fact defeated, that there happened an event of such a magnitude and with such implications that the whole face of the battle was changed. At first sight it seemed to offer a wonderful opportunity for the opposition. But they found that the present which Fate had tossed to them was a hand-grenade about to explode. They were only just quick enough to get rid of it.

On 13 August 1553, a Sunday, a fugitive from justice in southern France came to Geneva. In the afternoon he went to hear Calvin preach in Saint Pierre. He was recognized, arrested, and imprisoned. This was the beginning of the final act in the erratic career of Michael Servetus.[1]

Servetus first swam into notoriety when, after reading law at Toulouse and being secretary to the Emperor's Spanish chaplain, he lived in Basel and poured his views on the Trinity into the unwilling ears of Oecolampadius. These views he put into a book, published in 1531, *de Trinitatis orroribus libri septem*, 'Seven books on Errors about the Trinity'. From Basel he went to Strasbourg, where his main target was Bucer, and where he began to get the city a bad name among other Reformers. Bucer asked him to leave. He returned to Basel, but there the magistrates ordered him to retract the opinions in his book. The way in which he obeyed was typical of the lack of candour which he showed throughout his life. He wrote a new book, *Dialogorum de Trinitate libri duo*, 'Two books of Dialogues on the Trinity', in which he retracted what he had written in the sense that it had been an immature work whose ideas needed further development. The Inquisition in Spain ordered his arrest. Servetus as such ceased to exist, reappearing in Paris as Michael Villeneuve, lecturer in mathematics. He took up the study of medicine with outstanding success. It is said that he anticipated Harvey's discovery of the pulmonary circulation of the blood. Certainly he wrote a very popular work on medicinal syrups, *Syruporum universa ratio*, 'The universal use of Syrups' (1537). In the mid thirties Calvin arranged to meet him in Paris, at risk to his own life, that he might 'gain him for the Lord'. Servetus failed to keep the appointment. This is an obscure business, and we do not even know whether to Calvin he was then Servetus or Villeneuve. From Paris he went to Lyon where he edited Ptolemy's *Geography* in Latin (Erasmus had edited the Greek text in 1533). But when he returned to Paris, a book on Astrology was condemned and suppressed by the Faculty of Medicine. As Villeneuve he became personal physician to the Archbishop of Vienne, whose friendship he had gained in Paris. Nor could his patron, a great hater of Luther and Calvin, have known of his correspondence with Calvin or of a strange book that he was preparing. Of two other books the archbishop, an amateur of literature, must have approved, for now Servetus brought out the second edition of his Ptolemy and a new edition of Pagninus' Latin Bible.

It was in 1545 that he took up again his connection with Calvin, asking him through a common acquaintance, the bookseller Jean Frellon of Lyon, for help in understanding three difficult points. (1) Whether the crucified man Jesus was the Son of God and what was the manner or type of this sonship? (2) Whether the kingdom of God is in men, when it begins, and when a man is regenerated? (3) Whether Baptism demands faith like the Supper, and why Baptism was instituted in the new covenant? Calvin sent replies to the questions. Servetus was dissatisfied and disputed his answers. Calvin replied again, this time at greater length, and also sent him a copy of the *Institutio*, where he would find his doctrines set out fully. Servetus again disputed, returning the *Institutio* scribbled with his criticisms. He also sent him part of the book he was writing and an essay consisting of thirty 'letters' or chapters. It is hard to believe that a man was completely sane who could accuse Calvin of teaching that Abraham was justified by works,[2] or who could write such violent rudeness to a respected scholar whose advice he was asking. 'I have often told you that that triad of impossible monstrosities that you admit in God is not proved by any Scriptures properly understood';[3] 'John himself says: "By this we know that we know him, because we keep his commandments. He who says, I know him, and keepeth not his commandments, is a liar; for his commandments are not grievous." This shows that your knowledge is ridiculous, nay, a magical enchantment and a lying justification.'[4] And so on. Even Bolsec called Servetus 'homme vrayement fort arrogant et insolent'. Calvin wrote to Frellon that unless 'a certain person' could learn to write a little more humbly, he need not send on any more letters. But on the same day a letter to Farel sounded a very different strain:

Servetus lately wrote to me and coupled with his letter a long volume of his delirious fancies, with the Thrasonic boast that I should see something astonishing and unheard of. He would like to come here if it is agreeable to me. But I do not wish to pledge my word for his safety. For, if he comes, I will never let him depart alive, if I have any authority.[5]

The history of this letter and its publication will be found in Doumergue VI,

118

261–5. The final sentence may be read as a threat or as a warning. If a threat, then it was communicated to Farel and not directly or indirectly to Servetus. If a warning, then he had also conveyed it to Servetus, either directly by telling him that he refused to give him safe conduct, or indirectly by not telling him that he would give him safe conduct. The correspondence ceased, Calvin determined that 'he shall not henceforth wring one word out of me'.[6] We must note that Calvin was aware of the identity of M. de Villeneuve and that he could at any time have unmasked him. He had, however, a settled policy of having no dealings with the Romanists as a body.

In January 1553 the book that had been ready for some years had other material added to it and was published as *Christianismi Restitutio*: 'The Restoration of Christianity. A calling of the whole Apostolic Church to make a fresh start, restored completely in the knowledge of God, the faith of Christ, our justification, regeneration, baptism, and the Lord's Supper. Our restoration finally in the kingdom of heaven, with the loosing of the captivity of ungodly Babylon and Anti-christ and his own destroyed.' The *Restitutio* (the title is a deliberate hit at the *Institutio*) consisted in fact of several books in one; a revised edition of the *de Trinitatis erroribus libri septem*, seven more books on faith and the kingdoms of Christ and Antichrist, and regeneration, the thirty 'letters', sixty signs of the Antichrist, and an apologia to Melanchthon on the Trinity and on Church discipline. A Basel publisher having refused to have anything to do with it, he got the Vienne printers, Arnoullet and Guéroult, to print it for him. These men, brothers-in-law, were Genevese, the latter a Libertine who 'a few months before had left Geneva to escape punishment for his fornication and other crimes'.[7]

But it was still not known in Vienne that the author of this anonymous work was none other than M. de Villeneuve, physician to the Archbishop, or that M. de Villeneuve was none other than the heretic Michael Servetus. How he escaped detection is a marvel, for certainly some of the Swiss Reformers knew of his identity. It became known through Guillaume de Trie, a French refugee at Geneva, the son-in-law of Guillaume Budé, and a personal friend of Calvin's. Servetus had sent a copy of the *Restitutio* to Calvin, who had, as we have seen, read parts of it in manuscript and knew its author. He seems to have spoken about it to his trusted colleagues and friends (for its opinions were not those that he would wish to spread abroad). De Trie was one of these, and he had a cousin living in Vienne whom he was trying to win for the evangelical faith. In his next letter he indulges in some apologetics and contrasts the purity of theology in Geneva with the laxness of Rome, which lets anybody say what he likes. Why! in Vienne at this present time there is living an arch-heretic, and not merely living, but actually in the employ of the Archbishop himself. 'The man of whom I speak has been condemned in all the Churches that you reprobate. Yet he is suffered among you . . . He is a Portuguese Spaniard named Michael Servetus in his real name, but he calls himself Villeneuve at present'.[8] And he sent him page 1 as a sample. This was 26 February. The cousin, Antoine Arneys, at once passed on the letter to the authorities and within three weeks the Inquisitor General of the Kingdom of France was writing 'très-secrètement' to the secretary of the Archbishop of Lyon, Cardinal de Tournon, asking him to look into the matter. The Cardinal wrote to the Lieutenant-General of Dauphine, saying that this affair was of 'grande importance' and must be dealt with at once. M. Arneys was asked for further information, for which he wrote to M. de Trie, who sent a further batch of papers:

but I will tell you one thing; I had the greatest difficulty in getting them out of M. Calvin. Not that he wants such execrable blasphemies to go unreproved, but because it seems to him that his duty, as one who does not bear the sword of justice, is to convict heresies by doctrine rather than by pursuing them with the sword. But I was so importunate with him, remonstrating that I should be accused of levity unless he helped me, that in the end he agreed to let me have what you see.[9]

M. de Villeneuve was therefore interrogated in prison by a commission headed by Matthieu Ory, Inquisitor General. After taking the oath on the Gospels to tell the truth, the prisoner said that his name was Michel de Villeneuve, Doctor in Medicine, and a native of Tudelle in Navarre. He gave a short account of his career, omitting his period in Basel and Strasbourg. He had written the *Syruporum universa ratio*, the book on Astrology, and the *Apologia pro Campeggio*, but no other book by him had been printed, although he had corrected several. He was shown two printed sheets with manuscript notes in the margin, where in effect infant baptism was called a demonic monstrosity. He replied that he believed infants to be saved by baptism. It was pointed out to him that he must therefore correct some notes in his own hand to the contrary. He promised to do so, but said that he could not tell off-hand whether this was his letter or not. Then he said that he thought it was and that if it contained anything against the faith he would 'submit to the determination of our Mother Holy Church', and would, if he were allowed to read it more carefully, correct any errors.

The next day he was again interrogated on oath. He was now shown the 'letter' on free will. He began to weep and said: 'Messieurs, I want to tell you the truth. When these letters were written, at the time I was in Germany, about twenty-five years ago, there was a book printed in Germany by a man named Servetus, a Spaniard—I do not know what part of Spain he came from nor where he lived in Germany . . . And after I had read the book in Germany, being very young, about fifteen or seventeen, it seemed to me to be good, in fact better than others.'[10] He had written to Calvin, he said, and sent him some questions that Servetus had asked him, and for the purpose of the correspondence, he had taken the name of Servetus, although he had made it clear to

Calvin that he was not Servetus. When he saw that Calvin had got angry he had broken off the correspondence. On infant baptism he had long changed his opinion and now wished to keep in step with the Church. As for the 'letter' on the Trinity, that merely expressed the views of Servetus.

After the second interrogation, Servetus sent his servant to collect some money due to him. The next morning he rose very early, got the key of a little garden from the jailer, climbed the wall, and, as the Genevan Council derisively wrote to the court at Vienne, 'left prison without saying goodbye to his host'.[11] All that the tribunal could do was to sentence their lost prisoner, and this they did on 17 June. He is 'to be burned alive in a slow fire until his body becomes ashes. For the present [that is, until he is caught] the sentence is to be carried out in effigy and his books are to be burnt.'[12]

Servetus now did such an incredibly foolish thing that we can only suppose that his twenty years of play-acting had transported him into a state where he could not distinguish fact from fantasy. Quite unnecessarily, so far as we know, *en route* for Italy, he went to Geneva and attended Calvin's sermon in Saint Pierre. He was arrested at Calvin's demand through his secretary Nicolas de la Fontaine, under the Genevan system whereby an accuser had to go to prison as well as the accused until he could furnish proofs. Calvin composed a list of accusations on theological points which de la Fontaine submitted to the court. The first hearing, before the Syndics, with Pierre Tissot as prosecutor, took place on 14 August, Servetus being tried under his own name. The accusations were read, together with Servetus's replies. De la Fontaine declared himself dissatisfied and they returned to prison. The next day Antoine Calvin relieved de la Fontaine as accuser. On the 16th Philibert Berthelier appeared as substitute-Lieutenant for Tissot. Germain Colladon, uncle of Nicolas, and formerly a well-known lawyer in the Duchy of Berry, was prosecuting counsel. The next day Calvin appeared before the *Little Council* with a complaint against Berthelier as trying to excuse Servetus in some way (the sentence in the minutes is obscure). For the next several sessions the first Syndic, Perrin, was absent, and Tissot resumed his place as Lieutenant. It would be wearisome to drag the reader through the many interrogations. The points that had to be proved were as follows:

1. That the writings in question were heretical; that is, that they were contrary to Scripture as understood by the Catholic fathers and councils, and heretical, moreover, on principal heads of the faith. Thus, much time was spent on early Church Christology.
2. That Servetus was the author of the writings in question.
3. That he had written them intending that they should be sold and that therefore the views expressed in them should be communicated to others.
4. That he had verbally or in writing communicated these heretical opinions to other persons, among them M. Calvin, M. Viret, and M. Poupin.
5. It had also to be established from Roman Law that heresy was a criminal

offence in the empire. There was therefore much talk of the Codex of Justinian and of examples or supposed examples of the punishment of heretics by the civil power.

As the Registers of the Venerable Company of Pastors say, it was clear that the trial was going to drag on interminably. Not so much because of the intricacy of the case, for in fact there can be no doubt at all that Servetus' books were, according to the standards of Catholic Christianity, grossly heretical. But the Libertines were using the trial to harass Calvin. Their difficulty was that the Romanists had already condemned Servetus to death and their own conduct was being observed all over Europe. To re-open all the old brothels in Geneva—the election manifesto, so to say, of Gaspard Favre —would not compensate, as Perrin well knew, for the possible effects, religious, political, and social, of siding with a most notorious heretic. All they could do was to keep the case alive. Servetus by now knew that his judges were the sworn enemies of his accuser and all his old insolence crept back into his dealings with Calvin. His replies to Calvin, indeed, stand in most distasteful contrast to his mealy-mouthed cringing to the Inquisitor at Vienne. Thus Bonivard:

Calvin's enemies, who had at that time gained control in the city, incited Servetus against Calvin through 'le bastard de Genève' who was the jailer and a follower of Perrin. They held out hopes of supporting him, and so persuaded him, not only to dispute with Calvin but also to insult him when he went with them to the prison.[13]

On 21 August the *Little Council* thought of an ingenious way out of their dilemma. They would write to Vienne 'to learn why he was detained and how he got away' and they would write also to certain Swiss Churches and cities for their opinion. They could hardly have believed that the other Churches would take Servetus' side, but they were perhaps relying on receiving some lukewarm replies as in the Bolsec case. Even if the opinion were uniformly adverse to Servetus, they would be following others rather than Calvin in condemning him. While awaiting the replies, they thought of another solution and asked Servetus whether he would rather continue with the present trial or be returned to Vienne. 'He threw himself on the ground, begging with tears to be judged here, and let Messieurs do with him what they would, but not to let him be sent back there.'[14]

On 20 October the replies were read in the Council. One and all, Zürich, Basel, Bern, Schaffhausen, condemned Servetus' opinions as heretical, blasphemous, a pestilence. This was really the end of the trial, and on 26 October the *Little Council* gave their decision, but not before Perrin had made a last effort to save Servetus by getting the case transferred to the *Two Hundred*. The next day sentence was pronounced, the same sentence as in Vienne: Calvin and other ministers asked that he should be spared burning and be beheaded instead. This was refused. After a painful final interview with Calvin, Servetus was burned, Farel attending him.

Should the State punish heresy as a crime? Calvin's doctrine of civil government stands almost unaltered from the first edition of the *Institutio* to the last, and it is restated in the *Defensio orthodoxae fidei*, which he wrote on the Servetus affair at the request of the German cities. 'Is it lawful for Christian princes and judges to punish heretics?'[15] The purpose of civil government is not only that 'men may breathe, eat, drink, and be warmed, although it certainly includes all these when it provides for human society. But it also exists so that idolatry, sacrilege of the name of God, blasphemies against his truth and other public offences against religion may not emerge and may not be disseminated . . . Finally, that among Christians the public face of religion may exist and among men humanity'.[16] Thus it is the duty of the State to establish true religion and to maintain that religion once it is established. The State and its administration are in no way secular or unclean, a neutral or antagonistic realm to the Church. On the contrary, the laws and those who administer them are ordained by God for the economy of his world. The rulers are ministers and servants of God and as such bear the authority not only of an earthly office but of the Lord by whom and for whom they execute their office. Granted that it is the duty of the State to establish and maintain true religion, what is a government to do if it sees true religion fundamentally attacked? On the toleration or the punishment there will be a difference of opinion between the consensus of opinion in the twentieth century and the consensus of opinion in the sixteenth century. Our imaginations shudder at the terror and agony of the wretched victim. Their sense of order was horrified by the thought of souls destroyed by false doctrine, of Churches torn asunder into parties, of the vengeance of God displayed upon them in war, pestilence, famine.

The case of the Italian refugee, Valentin Gentile, is an instructive parallel to that of Servetus. The Italian congregation in Geneva was divided on the doctrine of the Trinity. Accordingly a confession of faith was drawn up, to be subscribed on pain of banishment. All save two subscribed. Gentile, a subscriber, continued nevertheless to propagate his Trinitarian and Christological heresies. In July 1558 he was arrested and imprisoned. The statement which he drew up was considered insufficient and condemned. Not wishing to suffer Servetus' fate, he professed repentance. A commission of lawyers was deputed to determine the genuineness of his profession. On 15 August they pronounced against him, recommending that he should be executed by beheading. As other persons, however, testified to his penitence, the death sentence was commuted to making reparation and the *amende honorable*—in other words, to public penance. Eight years later Gentile repeated his views in Bern, whose authorities had no compunction about doing what Geneva had left undone, and he was beheaded on 10 September 1566.[17]

2. THE FALL OF THE PERRINISTS

While the Servetus trial had been going on, the persecution of Calvin by the Libertines had not abated. We left him in despair, asking permission to resign his ministry. At the beginning of September 1553, with an eye to the Lord's Supper shortly to be celebrated, the *Little Council* debated Philibert Berthelier's request to be absolved and Calvin's insistence that excommunication lay with the *Consistoire* and not the Council. The Council agreed that Berthelier be given permission to communicate, but asked him not to make use of it on this occasion. On Communion Sunday, 3 September, at the end of his sermon, Calvin reaffirmed the non-competency of the Council in excommunication and warned any who were excommunicate not to present themselves. He spoke so bluntly that he believed his resignation would now be accepted or that he would be summarily dismissed. In the afternoon sermon, then, it happened that in preaching through Acts he had now reached Chapter 20, where St Paul bids farewell to the elders of Ephesus in a touching scene on the sea shore: 'And now, brethren, I commend you to God, and to the word of his grace, which is able to build you up, and to give you an inheritance among all them which are sanctified' (v. 32). He was always ready to serve the Church, he said, but he saw that things were so disposed that he did not know if this might not be his last sermon in Geneva, for those in power wished to force him to do something that was not lawful in the sight of God. When he was gone, the people must not cleave to him personally but to the Word of God which had been preached to them. And so, brethren, like St Paul, I commend you to God and to the word of his grace.

Instead of dismissing him, however, the Council acted sensibly and decided that the *Ordonnances* should be carefully studied to see what they actually said. At once, however, a difficulty arose. The copy made by the clerk Trolliet, a man who had been a great nuisance to Calvin, differed from the original written by the secretary to the Council, and this original was lost. The Syndic Darlot was therefore deputed to search for it. After he had found it, a fortnight of discussion passed. On 18 September the fateful motion was put: 'whether the Council could command that the Supper be administered to him who asks for it in the Council without his showing repentance in the *Consistoire*'. A majority voted that 'we should keep to the edicts as in the past',[18] that is, 'the *Ordonnances* are to be interpreted in the sense in which they have been exercised since 1541'. Excommunication is the jurisdiction of the *Consistoire*.

By the beginning of November the Libertines had been defeated in their effort to make use of Servetus. In the result Calvin was being acclaimed as the defender of the faith, a champion of Christendom. Moreover, there were signs that the common people in Geneva had begun to compare the ministers with the Libertines and to decide that they preferred the sort of city the ministers would give them. For when Farel preached a fierce sermon against *les enfants de Genève*, that they were worse than brigands, murderers, thieves, adulterers, atheists, and was cited before the Council by some of them in the name of the citizens of Geneva, another group of citizens presented themselves to speak on his behalf also in the name of the citizens of Geneva.

The persistent Berthelier, as if he could not live without the means of grace, again applied for reinstatement on 3 November. Four days later the question of excommunication was debated in the *Two Hundred*. By a large majority it was decided that the *Ordonnances* should be exercised thus: An offender should first be admonished privately. If he failed to amend, he should then be admonished by two or three from the *Consistoire*. Still unrepentant, or if he has committed a fault serious enough, he should then be sent to the Council. 'And as for the Supper, the *Consistoire* has not the power to forbid anyone without the commandment of the Council. But if there is someone that the *Consistoire* feels should not receive the Supper, it should be told to the Council, who will discuss it and will determine whether he should be forbidden or not.' [19] The Council will act in conjunction with two or three ministers, 'but in such a way that the final word shall be with the Council'.[20] The ministers, for that they could not accept the decision, asked for a further debate in the *Two Hundred* and also in the General Council. This was granted and the outcome was that the opinions of the Churches of Bern, Zürich, Basel and Schaffhausen should be sought. These, when they arrived, decided nothing.

The trouble dragged on, with the Berthelier brothers at the heart of it. When 1554 came Calvin was still thinking he would have to leave. But he also both began to feel a gleam of hope and to notice that the Libertines were, as he had done earlier, beginning to lose heart. Philibert Berthelier was refused Communion again in the spring and summer of 1554, but made another application for the September celebration. After a long and fruitless argument in the Council it was decided to appoint a commission to enquire into the matter once more. Their report was made on 22 January 1555: 'The Council assembled under oath at 7.0 a.m. The letters from Germany [i.e. the Swiss Churches] were read word for word, as also were the edicts on excommunication. Decision: *On se tient aux editz*—we will keep to the edicts.' [21] This decision was confirmed on the 24th by the *Sixty* and the *Two Hundred*. The Church settlement of 1541 was now ratified. The opposition of the Libertines was declared to be what it had always been, illegal.

But all was not yet peaceful. The Perrinists had not changed their minds and they were still in power. They could still annoy Calvin in many ways. For instance, they made him submit his treatise on the Eucharist against Westphal to censors: 'At this I lost my temper and told the four Syndics that if I lived for a thousand years I would never publish anything else in their city.' [22] Even as late as May the victory over the discipline seemed to have been short-lived, for Calvin was writing to Farel: 'Here at home everything is in fearful confusion . . . On the inner discords of our city I am afraid that you will soon be getting bad news.' [23]

His judgment was at fault. The February elections had already thrown out the Perrinists, who had held sway for so many years. All four Syndics were now supporters of Calvin. They proceeded to oust from the *Little Council* the Libertines, and that under the same law by which they had obtained control. The *Sixty* and the *Two Hundred* were similarly purged. About the same time a large number of French refugees were given citizenship. The *Little Council* was closed to them as not Genevan born, but they could be elected to the other Councils. That this was for the economic good of the city cannot be doubted. Whether it was either wise or quite fair is another matter. At any rate it was to revive the fears, real or pretended, of French infiltration.

The Libertines had awoken to find themselves without the power which they had held long enough to consider theirs by right. The knowledge drove the wild men among them to insurrection, and they carried the more prudent or fearful with them. On 16 May they made a remonstrance to the General Council on the granting of *bourgeoisie* to so many Frenchmen. The Council refused to take any action. That evening the discontented ringleaders met for supper in a tavern. Perrin was host; among the others there were Vandel, Sept, and François Berthelier. Calvin believed that an armed uprising was plotted; most historians think that the company drank too much and got carried away by a lot of wild talk about Geneva for the Genevese. At any rate, they set out to burn down a house which they thought was full of armed Frenchmen. Meeting the servant of one of their enemies, Berthelier threw a stone at him and hurt him. Arrived at the house, they were ordered to disperse by the Syndic Aubert (who lived next door), carrying his bâton of office. Perrin snatched the bâton from him, with the implication that he was assuming power. But another Syndic arrived on the scene and ordered Perrin to go with him to the Hôtel de Ville. By now the patriots were somewhat uneasy; the half-hearted and the uneasy were slipping away down dark side streets, and soon all was quiet. The insurrection was over.

But an armed insurrection had been made. Perrin had dared to seize power by force. The authority of the republic had been attacked and insulted. Some of the leaders fled the city, Perrin and Philibert Berthelier among them. They were tried and condemned to death in their absence. Others less fortunate were tortured and executed. The living continued to make what mischief they could from a distance. But the organized and protracted opposition to Calvin's Church polity was at an end.

3. THE UNIVERSITY OF GENEVA

One part of the *Ordonnances* had yet to be satisfactorily implemented. There was preaching private and public. There was discipline. The deacons seem to have been doing their work conscientiously; the fact that we hear so little about it suggests that there were no serious complaints in an area which is usually the first to produce complaints (Acts 6: 1!). There was considerable activity in academic theology, in writing, lecturing and publishing. But the provisions for education had not been satisfactorily met. We have already seen that there was a school with Saunier, Cordier, and Castellio some time masters. This had been the successor to a late fourteenth-century school for grammar, which in the fifteenth had developed into a school to teach the *trivium* and the *quadrivium*. It fell on evil days and closed down in 1531 because no master could be obtained. In 1535 the new school had been opened in the former convent of Rive. This seems to have declined during Calvin's exile and on his return he had experienced great difficulties in getting masters and in procuring them adequate salaries. Calvin's efforts to set up a proper educational system in the city came to nothing, probably in face of the Council's unwillingness or inability to raise sufficient money. Claude Baduel, himself interested in establishing a college at Nîmes wrote to him in June 1550:

I see from your letter [a circular letter, now lost] that your city magistrates will take no great care or thought for setting up a college for the arts [*Gymnasio literarum*], and I see also that this negligence is very distressing to you. [24]

It was not until January 1558 that the Council agreed to take the matter in hand seriously.[25] Then things went very slowly ahead. On 25 March the Syndics decided that they would go down after dinner to look at a site, inviting 'M. Calvin et autres gens desprit' to accompany them. The next Monday they are quite enthusiastic:

They report that we can build six classes in the garden de Bolomier [a garden so called after the fifteenth-century founder of the hospital of Bourg du Four], still leaving room for students to walk at the side of *byse*, from which will be the entrances. This place has a fine view and plenty of fresh air, so it is healthy and wholesome for the students . . . It must be done as soon as possible.[26]

Anyone who has been concerned with getting a public building erected will be able to predict the course of events. They did not start digging the foundations until the end of 1558. They ran out of wood; they ran out of stone; they ran out of ready cash. This last was the most serious, but the Genevan Councillors were old hands at raising funds, for they had had practice in the days when they were rebuilding the city walls. Now they not only levied generous fines on offenders 'for the Collège' but also ordered all lawyers to impress on their clients the need for generosity both alive and in their wills. In the end, of course, everyone gave something, from the wealthy Robert Stephanus with his three hundred and twelve florins down to the few sous of the very poor. Part of the proceeds of the sale of the property confiscated from the Perrinists was also devoted to the Collège. So the Collège got built. It was not finished in time for the opening ceremony, but then, what building ever is? Indeed, it was not until 1563 that the workmen finally moved out; and then the glaziers had to come the next year to replace with glass the paper windows blown out in a storm. But when it was completed this quiet place stood almost as it stands now, one of the pleasantest corners in the Old City.

Already Calvin had been looking for professors, and he had been flying high. Cordier had been his first choice, but Cordier still felt committed to Lausanne. Then he asked Mercier, the Hebrew professor at the Collège de France in Paris, but he could not come. Next it was Emmanuel Tremellius, who taught Hebrew for a time in Cambridge and who was later to edit a famous Syriac and Latin Bible. He too could not come. At last he was fortunate in securing Théodore de Bèze as Rector. Beza had not yet written anything outstanding apart from his Latin translation of the New Testament in 1557; but his edition of the Greek Testament was to be published in 1565 and was enormously to influence Protestant New Testament studies. Besides Beza, however, Calvin now had a stroke of luck in that at this very point, in protest against the Council of Bern under whom they served, the entire teaching staff at Lausanne resigned and, at Calvin's invitation, migrated to Geneva, bringing some of their students with them. François Bérauld—son of the learned Nicolas Bérauld of Orléans the tutor to the Admiral Coligny, and himself a poet in Latin and Greek and the translator of Appian into Latin—became Professor of Greek. Antoine Chevalier, who also a little later taught at Cambridge, was to be Professor of Hebrew.

The Collège was opened with great ceremony in Saint Pierre on 5 June 1559. Calvin presided and made the final speech, and Beza sketched in a Latin speech the history of higher education from the Old Testament patriarchs to the modern universities. In spite of misgivings, the enterprise flourished. Within five years the numbers had risen to over one thousand in the Collège, the so-called *schola privata*, and three hundred in the Academy, the *schola publica*. The former corresponded to the preparation to the course in a university, something akin to what we have sketched in Chapter One § 2. By the time boys had passed through the seven classes they would have read some Virgil, Cicero, and Livy in Latin, Polybius, Xenophon, and Demosthenes in Greek, not only for the language but also for classical history. They would also have made a start on philosophy. In the Academy were taught theology, Hebrew, Greek verse and philosophy, dialectics and rhetoric, the physical sciences and mathematics. There were also some classes in medicine and later in civil law. But, lest we lose ourselves in thinking that Calvin was simply founding a university where all the subjects stood on a level, we will turn back to the *Ordonnances* and remind ourselves of the purpose of education:

The order nearest to the minister . . . is the lecturer in theology, of which it will be good to have one in Old and one in New Testament. But because it is only possible to profit from such lectures if first one is instructed in the languages and humanities . . . a college should be instituted for instructing children to prepare them for the ministry as well as for civil government.[27]

Here theology was still *regina scientiarum*, the crown of education, for which all arts and sciences were a preparation. Students were trained, not to get degrees or lucrative employment, but that they might serve God as preachers of the Gospel or as godly magistrates.

4. OLD TESTAMENT COMMENTARIES AND THE FINAL INSTITUTIO

Calvin himself was one of the two theological professors, with, no doubt, responsibility for the Old Testament lectures. These are the source, in fact, of most of his commentaries on the Old Testament. From about 1552 some of his younger friends agreed to act together to make his task easier. Instead of dictating to a secretary in his own room, he was now able to rely on transcripts of his lectures. Already *Isaiah* had sprung from lectures, although the first edition might be said not properly to be Calvin's own work; for Nicolas des Gallars, acting as stenographer, took down from lectures (up to 1549) the main heads of his argument, wrote them up, and read back the result to Calvin who accepted or corrected as necessary. But now a scheme was evolved to take down the lectures verbatim. None was able, apparently, to match Denis Raguenier's achievement with the sermons, and no doubt it was thought that these kept him too busy to attempt also the lectures. Yet it seems that he helped with them also, co-operating with Jean Budé and Charles de Jonviller (or Jonvilliers). In the preface to the *Minor Prophets*, Budé relates how, in the lectures on the Psalms (1552ff.) some of them, who already made notes for their own use, thought it would be good to conflate their notes and, with Calvin's cooperation, publish a commentary on the Psalms. Their plan came to nothing, for Calvin would not hear of a commentary on a book that Martin Bucer had expounded so well. Later he changed his mind and wrote a commentary (not, it would seem, a transcript of these lectures). The printer Jean Crispin explained in a preface how they performed their task:

In copying they followed this plan. Each had his paper ready in the most convenient form, and each separately wrote down with the greatest speed. If some word escaped the one (which sometimes happened, especially on disputed points and on those parts that were delivered with some fervour) it was taken down by another . . . Immediately after the lecture, de Jonviller took the papers of the other two, placed them before him, consulted his own, and, comparing them all, dictated to someone else to copy down what they had written hastily. At the end he read it all through so as to be able to read it back to M. Calvin at home the following day. When any little word was missing, it was added; or if anything seemed insufficiently explained it was easily made clearer.[28]

Budé's whole preface will repay study, not least for his critique of Calvin's lecturing style. It is, he suggests, rather in the old-fashioned, pre-Renaissance manner, 'more in the scholastic than in the oratorical style', in a 'simple though not uncultured mode of speaking', 'much like that which was used in lectures in former days'.[29] This plain and unadorned style, as Budé sees, is admirably suited to clear exposition. From a preface to *Daniel* by the printer, we have a little interesting information about Calvin's lecturing method. As we have already said, he lectured directly from his Hebrew Bible. Each verse he first recited in Hebrew and then translated into Latin. Thus, just as his New Testament commentaries are firmly anchored in the original Greek, so are his Old Testament in the Hebrew.

With the help of these enthusiastic stenographers, Calvin's Old Testament commentaries flowed fast from the presses of Geneva. In the same year as the second volume of *Acts*, *Genesis* was published. *Psalms*, however, in 1557 was not a transcript of the lectures but a commentary written or dictated by Calvin himself. In 1557 also came *Hosea*; two years later the *Minor Prophets* and a rewritten *Isaiah*, dedicated to Queen Elizabeth of England, as the first edition had been to her brother. The commentary on *Daniel* in 1561 was followed by the *Harmony of the Pentateuch*, *Jeremiah* and *Lamentations* in 1563. Two others were published posthumously, *Joshua* in 1564 and *Ezekiel 1–20* in 1565. Beza said that if he had lived longer he would have written commentaries on every book in the Bible.

It is not without significance that this professor of theology did not lecture on what we should call dogmatics. All his lectures were expositions of Scripture. The dogmatic theology was being pursued in the ever-expanding *Institutio*. We left this book in the 1550 edition with its twenty-one chapters. How soon Calvin became dissatisfied with it or how soon he took the revision in hand we do not know. But in the autumn of 1558 he became very ill with a quartan fever. Afraid that he would die with the *Institutio* unrevised, he forced himself to make the alterations he wanted.

Now a double form rules, on one side theological, on the other literary. The literary was the simple device of adopting the Apostles' Creed, already forming four chapters in the earlier edition, as the framework for the whole. The *Institutio* was therefore divided into four books, to every division of the Creed a book. 'I believe in God the Father almighty . . .'; Book I, *On the Knowledge of God the Creator*. 'And in Jesus Christ his only Son our Lord . . .

to judge the quick and the dead'; Book II, *On the Knowledge of God the Redeemer in Christ*. 'And I believe in the Holy Ghost'; Book III, *On the Mode of Obtaining the Grace of Christ*. 'The holy catholic Church . . .'; Book IV, *On the External Means or Helps by which God invites us into Fellowship with Christ and keeps us in it*. The material which had stood in the twenty-one chapters is now completely rearranged under these four books, each book divided into chapters, each chapter into numbered sections. By adopting this form Calvin had ranged his work with the earliest of the Catholic creeds. He is making it plain formally that he wishes to stand within the tradition of the Catholic Church.

Through this literary form there runs also the theological form, the treatment of doctrines in terms of the knowledge of God.[30] But it is a mistake to interpret this theological form of the *Institutio* as governed by the doctrine of the knowledge of God the Creator and the doctrine of the knowledge of God the Redeemer in Christ. In this way violence is done to Calvin's intention and his theology is misinterpreted. Rather, the twofold knowledge which governs the *Institutio* is that which has been the first sentence since 1536: 'Well-nigh the whole of sacred doctrine [all our wisdom 1539ff.] consists in these two parts, the knowledge of God and the knowledge of ourselves.' This most profound understanding of the relationship between God and man and therefore of theology is not exhausted with the first chapter. It accompanies us throughout the *Institutio*, as the presupposition of whatever doctrine is under discussion.

Besides the new form, there were also considerable additions of new material. The title tells the truth: '*Institutio Christianae religionis*, now first arranged in four books, and distinguished by chapters, by the best method; and so greatly enlarged by new material that it can almost be regarded as a new work'. From six chapters to seventeen; from seventeen to twenty-one; and now to eighty. This increase was due less to new topics demanding chapters to themselves than to the extended treatment of existing topics and the necessary sub-dividing of chapters. One of the most remarkable examples is Chapter 6 in 1536. Here we have one chapter, entitled *On Christian Liberty*, dealing with three topics, Christian liberty itself, the authority of the Church, and civil government. In 1539 this became three chapters (13, 14, and 15) dealing with these topics respectively. In 1543, however, the chapter on the authority of the Church was transferred to make part of Chapter 7, under the exposition of the Creed on the Church; Christian liberty was also placed earlier as Chapter 12; and civil government, now called *On Political Administration*, became Chapter 20. In 1559 *On Christian Liberty* appears as Book III, Chapter 19; *On Political Administration* comes, not much changed from 1536, as the last chapter of Book IV; but the material on the Church, one third of a chapter in 1536, just over one chapter in 1539ff., becomes no less than twelve chapters in Book IV.

On 2 May 1559 permission was given by the Council for its publication; and Robert Stephanus finished printing it, a most noble folio, on 16 August 1559. The *Institutio* had reached its final form. It only remained for Calvin to translate it into French like its predecessors. Colladon described how Calvin prepared this translation:

He dictated a heap of things both to his brother Antoine and to a servant who acted as secretary. He put, in various places, pages torn out of an earlier French edition. He frequently made use of the bookbinders. But in the end it was quite necessary for someone to go through the work again. In many passages there had been considerable alterations; erasions and insertions muddled the text from one end to the other, making it difficult to read, often faulty where the secretaries did not get the word that he said. At the request of Antoine, who paid for the printing of this edition ... I revised all this muddle of Latin and French as it stood in Calvin's papers, and I undertook to read it over again, to correct it and compare it, to make it surer, clearer, easier and less confused for the printing.[31]

The difficulties of printing such confused copy resulted in a somewhat faulty edition, which was not recognized as Calvin's own translation until 1921.[32]

The *Institutio* began as an oratory and ended as a cathedral. What has led to the development of the work? First and foremost, Calvin's attention to the Scriptures through so many years of lecturing, preaching and writing commentaries. As his understanding of the Bible broadened and deepened, so the subject matter of the Bible demanded ever new understanding in its interrelations within itself, in its relations with secular philosophy, in its interpretation by previous commentators. Secondly, his study of Church history and the great theologians of the Church opened up a wider view of the problems with which he was himself engaged and which he saw had, *mutatis mutandis*, been their problems also. The 1559 *Institutio* is formally a less 'modern' work than its earlier editions and bears resemblances to some patristic and early scholastic dogmatic writings. Perhaps what Budé said of his lecturing is true here also, that he is tending again to a somewhat old-fashioned form. And thirdly, the controversies in which he had been embroiled as well as his reading of the contemporary theological and religious situation compelled him to deal more and more fully with certain topics. And it is here, in contrast to what we have just said, that the 'modernity' of the *Institutio* appears most clearly. Calvin deals with the wisdom of the Christian ages, and he casts his book in a somewhat antique mould, but no-one could mistake the age in which and for which he wrote, the age of a stiff Romanist theology, of a bewildered Western Christendom, of a world taking its first steps outside the Church in the apparent freedom of secularity.

Chapter 9

Caring for the Churches

1. THE ONE BODY

A map depicting the world in about 1500 would show us all Europe coloured scarlet for the Papacy. From the Spanish peninsula to Poland, from Sicily to the Shetlands, one uniform red. Of course, a large-scale map would betray tiny patches of white here and there; in south-east Buckinghamshire and in Essex, where there still existed obstinate Lollards; in Bohemia the white of the Hussites; in 'the Alpine mountains cold' of north-western Italy, the home of the Waldensians. It is also true that the red was unstable. Looked at from another angle it wavered into the uncertainty of shot silk. What colours were they, the quasi-religious or irreligious philosophies of the Renaissance, the devotional Augustinianism of the Brethren of the Common Life, the utopias of the anabaptists and the paradises of Hieronymus Bosch, the Herculean attempts of cardinals and councils who would make the stables fit for the crib? But another turn of the map incarnadines Europe again.

Given another fifty years and the colours are more fast. Spain and Italy still scarlet as ever; but England, Scotland, Switzerland, white; France, Germany, the Netherlands, Poland, barred red and white. The Western Church has split into two opposed bodies, the Romanists and the Evangelicals. But like some great rock that falls from the cliff and breaks on the boulders below, the Evangelicals are not entire. Anglican, Lutheran, Reformed; the charitable titles cover a multitude of dissensions. Lutherans so Lutheran that they make the young Martin Luther look like the Pope, savage the moderate Lutherans whom they call crypto-Calvinists. Zürich, faithful to its warrior-theologian, distrustful of Geneva; Bern through her Boanerges Zebedee calling down fire from heaven on the writings of Calvin. And in England they are measuring out the ground for the duels of the next reign.

'I believe . . . the holy, catholic Church, the communion of saints'. 'The Church,' says Calvin, 'is called "catholic" or "universal" because there could not be two or three Churches, unless Christ is torn asunder, which is impossible.'[1] This unity is unity within the one Christ. The foundation of the Church is the election of individuals. Chosen and engrafted into Christ, they are therefore one with him; and because one with him, one also with all others who are engrafted into him. It would clearly be an absurdity to imagine a number of warring elements within Christ who were yet all in harmony with him. The concept of unity is at the very heart of Calvin's doctrine of the Church. It has been said that Calvin's thinking is collectivist throughout. Better to say unitive. We think of his insistence on the unity of God, on the unity of Christ, on the initial unity of creation, on unity with Christ and therefore on unity in Christ. He regarded nothing so unchristian, ungodly, and against the true order of things as disunity:

> all the elect are so united in Christ that, as they are dependent on one Head, they also grow together into one Body, being joined and knit together as are the limbs of a body. They are made truly one since they live together in one faith, hope and love, and in the same Spirit of God. For they have been called, not only into the same inheritance of eternal life, but also to participate in one God and Christ.[2]

There is a vital corollary to this. To be one with Christ means that he and the believer have everything they possess in common. So it is between believers. 'The communion of saints' means that any gifts bestowed by God on one believer are not his private endowment but for the common good. This is true not only of spiritual goods, but also of material. Not, he hastens to add, that private possession is forbidden, but that the believer should regard himself as the steward of what he possesses for the welfare of the whole Body: 'If they are truly convinced that God is the common Father of all and Christ the common Head, those who are united in brotherly love cannot but share their blessings with one another.'[3] This oneness, he says, is not to be disturbed by any false predestinarianism of doubting whether a fellow member is elect, so that, if he is not, we are absolved from sharing our goods with him. The elect are known to God alone. For us it is sufficient that profession of Christ is made.

Since the Church is the society of those who are or who profess to be in Christ, it follows that to be outside the Church is to be outside Christ, and hence, according to St Cyprian's famous dictum, to be without salvation. For Calvin the Christian life is Church life. He expands the old image of Mother Church: 'There is no way to enter into life except this mother shall conceive us in her womb, bring us to birth, nurse us at her breast, and keep us under her care and protection until we put off our mortal flesh and become like the angels of God.'[4] And in this case, a man does not leave his father and mother; for God is our Father and the Church our mother all the days of our life. The maternal power, however, does not lie in the Church itself, but in the Christ who by his Spirit is present in his Church in preaching and Sacrament.

The consequence is that none may separate from the Church. To separate from the Church is to separate from Christ. There will always be much to

134

grumble at in any Church; but faults do not justify separation so long as the Word of God is preached and the Sacraments are administered. The faults to which he refers may be practical, that is, abuses of one sort or another, faults in ministers or in the inner circle of Christians; or they may be fringe doctrines. There are fundamental doctrines like the Trinity, the deity and humanity of Christ, justification, or Christian love, the denial of which may not be tolerated. And there are also non-fundamental doctrines (the example he gives is where the soul goes immediately after death) for the sake of which one may not separate from the Church.

We may ask simply at this point why Calvin left Rome. Precisely because he regarded this institution as no longer the Church of God. If the Church is recognizable by the presence of Christ in his Gospel and in the Sacraments of his Gospel, then Rome was not recognizable as Church. The Gospel, he claimed, was conspicuous for its absence under the Papacy; the Sacraments had been twisted out of their genuine signification into a form and meaning that contradicted their true character. Hence the Papacy lacked the presence of the Redeemer and Lord, the Head, without whom it could not be the Body. Thus he bluntly says: 'We had to leave them in order to come to Christ.'[5] Although vestiges of Church-hood are to be found here and there under the Papacy, 'I say that every individual congregation and the whole body lack the form of the genuine Church'.[6]

For the evangelical Churches to reunite with Rome while she kept and canonized her medieval theology and constitution, Calvin soon saw to be an impossibility. Nor did he set much hope on the conferences called for this purpose. He himself was present, without playing much part, in those organized by the Emperor at Worms and Ratisbon in 1540 and 1541. There he became ashamed of the attempts to arrive at a compromise by Melanchthon and Bucer:

So far as I can understand it, if we could be content with a half-Christ we might easily come to understand one another. Philip and Bucer have drawn up ambiguous and insincere formulae on transubstantiation, to see whether they could please our opponents without themselves surrendering anything. I do not agree with this scheme . . . They do not fear equivocation in matters of conscience, than which nothing can possibly be more hurtful.[7]

He himself attended no more conferences between Romanists and Evangelicals, but urged the need for reform, showed the lines that should be followed, and criticized the weakness of the attempts that were made, in a series of treatises—*On the Necessity for Reforming the Church* (1544), *On the Fatherly Admonition of Paul III to the Emperor* (1544), *The Acts of the Synod of Trent, with an Antidote* (1547), and *The Adultero-German Interim and the true method of reforming the Church and healing her dissensions* (1549). In all, the central

135

message is clear: union lies in Christ and can be achieved only by obedience to Holy Scripture.

For the rest he pursued a settled policy towards Rome. He would have no private dealings with the institution. He maintained, so to say, no embassy in Rome. With individuals he might remain on good terms personally, while calling on them to drag themselves out of the miry clay with no long tarrying. And he will use all the devices that the sixteenth century learned from Demosthenes, Quintillian, and Cicero, to expose the abuses of the Papacy. One of his most brilliant pieces of French writing, but one in which his satire is at its most savage, is the *Traité des Reliques*. The subtitle promises 'an inventory of all the sacred bodies and relics which are in Italy, France, Germany, Spain, and other kingdoms and countries'.[8] And so he goes through the long list of the relics associated with Christ, with the Virgin, with the saints. The nails of the cross, for example. One in Milan and another in Carpentras, two in Rome, one in Siena and one in Venice, two in Germany, 'in France, one at the Sainte-Chapelle de Paris, the other at the Carmelites, another at Saint-Denis, one at Bourges, one at La Tenaille, one at Draguignan. And so there you have fourteen'.[9] The heads of St John the Baptist, the too many bones of St Peter and St Paul, the miraculously preserved water-pots (but the wrong size) from Cana in Galilee, the two bodies of St Anne and the three of Lazarus, the hair and the milk of the Virgin; Calvin knows where they all are, exposes them as sham, and asks whether any serious man will wish to place his faith in the counterfeit rather than entirely in the truth of God, the Jesus Christ of the Scriptures.

By the time Calvin appeared on the scene in 1536, Luther had another ten years to live; Melanchthon and Bucer were at the height of their influence; Zwingli had been dead for five years and Bullinger had taken his place in Zürich. Between Luther with his devoted followers and the men of Zürich was open animosity. Bucer's reputation at Wittenberg was of a foxy intriguer; and all the Swiss Churches had, in Luther's eyes, been tarred with the one brush. Although, no doubt, cultural and national differences contributed to the dissension, the immediate cause was the doctrine of the Eucharist. The conference at Marburg in 1529, called in the hope of settling differences or arriving at a compromise, merely confirmed and sharpened the disagreements. In this particular situation, Calvin early took Luther's side and even conceived such a dislike for Luther's sake against the writings of Zwingli and Oecolampadius that he would not read them. As between the two men themselves, he had no doubt of Luther's superiority: 'They flare into a rage if anyone dares to prefer Luther to Zwingli . . . This is not harming Zwingli in any way, for if they are compared with each other, you yourself know how much Luther is to be preferred.'[10] It was in an effort to resolve the Eucharistic controversy among the Evangelicals that he wrote his *Little Treatise on the Lord's Supper* (1540). Luther is reported to have said to a friend as he read it:

'This is certainly a learned and godly man, and I might well have entrusted this controversy to him from the beginning. If my opponents had done the same we should soon have been reconciled.'[11] But even before this, Luther had read the *Institutio*, probably the 1539 edition, and had sent friendly greetings through Bucer: 'Salute for me respectfully Sturm and Calvin whose books I have read with special delight.' 'Now,' says Calvin, 'just think what I have written there about the Eucharist and see the ingenuousness of Luther. It will be easy for you to see how unreasonable they are who obstinately dissent from him. Philip wrote to me: "Luther and Pomeranus have asked that Calvin should be greeted. Calvin has acquired great favour in their eyes."'[12] Some mischief makers, however, showed Luther a passage where Calvin criticized him. All he said was: 'I hope that Calvin will one day think better of us; but in any event it is good that he should even now have some proof of our good will towards him.' 'If we are not affected by such moderation,' Calvin went on, 'we are surely of stone. For myself, I am deeply moved by it, and have taken occasion to say so in the preface to *Romans*.'[13]

The friendliness lasted only a little while, however. Luther's fury with the men of Zürich in 1544 embraced Calvin also. Unjustly, for, as he told Farel, he had not even read the books that made Luther so angry. To Bullinger he counselled restraint:

Consider how great a man Luther is, and what excellent gifts he has; the strength of mind and resolute constancy, the skilfulness, efficiency and theological power he has used in devoting all his energies to overthrowing the reign of Anti-christ and to spread far and near the teaching of salvation. I have often said that even if he were to call me a devil I should still regard him as an outstanding servant of God. But with all his rare and excellent virtues he has also serious faults. Would that he had studied to curb his restless uneasy temper which is so ready to boil over everywhere . . . Flatterers have done him much mischief, since he is by nature too prone to be over-indulgent to himself.[14]

To Luther also Calvin wrote in an attempt to heal the dissension, addressing him as 'my much revered father', and 'my ever-honoured father'.[15] In fact, the letter never reached him. It was sent by way of Melanchthon, who thought it unwise to provoke Luther's wrath by showing him a communication from the enemy. The two Continental parts of the evangelical Church had set out on their separate paths and within a few years Lutheran theologians were writing their polemics against Calvin's doctrine of the Eucharist, and he was replying with an equal asperity.

Joachim Westphal of Hamburg—a man so Lutheran that he would not permit his congregation to shelter derelict non-Lutheran Evangelicals fleeing from persecution in England—opened the attack on Calvin in 1552 and 1553 with treatises that not merely taught the Lutheran doctrine of the ubiquity of Christ's body but unchurched all who did not agree with it. Calvin replied with *A Defence of the Doctrine of the Sacrament* (1555), and thereafter the controversy followed its predetermined sixteenth-century course with Westphal's answering *Defence*, Calvin's *Second Defence* (1556), Westphal's reply and Calvin's *Final Admonition to Westphal* (1557). Melanchthon suffered the fate of many non-combatants by being caught in the cross-fire and rather severely wounded. Where Westphal left off, Hesshusius, of awkward name and awkward nature, took up the quarrel with tracts against Calvin in 1560 and 1562. Against the first, Calvin, now thoroughly tired of the whole matter, replied in 1561 with *On the True Partaking of the Flesh and Blood of Christ*. It is here that he wrote his no doubt romanticized appeal to Melanchthon, who had died in the previous year:

O Philip Melanchthon! I appeal to thee, who now livest in God with Christ and there awaitest us until we are gathered with thee into blessed peace. A hundred times, wearied by the battle, and overcome by the trials, and resting thy head on my breast, thou hast said, 'Would, would that I might die on this bosom!' I too have afterwards a thousand times wished that we had lived together. Thou wouldest then have shewn more courage for the battle.[16]

There was the problem to be met of the disarray among what we should now call the Reformed Churches, not merely the quarrels between persons and the non-theological discord between local Churches but also the theological and ecclesiastical atomization. The chief occasion was once again the doctrine of the Lord's Supper, although Church order and discipline also provided fuel for discord. Time after time in his letters Calvin bewailed the lack of unity, both for its own sake and because of the scandal it caused to the rest of the world: 'What ought we, my dear Bullinger, to correspond about at this time rather than the preserving and confirming, by every possible means in our power, brotherly kindness among ourselves?'[17] It was with Bullinger principally that Calvin negotiated. In 1546 Bullinger sent him the Confession prepared by the Zürich ministers, asking for criticisms, which Calvin supplied freely. Out of this grew a further exchange of letters in which we see Calvin's exaltation of unity over points of doctrine. Why did you not take up the points that I made? he asks. We can surely discuss the matter without quarrelling, and the fact that we hold slightly different doctrines of the Eucharist in no way destroys our unity. 'In whatever way I may hold the firm persuasion of a greater communication of Christ in the Sacraments than you express in words, we shall not on that account cease to hold the same Christ and to be one in him. Some day, perhaps, it will be given us to unite in fuller harmony of doctrine.'[18] The Zürich theologians were still suspicious of him, attributing to him, he said, ideas that had never entered his mind. Agreement was at last reached when Calvin and Farel went to Zürich in the late spring of 1549. The so-called *Consensus Tigurinus*, the Agreement of Zürich, was drawn up and signed by the representatives of Zürich and Geneva and accepted by two other Swiss Churches.

The most ambitious attempt to secure evangelical unity came, however, not from Calvin, but from Thomas Cranmer. He sought to assemble in England or elsewhere a general synod of all the evangelical Churches, to discuss doctrine and especially to try to reach agreement on the Eucharist and on a form of words to express it. This was to provide the evangelical counterpoise to the Council of Trent. Accordingly, he wrote to Bullinger, Calvin, and Melanchthon, the acknowledged leaders of the Zwinglian, Calvinist and Lutheran Churches. Calvin praised the scheme, so much in accord with his teaching and his wishes, and promised 'if I could be of any service, I would not grudge to cross ten seas if it were necessary'.[19] The project came to nothing, and the sixteenth century left the Body of Christ, as Calvin put it, 'bleeding, its members severed'.[20]

2. LETTERS PRIVATE AND PUBLIC

By 1550 Geneva had taken the position formerly occupied by Zürich and become the centre of evangelical Christianity, Calvin the leader of the non-Lutheran evangelical Churches on the Continent. As we look through the eleven volumes of the letters printed in the *Corpus Reformatorum* edition, we are bewildered by the variety of the names and nationalities of the correspondents. From France and Germany, from Switzerland and the Netherlands, from Italy and Scotland, from Poland and England, come the requests for help; to them go out faithfully the long and careful answers. It is quite staggering that until the fifteen-fifties he could not be persuaded to write letters through a secretary, thinking that people might be offended if he did not write in his own hand. Jonviller it was who not only helped to preserve the Biblical lectures but lightened also this burden:

Some years ago, I saw that Calvin was almost overwhelmed with the labour of writing letters himself, without a secretary. I begged him to spare himself, and said that his letters would be no less acceptable if he signed them himself, no matter who wrote them. He replied that he thought that offence would be taken and that he would be considered careless unless he wrote with his own hand. When I gave good reasons to the contrary, he gave way, and now uses [me and] other secretaries.[21]

A few of his letters were written for purely personal reasons, but these were mostly in earlier days. There is the charming little gesture when, sending a letter to Viret by one of a pair of students and seeing that the other is a little jealous at not being the messenger, he sits down and writes for him another letter of no substance but asking Viret to pretend that it contained most important tidings.[22] He enjoyed writing to his friends. With Farel he was most free, telling him his inmost thoughts, his private opinions of other persons, pieces of secret information (although he knew that Farel was indiscreet), rebuking him with the utmost freedom, laughing with him and at him. In the letters to Farel we see Calvin unreserved and uninhibited. Later in life Bullinger took Farel's place in Calvin's correspondence, but the letters to him were never so warmly intimate.

Some of his most interesting personal letters are those to Monsieur de Falais, properly Jacques de Bourgogne, in the descent, although illegitimate, of the ducal house of Burgundy, and who had been brought up in the Imperial Court. In the early fifteen-forties he had embraced the evangelical faith and had written to ask Calvin's advice. To stay on his estates in the Netherlands would create the problem of conforming to Rome. To leave would mean giving up a great deal for an unknown and insecure future. Calvin replied in his usual direct way. 'What you should do is to leave before you are sunk so deep in the mire that you cannot get out; and the sooner you leave the better.' [23] De Falais so far acted on the advice as to seek refuge first in Cologne, under the protection of the reforming Cardinal-Archbishop Hermann, and then in Strasbourg. But in the middle of 1545 Calvin was looking out for a good house for him and his wife in Geneva. The next year he dedicated his *I Corinthians* to him as one whose life and household management admirably corresponded with St Paul's ideal for the believer. M. de Falais was much taken with his commentary, so that Calvin wrote to Madame to tell her to be patient and not complain that her husband 'enjoys himself all alone reading my commentary'. [24] He promises, too, to consider her suggestion for publishing some of his sermons, but thinks that there would not be sufficient demand for them. In February 1547 he was again seeking a house in Geneva for them, and thought that he had got one with a good garden and a fine big drawing-room. This fell through, but in May he had rented a house from Perrin, on rather stiff terms. This also was let slip, perhaps because Madame had a baby in August. In the style of the times, Calvin wrote that he would like to spend half a day with them waiting for its first smile, but putting up with its tears and cries, which are the keynote, the first note sounded at the beginning of this life, 'that we may smile from the heart when we are about to depart from it'.[25] Alas! the poor little thing was given no time to learn to smile, for she did not see September. At last the house-hunting bore fruit and in February 1548 Calvin fixed them up with an estate in the village of Veigy. After further delays, they were in Geneva by the August and apparently lived with Calvin for the rest of the year before moving to Veigy, some eight miles out on the road to Thonon.

Most of the letters, however, concerned Church business of one sort or another; and many of them are theological treatises running to several thousand words. He found himself in the black books of Queen Marguerite of

Navarre. The logic of her religion, learned largely from Lefèvre and Briçonnet, had opened her heart to the spirituality of the so-called Libertines. This name (they have nothing whatever to do with the Genevan Libertines) signifies an antinomianism and a freedom from religious forms, including the Scriptures. Calvin had written a tract *Against the Fanatical and Furious Sect of the Libertines who call themselves Spirituals* (1545); Marguerite was sheltering two of them in her court. In attacking them, she said, Calvin was attacking her. A long letter had to be written.[26] To rulers or influential ministers of state in Britain, Poland, France, flowed out from Geneva the recommendations on Church reform, the exhortations to act boldly. The one message to all was: Unconditional obedience to the Word of God in place of political and personal considerations.

This was the burden, too, of the two early open letters, supposed to be addressed to his Orléans friend Du Chemin and to the reformist Gérard Roussel, on fleeing idolatry and on renouncing the Roman priesthood (for Roussel had just been offered a bishopric). And in the many letters to commoners, to nobility, to royalty, there was again but the one theme. No compromise! he wrote to the Duchess Renée, whose evangelical chaplain had suggested that it would be politic for her to attend Mass and then have a nice quiet little Lord's Supper afterwards. No compromise! to Madame de Cany, the Picard lady won for the faith by Laurent de Normandie, and who was being persecuted by her husband. No compromise! to the King of Navarre, son-in-law of Marguerite: 'although according to the world it would seem neither useful nor expedient to confess the truth of God, yet you have to consider, Sir, what he demands of you who is entitled to be obeyed without contradiction.'[27] To M. d'Andelot, younger brother of the Admiral Coligny, who had capitulated during his imprisonment, he wrote bracingly and without pity: 'God has been defrauded by your overgreat deference to men, whether from favour, fear, or respect . . . Your fall has been very grievous, and you ought to remember it with bitterness of heart.'[28] He was infuriated by the weakness of Navarre, who was being drawn away from his duty by 'foolish *amours*', by '*jeunes filles*', and with his brother the Prince of Condé for his flirtations—a source of scandal in one who should be setting an example to the rest. While the fate of the Gospel hangs in the balance, these leaders think they have time to chase after women.

In among such letters an old correspondence was resumed. Who should turn up in Geneva in 1559 but the son of François Daniel, run away from home to join the army of the Lord in Geneva! It was not the first time that Calvin had been called upon in the difficulties of the Daniel family. I am sure you will be angry, he wrote, because he has disappointed you and disobeyed you. But do not be too angry. 'If you had had the courage to do your duty that you ought to have had, you would long ago have set him an example.'[29] He is obviously a good lad, and has only left France because he cannot bear the superstitions of the Papacy. You ought to be pleased with him, and I affectionately beg you to treat him friendly. The letter was successful, not only in gaining forgiveness for the young man, but also in reviving the friendship dormant over twenty years. François wished his son to study civil law; he would do so, but without enthusiasm. Calvin would also see to it that he studied the humanities and theology, but above all that he be trained in godliness. Calvin also hopes that François will now follow his son's good example and extricate himself from the snares in which he is entangled.[30] Early in the New Year the young Daniel returned home, followed by a letter from Calvin on his aptitude and promise, and with greetings to old Madame Daniel, who was still alive, and presents for the lad's sisters.

He was by no means the only one to go to Geneva, nor the only one soon to leave. It was reckoned that in 1557 the refugees outnumbered the inhabitants. More than three-quarters of them were of French nationality, and of the rest there were comparatively few who were not French-speaking, either from the southern Netherlands or from the French-speaking Churches in the Rhineland, forced out from both places by persecution. The internal political consequences of this vast influx of Frenchmen we have already seen and no one will wish to blame the Genevese for their anxiety. If, however, their fear was based on the dangers to the economy, it had more justification. A Robert Estienne, a Jean Crespin, a Laurent de Normandie, would create prosperity and confer honour on the city. But these famous business men were not going to give work to some thousands of extra hands in a city that had numbered ten thousand only twenty years before. Nor, as we have already seen, could Geneva expand beyond its walls. A very serious housing shortage resulted. The man (perhaps with a family) who could not get work and who had no satisfactory accommodation drifted off to some other city. The English refugees who had flocked to Frankfurt, Zürich and Geneva in 1554 and 1555, as soon as they heard that Queen Mary was dead and Elizabeth on the throne returned to the England that they knew would welcome them.

Where they were numerous enough, the non French-speaking refugees formed their own Church. The English, indeed, tended to keep themselves to themselves so far as Genevese were concerned, and to form a community of their own. Besides the ministers like John Knox and William Whittingham, the future Dean of Durham, there were the families of John Bodley, father of the founder-to-be of the Bodleian, of Sir William Stafford and men like Sir Richard Morrison and the printer Rowland Hall. They carried out an important activity of publishing which was to culminate in the Geneva Bible of 1560, the most widely used Bible in England until the Authorized Version.

Mixed with the immigrants who had genuinely fled from persecution there were also some strange characters and, we may conjecture, not a few French secret agents. One of the most curious lived next door to Calvin from 1559. This was Jacques Spifame. An entry in the *Registres de Conseil* for 17 April in that year tells us that Jacques Spifame, formerly Bishop of Nevers, and 'président et maistre des requestes du roy', had come to Geneva for the sake of the Gospel and was asking for asylum. Granted. He also mentioned that 'he had kept *une femme* for some years whom he had never married'.[31] This last matter was referred to the *Consistoire*, who gave their blessing to the union. Before long he was admitted *bourgeois*. Then this former bishop became a pastor. Unfortunately, a few years later he was sent as a minister to France, and there, the Council heard, he was negotiating for another bishopric. It also came out that he had not told all the truth about his wife and that he had made a false marriage contract. For these crimes, or more probably for intrigues with France or Savoy which were never made public, he was beheaded in Geneva in 1566—but that takes us beyond our story.

The Italians had their own Church from 1542. Its first minister had been Bernardino Ochino, formerly General of the Capuchins, who was warmly attached to Calvin and who found Geneva most congenial. Another close friend of Calvin's was one of the Italian deacons, but a man so highly placed that when he applied for asylum the Council suspected him of being a spy. This was Galeazzo Caracciolo, Marquis of Vico, head of one of the foremost families in Naples, a great-nephew of Pope Paul IV, and a chamberlain to the Emperor. He had left his country and career, his wife and family, to settle in Geneva in 1551, and there he remained for the rest of his life, in spite of urgings from Pope and family to return. In 1559 he obtained a divorce from his wife, apparently on the grounds of desertion, and married again. At the time this was something of a *cause célèbre*, both because of Caracciolo's connections and because it illustrated the Reformed attitude to remarriage after divorce. But the Italian Church was also to cause trouble by its Trinitarian heresies through Gentile.

3. OUTSIDE GENEVA

We come to the establishment and organization of local or national Churches. To some Calvin could offer advice only on the basis of such information about the local situation as he had been given, and he was not always well advised. Usually, perhaps always, he wrote only when it was suggested that his help would be welcome. But his advice was not invariably taken. Thus his letters to the Duke of Somerset, the first 'Protector' in England during the reign of Edward VI, contained a complete scheme for reforming the English Church. The first letter was, indeed, a little treatise running to some five thousand words.[32] Its chief recommendations were: (1) provision should be made for the preaching of the Gospel; (2) abuses should be eradicated; (3) some form of discipline should be established. He wrote Somerset other letters on specific points of Church organization and also dedicated to him his *I Timothy*. As we have already seen, to the young King he dedicated both his *Isaiah* and the *Catholic Epistles*; but Edward was never to have a chance to put into effect the advice he received, for he died in 1553, to be succeeded by his sister Mary. Some of the refugees escaping from her persecutions we have seen in Geneva, but the majority went either to Zürich or Frankfurt. On Elizabeth's accession in 1557 the situation had quite changed for Calvin. We may conjecture that his advice had been rather respected than regarded as practicable by the Edwardine councillors and bishops, and that, whatever had happened, the new queen would not have leaned Geneva-wards. But she had good excuse for her coldness. Not only had Calvin tended to support the Knoxians in the famous troubles in Frankfurt, calling some things in the 1552 Book of Common Prayer unsuitable even if endurable, but he had soon been gravely compromised by John Knox's book against women rulers, the *First Blast against the Monstrous Regiment of Women*. Although Calvin tried to mend matters by letters to William Cecil and although he dedicated the revised edition of *Isaiah* to 'The Most Serene Queen, splendid for her virtues no less than for her royal glory, the Lady Elizabeth, Queen of England and Sovereign Lady in Ireland and the circumjacent isles', the damage had been done. The influence wielded by Calvin in England for the next forty years was enormous, but it was by means of his numerous works, especially the *Institutio* (translated in 1561) but also the translations of his commentaries and sermons. Moreover, he never exercised a direct influence through, so to say, the official channels, even though leading statesmen and churchmen, including some archbishops, were strong Calvinists. In the controversies between the Church of England and the Puritans and Separatists, the position of Calvin is far from clear. A close study might well show that it was the champions of the established Church who claimed his support and that their opponents relied rather on Bullinger and Beza.

His influence in Scotland, immense as it was, was nevertheless still not direct but mediated through his personal relationship with Knox in Geneva and through his writings. After Knox had returned to Scotland in 1559, he organized reform according to the pattern of Geneva, with local adjustments; but he very rarely sought Calvin's advice. His liturgy was close to Calvin's and the Scottish 1560 Confession of Faith might be regarded as a restatement of Calvin's theology. How far Calvin's theology and the polity was transmuted as it passed through Knox's mind is another matter. Nevertheless, the name of Calvin was still honoured in Scotland when it had been forgotten in England.

In Poland there had been a long tradition of independence over against the Papal demands. Add that at the end of the fifteen-forties persecution drove many Evangelicals from Bohemia into Poland. Add also that there was a strong humanist influence in the country. It seemed for a time that King Sigismund II, urged on by his chancellor Nicolas Raziwill, might reform the Church on the lines of Calvin's recommendations in letters and book dedications. This failed to happen; and the Calvinian Church in Poland, at one time numerous in membership and powerful in influence, had been virtually broken by the early years of the seventeenth century.

But no land was so much the object of Calvin's pastoral care as his own homeland. He lived in Geneva and after many years was admitted to citizenship; but he remained always a Frenchman, striving to win his fellow-countrymen for Christ, to see the Church return to its origins in the evangelical faith. To understand Calvin's work towards France, it is necessary to know something of its immediate religious history. The persecution that had driven away Calvin and so many others in 1534 continued sporadically, with the persecuting edicts being enforced with less or more of rigour. Francis was a lazy persecutor in comparison with his successor Henri II, who, when on his accession in 1547 he saw the Evangelicals increasing in the country, set up a special court to deal with them, the so-called *Chambre ardente*. This operated for two years, when heresy trials were once again taken over by the ecclesiastical courts. The Churchmen proving too lenient, the trials were transferred by the Edict of Chateaubriand to the civil courts, and soon the *Chambre ardente* made its appearance again. A reign of terror ensued comparable to the fearful years in England under Mary Tudor. Attempts to establish an even tighter inquisition on the Spanish pattern were rejected by the *Parlement* of Paris, but this made little difference to the severity of the persecution.

Faced with such a situation, Calvin called upon French evangelical Christians to stand firm. This had been his message from the beginning. It was the burden of one of his most brilliant French treatises, *Excuse de Iehan Calvin à Messieurs les Nicodémites* (1544). 'Apologia of Jean Calvin to the Nicodemites, on their complaint that he is too rigorous'. There are many in France who wish to embrace the Gospel, but who fear for themselves or their families. There are others who are intellectually interested in the Gospel and half turn Christianity into a philosophy, but who see no need for reformation. There are the courtier clergy, *les délicats*, who want a charming and cultured religion which they can discuss pleasantly with *les mignons de cour*. And there are the time-serving clergy who gently move a little with the spirit of the times, not far, but just enough to attract attention as modern men, men with their ear to the ground, suitable men for good posts—for we must not forget that a reformist bishop, provided he kept in line, was a far better advertisement for Rome than some old diehard like Bédier. They are all saying that Calvin is too extreme. But 'it is not a question of their opinion or mine. I show what I have found in Scripture. And I have not made up my mind in a hurry, but have pondered the matter frequently. What is more, I say only what is well known, what none can contradict without blatantly denying the Word of God'.[33] They must give up their worldly wisdom, their being wiser than God, and become obedient to his Word. There is no need for them to seek persecution, no need to do wild things. Let them just be obedient to God's Word;

not a little obedient, excusing their weakness, but let them aim at a total obedience. Then they will stop playing with religion and start being religious in earnest. They will not try to hide themselves by outwardly conforming to the Papist religion. 'Nicodemus came to Jesus by night in the time of his ignorance. After he had been taught, he confessed him openly by day, even at the hour of the greatest peril.' [34]

Calvin did more than exhort and strengthen. He provided the local churches springing up in many districts with literature and where possible with ministers. At first these churches were just groups of Evangelicals meeting to pray and read the Bible together. But even in the fifteen-forties it becomes clear that some groups had moved out of this stage and had begun to adopt an organization and also, a significant step as we see in the English Separatist congregations, to make provision for the celebration of the Sacraments. Calvin's Church organization was generally accepted, no doubt adapted in details to suit local conditions. By the end of the next decade there were possibly as many as fifty organized Churches in France. How many were represented at the Synod in Paris in May 1559 is matter of debate. At this Synod there was framed, against Calvin's wishes, a Confession of faith, the *Confessio fidei gallicana*, based on his Genevan Confession. A system of discipline was also drawn up. Since this Church needed to be organized on a national scale, it had to go beyond the Genevan model intended for a city of three parishes with a few villages. In France the central authority in the evangelical Church was the national synod, to which representatives were elected from the local synod, or colloquy.

Already for many years Geneva had been sending help to the French congregations. This had largely taken the form of books smuggled into the country and sold by the colporteurs, who also sometimes acted as ministers. (One interesting by-result of this was that printing became the major industry in Geneva and the sale of books the major export, thus helping, but by no means resolving, the endemic balance of payment problem.) Besides the colporteurs, however, Geneva took the lead in sending regular ministers into France.[35] Between 1555 and 1562 upwards of one hundred ministers were sent into France. This was strictly the activity of the pastors in Geneva. The Council asked Calvin to tell them nothing about it. When the French authorities complained, they were able to disclaim responsibility.

It was from Lausanne, however, that there went out the five young men who were captured and imprisoned at Lyon. Calvin wrote to them with his same message to stand fast. In the meanwhile, we are both praying for you and making representations in the right quarters. Trust in God; he has never failed any. They were in prison for a year. A pardon seemed less probable, but not impossible. If God's good pleasure shall lead them to the stake, he now wrote, let them be confident that his grace will be with them to sustain them. 'And now, brethren, after having besought our good Lord to take charge of you, to help you in everything and through everything, to make you taste by experience how kind a Father he is and how careful of the salvation of his own, I pray to be remembered in your prayers.' [36] At last it was clear that they would be burned:

Since it seems that God would use your blood to sign his truth, there is nothing better for you than to prepare yourselves to that, praying him so to subdue you to his good pleasure that nothing may prevent you from following wherever he calls you. For you know, my brothers, that we must be mortified like this in order to be offered to him in sacrifice. You cannot fail to have hard conflicts, when what was said to Peter will be accomplished in you, that they will carry you whither you would not. You know, however, in what strength you have to fight. All those who trust that strength shall never be daunted, far less confounded. So, my brothers, be confident that you will be strengthened according to your need by the Spirit of our Lord Jesus, so that you will no more faint under the heavy weight of temptations than did he who won such a glorious victory that in the midst of our miseries it is an unfailing pledge of our triumph. Since it pleases him to use you to the death in maintaining his quarrel, he will strengthen your hands in the fight and will not suffer a single drop of your blood to be shed in vain.[37]

In 1559 a more sinister turn was taken in the evangelical affairs. The persecuted Church began to think in terms of armed resistance, even of armed revolt. The ranks of the Evangelicals now contained a large number of nobles, unused to suffering wrongs as patiently as the middle classes who had hitherto predominated. It seemed, too, that the doubtful political situation created by the sudden death of Henri II and the Council of regency set up because of the king's youth and weak intellect, might prove a favourable opportunity to overturn the established Church. Calvin was sounded as to his opinions on active revolt. He had already, in a letter to the Church in Paris, made it clear that he was aware of the new situation brought about by the change in the composition of the Church, and had spoken out strongly against the use of force: 'Let it be your care to attempt nothing that is not warranted by his Word . . . It would be better for us all to be ruined than that the Gospel of God should be exposed to the reproach that it had armed men for sedition and tumult.' [38] His teaching in the *Institutio* is clear, but it leaves a loophole for resistance. Rulers are to be obeyed, even when they are unjust and cruel. No private citizen has the right or the duty to resist or to seek to overthrow the ruler. But in a state that is not an absolute monarchy there will always be, alongside the chief ruler, his ministers of state, his nobles of royal blood, his parliament. Calvin therefore makes an exception and indeed declares it the duty of certain bodies to withstand the ruler when his government becomes intolerable:

I am speaking only of private men. For sometimes popular magistrates have been appointed to curb the tyranny of kings. There were the Ephori, who were opposed to kings among the Spartans, or the Tribunes of the people to the consuls among the Romans, or Demarchs to the Senate among the Athenians. And perhaps something similar exists in the power exercised in each kingdom by the Three Orders when they hold their primary assemblies. So far am I from forbidding these to use their office to moderate the undue licence of kings when they tyrannize and lord it over the humbler of the people, that I affirm that their dissimulation is not free from wicked treachery, because they fraudulently betray the liberty of the people, knowing that by the ordinance of God they are its appointed guardians.[39]

At first sight the situation in France seems precisely to fit the exception. Here was a powerful monarchy pursuing a tyrannical policy over the humbler people. Here too were the Three Estates of Clergy, Nobles, and Commoners, although they had not met for half a century. Among the many nobles who openly professed the evangelical faith were two princes of the royal blood, the King of Navarre and his brother the Prince of Condé. The King of France, whether in his own person or through a regency, was oppressing the Evangelicals. Little or no help was to be expected from the Clergy. The nobles were therefore clearly the most fitted 'to moderate the licence of the king'. And yet Calvin would not sanction armed force. Plainly, everything hinges on what he means by 'moderating' and 'curbing'. Taken in the context of the fact that in Geneva he took no steps to overturn the Perrinist régime by force, and that now in France he rejected this policy, it would seem that he was not advocating armed resistance but pressure on the ruler through constitutional means.

The use of constitutional means, however, had been let slip by the political foolishness of the King of Navarre, who had allowed himself to be manipulated by the Queen Mother, Catherine de Medici. Power had thus passed into the hands of the Guises, that is, the Cardinal of Lorraine and his brother the Duc de Guise. They continued the persecutions of Henri II. Now Calvin was asked about a specific conspiracy. The plan was to arrest the Guises and for Evangelicals to supply their place. The leader of the conspiracy was one Godefroy de Barry, the Seigneur de la Renaudie, regarded by Calvin as 'a man of no personal merit'. He went to see Calvin, to gain his support and to raise some troops in Geneva. 'I immediately,' wrote Calvin to Bullinger, 'put a stop to his bragging and professed my utter abhorrence for his conspiracy.'[40] De Barry nevertheless gave it out that he had Calvin's blessing. In the manner of all these amateur conspirators, he held what he supposed to be secret meetings with sympathizers in the city. Volunteers were enrolled. Calvin told them they must be bewitched and asked them what they thought they were going to achieve. They replied that the Prince de Condé was going to present the Genevan Confession to the King as a sort of manifesto for evangelical liberty and that a large force would be assembled to defend the Prince in case the Guises should try to arrest him. Calvin said that he was still not happy unless they took good care that no bloodshed should result, 'for I declared that the inevitable result would be that from a single drop there would at once flow streams that would drown France'.[41] The conspiracy was bungled, of course. To John Sturm of Strasbourg Calvin expressed his disgust, not only at the principle but also at their amateurish execution; 'what they resolved foolishly they planned childishly'.[42] From this Conspiracy of Amboise flowed the rivers of blood which Calvin had foretold, the wars of religion in France.

He was, during the events which followed, not only well informed but also in close touch with the leaders of the Evangelicals. A very large part of his correspondence during the last years of his life dealt with the troubles in France. During the civil war of 1562 he accepted the *fait accompli* to the extent of asking from the Genevan Council a loan for the Huguenots (which they could not give) and of countenancing the sending of volunteers from Switzerland. When the war ended with the Peace of Amboise in April 1563, he was again angry at the bad terms that the Huguenots had accepted. But when he spoke of God giving his followers a second chance of employing themselves in his service,[43] he did not mean another war, for 'I shall always give my advice to abstain from arms, and that all of us should perish rather than have recourse a second time to the disorders which we have witnessed'.[44] This to the Comtesse de Roye, the sister-in-law of Condé. The armed truce lasted beyond Calvin's lifetime, so that he never saw the second civil war in his France.

Chapter 10

Christ is Gain in Dying

In September 1558 a bombshell burst. Farel announced that he was going to get married. Calvin was much in demand for suggesting brides for young men. Only a couple of months before he had been writing to Farel himself on behalf of such a young man and saying that he can think off-hand of only three girls who are beautiful, virtuous, and well-dowried, although there are certainly two very pretty girls living near him, but their dowries are not very large. Ride over one day, he says, and we will talk about it. He little expected, when Farel did ride over, what he was going to hear. Farel, now aged sixty-nine, was engaged to a mere girl, the daughter of his refugee housekeeper. What is more, she had been for some time, and still was, living under the same roof with him. Would Calvin, his best and oldest friend, take the wedding? No, Calvin would not, and told him so bluntly. Farel, living perhaps, poor fellow, in a dream world of passionate love, could not believe that he meant it and when he got home wrote and asked him to change his mind. Calvin replied: 'I told you to your face that I would come neither to your engagement ceremony nor yet to your wedding, both because it was impossible and also because I thought it unwise. I am therefore surprised that you should invite me again.' [1] Farel should get married as soon as possible so as not to make a bad matter worse, for enough scandal had been created as it was. Farel's colleagues wrote to Calvin. They were flabbergasted. What should they do? Could they force him to break off the engagement? Calvin's answer is full of embarrassment, anger and pity—'le pouvre frere maistre Guillaume', 'we blush for his weakness', 'I am dumb with astonishment', 'only six months ago le pouvre frere would have said that an old man who wanted to marry a young woman should be tied up as a madman', 'I have reproached him very sharply'. But no, nothing can be done about it. Farel has given his word to the girl and he must keep it. The marriage is not illegal and no one has a right to break it off. But do not forget his past life as you judge him, 'how he has for thirty-six years and more served God and edified the Church, how profitable his labours have been, with what zeal he has striven'.[2] Calvin himself did not entirely cast him off, but his letters become infrequent and brief.

No sooner had Calvin recovered from the quartan fever of 1558–9, than he aggravated his lung trouble. He overstrained his voice preaching in Saint Pierre, and brought on a violent fit of coughing at home afterwards, so violent that he broke a blood-vessel in his lungs and had a bad haemorrhage. From this time his delicate health declined. He suffered great pain from the stone and from piles, and was weakened more and more by pulmonary tuberculosis. He continued with his usual work, however, although by the beginning of 1563 'he was often carried to his duties in a chair or on horseback'.[3] He kept going until February 1564, when he was in a pitiable plight, as his letter to the physicians of Montpellier, who had asked whether they could do anything to help, testifies:

I have no way of showing my gratitude other than recommending you to draw from my writings what may afford you spiritual medicine. Twenty years ago I experienced the same courteous services from the distinguished physicians of Paris, Acatus, Tagant, and Gallois. But at that time I was not attacked by gout, knew nothing of the stone or the gravel, was not tormented with the gripings of colic nor afflicted with piles nor threatened with haemorrhages. At present all these enemies charge me like troops. As soon as I recovered from a quartan fever, I was taken with severe and acute pains in my calves, which, after being partly relieved, returned a second and then a third time. At last they turned into a disease of the joints, which spread from my feet to my knees. An ulcer in the haemorrhoid veins long tortured me . . . Last summer I had an attack of nephritis. As I could not endure the jolting of horseback, I was carried into the country in a litter. Coming home I wanted to walk some of the way. I had hardly gone a mile when I was forced to stop, because of a feeling of lassitude in the loins, for I wanted to make water. And then to my surprise, blood flowed instead of urine. As soon as I got home I went to bed. The nephritis was very painful and remedies gave me only a partial relief. At last, with the most painful strainings I ejected a stone, and this lessened the evil. But it was so big that it tore the urinary canal and the flow of blood could be arrested only by an injection of woman's milk through a syringe. Since then I have ejected several others and the heaviness of my loins is sufficient symptom that there is still some stone there. It is a good thing, however, that minute or at least moderately small particles continue to be ejected. The sedentary way of life to which I am condemned by the gout in my feet prevents all hope of a cure. I am also prevented from taking exercise by the trouble in my seat. For although no ulcer appears, yet the veins are very swollen . . . But I am thoughtlessly taxing your patience, giving you double labour as the reward for your kindness, not indeed in consulting you but in giving you the trouble of reading over my trifles.[4]

And to Bullinger on 6 April 1564:

Although the pain in my side is abated, my lungs are so full of phlegm that my breathing is difficult and short. A stone in my bladder has been very troublesome for the last twelve days. Add to that our anxiety. For all remedies have so far proved ineffectual. Horseriding would have been best, but an ulcer in the haemorrhoid veins tortures me even when sitting down or lying in bed, so that I could not bear the agitation of riding. Within the last three days the gout has also been very troublesome. You will not be surprised, then, if so many sufferings make me lazy. I can hardly be brought to take any food. The taste of wine is bitter.[5]

On Wednesday 2 February he preached on I Kings in the morning and in the afternoon gave his sixty-fifth lecture on Ezekiel, concluding with the sentence:

And since that was said to his ancient people because they returned to the land of Canaan, how much more should God's free goodness be extolled by us, when his heavenly kingdom is at this day open for us, and when he openly calls us to himself in heaven and to the hope of the happy immortality which has been obtained for us through Christ?

And he ended with the prayer:

Grant, almighty God, since we have already entered in hope upon the threshold of our eternal inheritance, and know that there is a certain mansion for us in heaven after Christ has been received there, who is our Head and the first fruits of our salvation, grant (I say) that we may proceed more and more in the course of thy holy calling until at length we reach the goal and so enjoy the eternal glory of which thou dost afford us a taste in this world; by the same Christ our Lord. Amen.[6]

He was not well enough to preach or lecture for the remainder of this week, but on the Sunday morning he preached again on the Harmony of the Gospels. After this the pulpit of Saint Pierre knew him no more. Nevertheless, he still sometimes attended the Friday *Congrégation*, spoke briefly and closed with prayer.

In a touching but clumsy attempt to show their sympathy, the *Little Council* ordered the Syndics to visit him and gave him a present of twenty-five crowns. Calvin received the Syndics but refused the money, for he would not be paid when he was not working. Later in March he was a little better and even thought that he would live longer. But the exertion and excitement of holding the monthly meeting for mutual criticism at his house, and of discussing with the ministers some revisions in the French New Testament, set him back again. Once more he waited on the Council, and on Easter Day he received the Sacrament at Saint Pierre. He continued to dictate letters. 'What!' he would say when urged to rest, 'would you have the Lord find me idle when he comes?'

On 25 April he made his will. There was not a great deal to leave. To the Collège he left ten crowns and the same amount to the Compagnie des pauvres étrangers. To his niece, the daughter of Marie, ten crowns, to Antoine's two sons forty crowns each and to his daughters thirty each. Their brother David, a disobedient son, was left only twenty-five crowns. If his possessions when sold brought in more than the sum computed, the extra was to be divided among the legatees; but in fact his own computation had been about right. To Antoine, *frater meus carissimus*, he left, *honoris causa duntaxat*, a silver cup given him by M. de Trie.

As it was his wish to take leave of the *Little Council*, they visited him on the 27th. He told them that he believed his time was short and that he wished to thank them for their kindness to him; it would have been impossible for them to have shown more. It was true that he had had many conflicts in Geneva but this was not their fault. He asked their pardon that he had not done all he should have done; but his intentions had been good, and if he said that God had not used him at all he would be a hypocrite. He asked pardon, too, for his impatience and bad temper, which was part of his nature but of which he was ashamed. And it was right also that Messeigneurs should have a word of exhortation. In everything they must put their trust in God, when things are going well no less than in adversity, for 'we have an example in David, who confesses that when he was quietly settled in his kingdom, he forgot himself so far as to have stumbled mortally had not God taken pity on him'. Let them all do their duty in the commonwealth, each according to his calling, without envy or hatred, looking to God and praying him to lead by his Holy Spirit.[7]

The next day the ministers met at his house, and he delivered his last message to them. I have often been ill, he said, but now I feel quite different from anything I have felt before. I am so weak that I faint when I am put to bed, and all the time I cannot get my breath. 'I am quite different from other sick people. When they come near to their end, their senses fail and they become delirious. I certainly feel stupefied, but it seems as if God wants to concentrate all my inward senses. I believe I shall have much difficulty and that it will cost me a great effort to die.'[8] He was afraid that he might lose the power of speech.

And then he lived over again in a strange medley of devotion, self-justification, and bitterness, his life in Geneva:

When I first came to this Church, I found almost nothing in it. There was preaching and that was all. They would look out for idols, it is true, and burn them. But there was no reformation; everything was in disorder. There was, of course, the good man, Maistre Guillaume, and then blind Courauld. And besides them there was Maistre Antoine Saunier and that fine preacher Froment, who laid aside his apron and got up in the pulpit, then went back to his shop, where he chattered, and thus gave a double sermon.

I have lived here amid continual strifes. I have been saluted in derision of an evening before my door with forty or fifty arquebus shots. Just imagine how that frightened a poor scholar, timid as I am, and as I confess I have always been.

Then afterwards I was expelled from this city and went to Strasbourg; and when I had lived there some time I was called back here. But I had no less trouble when I tried to do my duty than previously. They set the dogs at my heels, calling out 'Wretch! wretch!', and they snapped at my gown and my legs. I went to the *Council of the Two Hundred* when they were fighting, and I kept back the others who wanted to go, and who had nothing to do there. They may boast that it was they who did everything, like M. de Saulx [Nicolas des Gallars], yet I was there, and as I went in, they said to me, 'Go away, Monsieur, they have nothing against you.' I replied, 'I will do no such thing. Come, wicked men that you are, come and kill me. My blood will rise up against you and these very benches will require it.' So I have been amid struggles. And you will find that there will be others, not less, but greater. For you are a perverse and unhappy nation, and though there are good men in it the nation is perverse and wicked, and you will have troubles when God shall have called me away; for though I am nothing, yet I well know that I have prevented three thousand tumults that might have broken out in Geneva. But take courage and fortify yourselves, for God will make use of this church and will maintain it and assures you that he will protect it.

I have had many infirmities which you have been obliged to bear with, and what is more, all I have done has been worth nothing. The ungodly will greedily seize upon this word, but I say it again that all I have done has been worth nothing, and that I am a miserable creature. But certainly I can say this, that I have willed what is good, that my vices have always displeased me, and that the root of the fear of God has been in my heart; and you may say that the disposition was good; and I pray you, that the evil be forgiven me, and if there was any good, that you conform yourselves to it and make it an example.

As to my doctrine, I have taught faithfully, and God has given me grace to write what I have written as faithfully as it was in my power. I have not falsified a single passage of the Scriptures, nor given it a wrong interpretation to the best of my knowledge; and though I might have introduced subtle senses, had I studied subtlety, I cast that temptation under my feet and always aimed at simplicity.

I have written nothing out of hatred to any one, but I have always faithfully propounded what I esteemed to be for the glory of God.

As to our internal state, you have elected Monsieur de Bèze to hold my place. Take care to help him, for the charge is great, and so weighty that he might well sink under the load. But take care to support him. I know that he has a good will and will do what he can.

Let every one consider the obligation which he has not only to this church but also to the City, which you have promised to serve in adversity as well as in prosperity. Let each keep to his vocation and not try to retire from it nor enter into factions. For when people go underground and intrigue, they may say indeed that they did not reflect, and that they did aim at this or that. But let them consider the responsibility that they have contracted before God.

And study, too, that there be no bickerings or sharp words among you, for sometimes biting gibes will be bandied about. This will take place, it is true, in fun, but there will be bitterness in the heart. All that is good for nothing, and is even contrary to a Christian disposition. You should guard against it, and live in good accord and all friendship and sincerity.

I had forgotten this point: I pray you make no change, no innovation. People often ask for novelties. Not that I desire for my own sake out of ambition that what

I have established should remain, and that people should retain it without wishing for something better, but because all changes are dangerous and sometimes hurtful.

On my return from Strasbourg, I composed the Catechism—and in haste; for I would never accept the ministry until they had taken an oath on these two points, that is, to preserve the Catechism and discipline. And while I was writing it they came to fetch pieces of paper the size of my hand and carry them to the printer's. Though Monsieur Pierre Viret was then in this town, do you think I ever showed him a word of it? I never had the time. I have sometimes indeed thought of putting some finishing touches to it if I had had the leisure.

As to the Sunday prayers, I adopted the form of Strasbourg, and borrowed the greater part from it. I could not take any of the other prayers from it, for it had none, but I took the whole from the Scriptures.

I also had to compose a formula of Baptism when I was at Strasbourg, where the children of anabaptists were brought to me from five or six leagues off to be baptized. I then composed this rough formula—which I would not advise you, all the same, to change.

The Church of Bern has betrayed this Church, and they have always feared me more than they loved me. I want them to know that I died in the opinion that they feared rather than loved me. And even now they fear me more than they love me, and have always been afraid lest I should upset their Eucharist.[9]

He turned again to Farel with a touching letter:

Since it is God's will that you should outlive me, remember our friendship. It was useful to God's Church and its fruits await us in heaven. I do not want you to tire yourself on my account. I draw my breath with difficulty and expect each moment to breathe my last. It is enough that I live and die for Christ, who is to all his followers a gain both in life and in death.[10]

(Thus Calvin's translation of Phil. 1: 21 in his *Commentary*: 'For Christ is gain to me in living and in dying'.) Farel, however, went to see him for the last time; but after this he asked that the many visitors should pray for him rather than visit him. For another fortnight he lingered in distress and pain, still trying to work, repeating verses from the psalms. He was, as he had foretold, in command of his mind until the end. On 27 May the *Registre de Conseil* recorded: 'Today about eight o'clock in the evening, *le sponsable Ian Calvin* has gone to God whole and entire in sense and understanding, thanks be to God.'[11]

At first his body lay in state; but so many came to see it that it was feared the Evangelicals would be accused of creating the cult of a new saint. He was therefore buried on Sunday 28 May in the common cemetery, without a tombstone, as he himself had wished. 'And there he lies today awaiting the resurrection which he had taught us and which he had so firmly hoped.'[12]

Appendix 1

Arguments for Re-dating

The dates usually assigned to Calvin's early years are as follows:

1509, 10 July	Birth
1523–1527 or 1528	University of Paris
1527 or 1528–1529	University of Orléans
1529–1531	University of Bourges
1531–1533	In Paris and Orléans
1533–1534	In Paris, Angoulême, and Noyon
1534	To Basel

His conversion is placed at dates varying between 1527 and 1534. Our present purpose is to examine the reliability of these dates.

1. AUTHORITIES

Beza 1 mentions only the birth-date and the year of going to Basel, to which year he also assigns 'sa premiere Institution' (OC 21, 30). Beza 2 is less precise, but he seems to keep to 1534 as the date for Basel. Colladon gives the birth-date, an approximate and incorrect date for the publication of the *Commentarius de clementia* ('il avoit adonc 24 ans seulement'—OC 21, 56), and the year of going to Basel, 1534. He also says that Calvin spent the year before leaving France in Orléans, where he composed *Psychopannychia*. Thus the earliest lives supply us with only three dates for this period, and one of these is certainly incorrect. If we had no other sources of information, we should know only that he was born in 1509 and went to Basel in 1534.

But we possess also the material relevant to Noyon, the selections and the digest of the Chapter Registers, as given in Lefranc, Desmay's *Remarques*, Le Vasseur's *Annales*, and the material on Orléans. Lefranc's dates should be corrected from K. Müller: *Calvins Bekehrung*. Finally, we have sixteen letters, written by and to Calvin, to be found in OC 10b, 1ff. and Herminjard volumes 2 and 3. (The English translation of Bonnet's collection of the letters is useless for serious study, abounding as it does in gross errors of translation and mistakes in dating.) Calvin's autographs of his early letters no longer exist (except for Nº. 18, OC 10b, 25–6) but are transcripts made by Pierre Daniel, a son of one of the correspondents. Calvin himself never

156

gives the year in these early letters. P. Daniel put dates to them, but nearly always a year or more earlier than Herminjard, who is chiefly responsible for the datings now generally accepted. The editors of OC have in the main been content to follow him.

The Noyon Registers determine the dates for Calvin's relations with the Chapter, but give only inferential help about his life outside Noyon. The letters, depending mostly on internal evidence, are a less reliable guide. More than one of Herminjard's dates rests on suppositions.

2. THE TERMINUS A QUO

When did Calvin begin his studies in Paris? '1523', is the general reply. This date is accepted, apparently without question by every scholar—the sole dissenter known to me is Imbart de la Tour. Let us trace this stream to its source. Those who feel it necessary to give an authority will refer us to Lefranc or Herminjard 2, p. 279, n. 2. If we turn first to Lefranc, we find that he also sends us to Herminjard. We have therefore no other modern source but Herminjard. What, then, are his authorities? They are Desmay and 'Calvin. Comment. sur I Thessalon'. By this latter he no doubt intends Calvin's dedicatory letter to Cordier. But the letter neither mentions nor even hints at any dates. Thus Herminjard's sole authority for 1523 comes in Desmay, writing a century later. But what is Desmay's authority? It is an entry in the Noyon Chapter Register for 5 August 1523, recording that Gérard Cauvin has been given permission to send Jean away from Noyon until 1 October that he might escape the plague then raging. There is no mention at all of Jean's destination. But what more probable, asks Desmay, than that it was on this occasion that he was sent to Paris to commence his studies? This is really such a feeble argument that, were it not for a certain apparent probability giving it some colour, surely no one would have paid any heed to it. The apparent probability is that in August 1523 Jean had just turned fourteen and this was the age at which one thinks of boys going up to the university in the sixteenth century.

Let us therefore look a little more closely at university entrance. We must say at once that this is a very uncertain subject and it would be foolish to pretend assurance. But we can at least elicit generalizations, which we may assume to be true of Calvin in the absence of evidence to the contrary.

In the early sixteenth century most students seem to have begun their university career as they were entering on their teens. Thus Thurot: 'When a scholar could read and write and had understood the elements of Latin grammar, he was judged capable of following the logic course. He could go to the University of Paris; and ordinarily one started to attend lectures in the Faculty of Arts before the age of fifteen' (p. 37). Fifteen is therefore normally the upper age limit. Thurot also gives us a lower limit: 'This teaching [i.e. the preparation for the arts course, explained on our pp. 4–6] finished at twelve or thirteen, the age at which boys entered the Faculty of Arts' (p. 94). Hence, 'one could be . . . a bachelor at fourteen' (p. 39).

We know that Paris was Calvin's first university. He was therefore not one of the exceptions, an older man, but within the twelve to fifteen age group. Since we must assume that a higher age in this group usually betokened backwardness, we should expect Calvin, with his 'extraordinaire memoire' and his 'singulier esprit' to enter the Faculty early rather than late. But it appears that he did not at once begin the arts course when he went to Paris, but spent some time on the preliminary grammar course. Hence, if he went to Paris in 1523, he would have entered the Faculty of Arts in 1524, at about the age of fifteen, when some clever boys are already bachelors. But Calvin is an outstandingly clever boy who, we are told, outstrips his fellows (Beza, Colladon, Masson). We are, then, immediately confronted by an improbability.

Let us apply Thurot's lower ages to Calvin. If he entered the Faculty of Arts at twelve or thirteen, the date would be either 1521 or 1522. We do not know how long he spent on the preliminary course at La Marche; but we must allow him time to suffer under the inadequate teaching of the Latin preceptor and time also (a few months, he himself says) to profit from Cordier. An academic year or the major part of it may be posited. This would fix his entry at La Marche in 1520 or 1521. Imbart de la Tour suggests that the gift to Calvin of the chaplaincy in May 1521, plainly an educational grant, immediately preceded his university entrance. This certainly makes better sense than the 'plague' theory; but it does not necessarily demand 1521 for university entrance, for the grant could have been given when he was already at the university. Nevertheless, although 1520 or 1521 are more probable dates than 1523, the arguments for 1520 (which seems rather more probable to me) are not compulsive in opposition to 1521.

3. THE LENGTH OF THE ARTS COURSE AT PARIS

Our authorities differ on details but show little disagreement in the end.

Hastings Rashdall: 'The time of those who kept their full residence of four years and a half at Paris appears usually to have been divided thus—they went up in October, took their B.A. in the spring of their second year, the licence two years after that, and 'incepted' towards the end of the same year . . . By the sixteenth century it had been reduced to three years and a half' (463–4). Renaudet gives a different time-table. The Faculty of Arts admitted to the philosophy course at about fifteen if the boys were competent in grammar (*Préreforme*, p. 26). This course, lasting two years, terminated in the baccalaureate. A further year of studies led to the master's degree. He says nothing of a licentiate. Thurot, to present a digest of his complicated account, tells us: (1) that to 'determine' for B.A. the student had to be at least fourteen and in the third year of the logic course (p. 43)—thus he could have begun at the age of twelve; (2) that in the fifteenth century the bachelors of one year usually became the *licenciés* of the next (p. 53)—but here is an inconsistency, for by the regulations of 1452 the *licencié* took an oath, not only that he had studied in Paris for three years (or rather, two years and a part of a year), but also that he was at least twenty-one; (3) that *licenciés* usually incepted M.A. at the end of the same academic year in which they received their licentiate; the *licencié* declared on oath that he was at least twenty-one and that he had studied in arts for six years. One does not have to be a very good mathematician to see that not all these statements can be correct.

There thus appears to be considerable variation between our authorities. But a table will show that the differences are not so great after all.

	Rashdall	*Thurot*	*Renaudet*
Matriculation to B.A.	1½ academic years	2½ years	2 years
B.A. to licentiate	2 years	1 year	} 1 year
Licentiate to M.A.	same year	same year	
Total	3½–4 years	3½–4 years	3 years

(But note Rashdall's final sentence, that in the sixteenth century the time had been reduced to 3½ years. This is confirmed by entries in the Archives of the University as given by Villoslada (pp. 22f.))

Let us apply these reckonings to Calvin's years in Paris.

He goes to Paris in 1520 or 1521, entering La Marche for the preparatory course in grammar.

He enters the Faculty of Arts for the philosophy course in 1521 or 1522.

He proceeds B.A. between 1523 and 1525.

He proceeds *licencié* in 1525 or 1526.

He incepts M.A. in 1525 or 1526.

There would appear to be a discrepancy between such an early date for the master's degree and the fact that he is not called *magister* in the Noyon Registers until 30 April 1529. But Müller points to omissions of the title in later entries (e.g. 1 May 1529, 20 June 1530, 7 January and 23 August 1533).

At this point Calvin leaves Paris.

4. THE LENGTH OF THE CIVIL LAW COURSE AT ORLÉANS

We enter now upon the period which Doumergue called 'une énigme chronologique' (1,127). Müller says more soberly: 'Von da an ist die Chronologie ungewiss'—as if it had been certain before this. I would suggest that the chronology is further and needlessly complicated by accepting 1523 and therefore being forced to date Calvin's migration in 1528 or at the earliest in the autumn of 1527.

On one legally attested fact about his law studies we can be certain. In the affidavit dated 14 February 1532 (N.S.) he is called 'maistre Iehan Cauvin, licencié-es-lois'. By this date, therefore, Calvin's law studies had taken him to a licentiate. Whether the university that granted him this degree was Orléans or Bourges is of little moment. Orléans is far more probable; but if Bourges is insisted on, then we shall have to infer that Bourges allowed the time spent at Orléans to count towards his degree.*

We turn to the statutes and customs of the University of Orléans. Bimbenet gives the time of the bachelor's course as five years up to 1512 (p. 323). He makes no mention of any curtailing of this period until 1679, when it was cut to two years— but that hardly concerns us. The period from baccalaureate to licentiate was, after 1512, three years (p. 325). Thus, according to Bimbenet, the whole course took eight years. Fournier's *Histoire de la science du droit en France* does not take into account the sixteenth century, and we must therefore be cautious about applying his times without confirmation. He agrees that the baccalaureate came at the end of five

---

* In Bourges the length of the course appears to have been forty months or at least three years for the baccalaureate and three for the licentiate.

years' study. Of the licentiate he says that it also was generally obtained at the end of five years (p. 115). In 1447, however, both baccalaureate and licentiate were reduced to forty months. Assuming (which we are not told) that the reckoning is according to the academic year of about ten months, this would allow four years for each part, and therefore again a total of eight years. But Fournier adds in a footnote: 'Les conditions de temps étaient dès ce moment un peu abrégées comparativement aux temps antérieurs' (p. 117 n. 1).

The doctorate was conferred on *licenciés* without further examination and soon after the licentiate. It is impossible to say what authority Herminjard had for imagining that a year and a half would suffice for a doctorate at Orléans (2,279 n. 2). It looks as if he merely worked from the assumption that Calvin went to Orléans early in 1528 and left for Bourges in the summer of 1529 and, by simple subtraction, was left with about a year and a half. Doinel's computations bear a certain air of verisimilitude about them, but they are contradicted by both Bimbenet and Fournier. According to him, the doctorate took three years, divided thus: *une année d'inscription* for the baccalaureate; a second year for the licentiate; a third for the doctorate.

If now we apply Bimbenet and Fournier to Calvin's law studies, we should expect him, starting in 1525 or 1526, to receive his licentiate in something less than eight years, that is, by 1533 or 1534. But this will not do, for he was certainly *licencié-ès-lois* on 14 February 1532,* and had probably graduated by March 1531, since it would seem that he was not at Orléans from then until 1532, except for brief visits. We have him, therefore, completing his law course in six years. The shortness of the time fits in with the accounts of his brilliance at Orléans in Beza and Colladon.

The duration of this period may also be used to determine the date of his migration to Orléans and therefore in confirming our dating of the start of his university career. Our hard date is 14 February 1532. Accept for the moment the up-to-eight years of Fournier or the full eight years of Bimbenet, and we find him going to Orléans in 1524. This is improbable, for it would mean his entering La Marche at the latest in 1519 and the Faculty of Arts in 1520, when he was only eleven. What, however, is clear is that Calvin could not have gone to Orléans as late as even the autumn of 1527. 1525 would allow him six years, 1526 five.

Thus not only the length of the arts course at Paris, but also that of the law course at Orléans makes 1523 for his entry at La Marche most improbable. It increases the probability of 1520 or even 1521.

In 1529, it would seem, Calvin migrated to Bourges. The year is an assumption based on (i) the fact that Alciati began to lecture there in April 1529, and (ii) a letter of Calvin's from Meillan, near Bourges, which Herminjard dates as September 1530, but which he believes to contain evidence of Calvin's presence in Bourges in 1529. We accept 1529, but without complete conviction. If we give him long enough in Orléans to take his bachelor's degree and make a start on his licentiate, that is three and a half or four calendar years, it can be fitted in between 1525 (and even 1526) and 1529.

---

* Battles and Hugo (*Calvin's Commentary on De Clementia*, p. 6*) are mistaken in following Lefranc's date of 14 February 1531. The French year began in March. Moreover, according to the document itself Gérard is already dead, and this had happened on 26 May 1531.

We may now tabulate the suggested re-datings:

1520 or 1521	enters La Marche.
1521 or 1522	enters Faculty of Arts.
1525 or 1526	incepts M.A.
1525 or 1526	migrates to Orléans.
1529–1530	at Bourges.
October 1530–March 1531	at Orléans.
Early 1531	takes licentiate.

In conclusion I would again emphasize that the arguments, although they are based on documentary evidence, are perforce probabilities and not certainties. To keep to the probable is the good advice that Aristotle gave to dramatists long ago. Historians and biographers (who are historians in little) must also follow the probable. But they have to remember that in real life it is not the probable impossibility that happens but the improbable possibility. I hope it may be agreed that my reconstruction is more probable than the accepted dating. But over it all looms Gibbon's judgment: 'the laws of probability, so true in general, so fallacious in particular'. But then, this applies to Desmay and Herminjard too!

Appendix 2

Calvin's Conversion

On no part of Calvin's life has so much energy been bestowed, so much ingenuity exercised, as upon the date, the manner, the causes, and the agencies of his conversion. The pieces of information with which our primary authorities furnish us are often inconsistent among themselves or with the assured or assumed knowledge we have of his early life. Such different views, such different datings have been advanced, and after nigh a century of Calvin-study so little certainty has been achieved, that one would wish a halt to be called were it not that in writing a life of Calvin it is not possible to describe the events of the decade 1525–34 without coming, however provisionally and hesitatingly, to some decision. The approach of two recent writers (P. Sprenger: *Das Rätsel um die Bekehrung Calvins*, and A. Ganoczy: *Le jeune Calvin*) has much to commend it. The one subjects Calvin's language about his conversion to a close investigation; the other examines Calvin's account theologically, seeking to understand what the conversion meant in relation to Calvin as a Churchman. With both the present writer feels in sympathy rather than with those whose aim is primarily to fix a date. But as a by-product of such investigations as Sprenger and Ganoczy have undertaken, it would seem that a certain period is indicated for the conversion.

It is of the utmost importance what we admit as evidence. It has been customary to use (i) a passage from Calvin's Preface to his *Commentary on the Psalms* (1557), (ii) a short passage from the *Second Admonition to Westphal*, (iii) a passage from the *Reply to Sadoleto*, (iv) the accounts in Beza and Colladon. To these Sprenger has added (v) Calvin's Commentary on Acts 9, the conversion of St Paul. Of these, I do not think that the *Admonition to Westphal* proves anything in terms of dates; the *Reply to Sadoleto* passage is a confession of faith put into the mouth of a lay convert from Rome. There is as little reason to identify Calvin with the convert as a dramatist with one of his characters. Sprenger's comparison of Calvin's language about his conversion in the Psalms commentary with his language about St Paul is both illuminating and misleading—illuminating lexicographically, but misleading in that it relates Calvin's conversion to Paul's. Now, Calvin himself does not do this, and his silence is pregnant. It is not difficult to see why he did not link himself to Paul. On the one hand, Paul before his conversion had been a persecutor of the Church: Calvin was never a persecutor of either the Evangelicals or the Romanists. And, on the other hand, Calvin did not wish to associate himself with any miraculous revelations from heaven, with their suggestions of 'les spirituels'.

Let us therefore take another look at the passage from the Preface in the *Commentary on the Psalms*:

God drew me from obscure and lowly beginnings and conferred on me that most honourable office of herald and minister of the Gospel. My father had intended me for theology from my early childhood. But when he reflected that the career of the law proved everywhere very lucrative for its practitioners, the prospect suddenly made him change his mind. And so it happened that I was called away from the study of philosophy and set to learning law: although, out of obedience to my father's wishes, I tried my best to work hard, yet God at last turned my course in another direction by the secret rein [*or* curb—*freno*] of his providence. What happened first was that by an unexpected conversion he tamed to teachableness a mind too stubborn for its years—for I was so strongly devoted to the superstitions of the Papacy that nothing less could draw me from such depths of mire. And so this mere taste of true godliness that I received set me on fire with such a desire to progress that I pursued the rest of my studies more coolly, although I did not give them up altogether. Before a year had slipped by anybody who longed for a purer doctrine kept on coming to learn from me, still a beginner, a raw recruit.

There is no need to spend time on the first three sentences. It is at the fourth that we begin.

And so it happened . . . Although no fast dates are set, we are given a certain period, in that he was taken from the study of philosophy (i.e. the arts course) and set to the law. This sentence surely forbids us accepting Beza's and Colladon's assertions that he began to move away from the Papacy at Paris.

I tried my best to work hard . . . that is to say, at the law. This is confirmation of what has just been said. The context of the conversion is his law studies.

Yet God at last turned . . . Calvin's course was set on some sort of a legal career. But God redirected his course.

What happened first . . . When is this 'first' to be placed? While he was working hard, for, according to the next sentence, the result of what happened was that he began to cool off from his studies. We have, however, to allow time for his working hard as well as for his working less hard. In any case, we see that the conversion happened during and not before or after his law studies.

He tamed to teachableness . . . The taming of a wild or unruly animal is a frequent metaphor in Calvin. Here the emphasis lies on 'teachableness', the opposite of 'hardened' in the next clause (see Sprenger, pp. 52ff. for a thorough treatment).

An unexpected conversion. Usually translated 'sudden'. But *subita* can mean either 'sudden' or 'unexpected'. That Calvin was aware of the ambiguity appears in his *Commentary on De Clementia:* '*Subita*—not only sudden [*repentina*], but also unexpected [*inconsiderata*]. For things which happen extemporaneously have hardly any purpose. Therefore *subitum* is taken for unadvised [*inconsulto*]' (Battles and Hugo, pp. 55–6). The context of our present passage seems to require *inconsiderata*—that is, the conversion was not the result of any wish or intention of Calvin's, but took place unexpectedly. Whether it happened suddenly is irrelevant in this context. The conversion itself (for Calvin's use of *conversio* see Sprenger, pp. 45ff.) occupies little space in this sentence. Had the phrase *subita conversione* been omitted, neither grammar nor logic would have suffered: 'he subdued my mind, too hardened for its years, to teachableness'. The conversion, however, is what happens 'first'. We are not told that now he is drawn out of the mire, freed from the superstitions of the Papacy, only that he has been tamed and made teachable.

I was so strongly devoted . . . In one respect the direction in which Calvin was going was towards a legal career; in another it was along the path of the late medieval religion. Sprenger refers 'superstitions' primarily to the veneration of relics and the cultic use of images. But this is treating the term too narrowly. 'Superstitions of the Papacy' is surely a general term to indicate what Calvin regarded as a degenerate form of Christianity. Superstition is not irreligion but false religion. It may mean holding a false concept of God in contrast to submitting to his self-revelation (thus *Inst.* I. iv. 1, I. xi. 1, etc.); or it may be the transferring to that which is not God of what belongs to God alone (thus *Inst.* II. viii. 16). Calvin is saying, not that he was devoted to certain superstitious practices or beliefs in the Papacy, but that he was devoted to this superstitious religion called the Papacy.

A mind too stubborn for its years. That is, stubborn in its adherence to the Roman Church. The clause is a useful pointer to the period of Calvin's life in which he was converted. We must not place the conversion at an age when his mind ought to have been settled and made up. Thus, bearing in mind the earlier mental maturity in that century, his mid-twenties (i.e. 1534, a date favoured by many) is too late. Q. Breen has an unhappy passage in this respect: 'Calvin was converted . . . rather late in life. He had been almost entirely committed to the humanistic ideal until his twenty-fourth year. As a rule young people experience their change before they are eighteen!' (p. 146).

And so imbued . . . The effect of his conversion on his law studies. The argument is: 'I tried my best to work hard: God tamed my mind by an unexpected conversion: I pursued my other studies more coolly.' *Imbutus* bears more than one meaning. The sense of a beginning fits best here (cf. Augustine: 'qui fide christiana primitus imbuti sunt'—*Catech.* 1. 1. See other examples in A. Blaise: *Dictionnaire Latin-Français des Auteurs Chrétiens*). Correspondingly, 'taste' is used in Calvin in opposition to being filled; in English we should say 'a mere taste' (see his commentaries on Heb. 6: 4–5, I Pet. 2: 3). 'True godliness' is to be taken in opposition to 'the superstitions of the Papacy'. That is *pietas* falsely so called: what Calvin now tasted was true *pietas*.

The rest of my studies. Calvin has not spoken of other studies since he mentioned the law. *Reliqua* can mean merely 'other' so that the phrase could be 'my other studies' whatever they might be. But if we follow the argument: 'the study of philosophy', 'learning law', 'I tried my best to work hard', 'an unexpected conversion', 'I pursued the rest of my studies with corresponding coolness', then the most probable sense of *reliqua* would be 'what remained' of his law studies. His work at the law is not given up altogether, but it is relativized, or lessened, by the desire to progress in true godliness. The comparative *frigidius* is therefore to be related to 'I set myself to work hard' as well as to *exarsi*. Thus: 'I burned to progress; I pursued the rest of my studies more coolly'; and 'I then set myself to work hard; I now pursued the rest of my studies more coolly'.

Before a year had slipped by. Must this be taken as indicating a calendar year, as it usually is? On the basis of this phrase, the conversion is placed as late as possible, for it is said that we do not find people coming to learn from Calvin until about 1534. Against this *argumentum e silentio* it is only necessary to say that we have too little knowledge of his early life to be certain. If *annus* here means a calendar year, we have to reckon with Calvin as a centre of evangelical activity earlier than we may have thought possible. This is the most likely sense of *annus*. But I will suggest another.

Still a beginner, a raw recruit. With some hesitation I would ask whether the words *conversio, docilitas, novitius, tiro,* and *annus* may not together form a single image, that of entry into the monastic life? The first entry into the religious house was the *conversio* from the world. The *novitius,* the novice, was the monk in his probationary period. *Tiro,* on the other hand, originally an army word for a recruit, was used by Christian writers of catechumens (cf. Commodianus, *Instruct.* 2, 4, 5; or Augustine: 'tiro Christi loquitur, cum accedit ad fidem'—*in Ps.* 26. 1. 1). The novitiate commonly lasted a year. Is Calvin then viewing his life in this metaphorical sense, and his conversion as a *conversio* into the life of a religious, a life in which all was dedicated and devoted to God?

From our reading of the Preface, is it possible to indicate a probable date for the conversion? One thing seems to emerge as necessary: if Calvin has remembered the sequence of events correctly, his conversion must be placed during his legal studies. A pre-Orléans date is inadmissible, as is also a date after he had taken his licentiate. If, then, 1525 (1526) and March 1531 are the termini, we must allow time for working hard and time (possibly less) for working more coolly. Something between 1528 and early in 1530 would be possible. If, however, the migration to Bourges indicates continued enthusiasm for the law studies, we must advance beyond the spring of 1529. If, on the other hand, there is substance in the stories of his preaching at Bourges, we must allow time for it. The latter end of 1529 or early in 1530 seem to be indicated. After this, Calvin does not break off his law studies altogether. He returns to Orléans in October 1530(?) for the final part of his course and takes his licentiate. He goes to Paris for further studies and finishes the *Commentary on De Clementia.*

As to the resignation of the chaplaincy in May 1534. Would, it is asked, a scrupulously honest man like Calvin have continued to profit from a gross abuse when once he had seen that it was an abuse? Therefore he was converted very shortly before this action. But the fact that he had received a taste of godliness does not mean that he saw all ethical issues clearly at once. Indeed, twenty-five years later he considered it the duty of the state to execute impenitent heretics. Surely it is far more likely that he regarded these sources of income as providing grants for his education. He was now almost twenty-five; his student days were over; he had no longer any thought of ordination to the priesthood. Therefore he had no right to retain his chaplaincy.

Notes

ABBREVIATIONS

OC   Opera Calvini (Corpus Reformatorum)
Op. sel. Opera selecta (Barth and Niesel)
CTS   Calvin Translation Society
ET   English Translation of Calvin's letters
LCC   Library of Christian Classics

INTRODUCTION

1. P. Bayle, *Dictionary* 1, 714.
2. For Lefèvre see Imbart de la Tour, *Les Origines* 3, *L'Évangélisme,* ch. 3; Dagens, *Humanisme et Évangélisme chez Lefèvre*; Renaudet, *Un problème historique*; Dörries, *Calvin und Lefèvre*; Carrière, *La Sorbonne et L'Évangélisme.*
3. For Briçonnet see Imbart de la Tour, op. cit.; Mousseaux, *Briçonnet et le mouvement de Meaux.*
4. Herminjard 1, 227.

CHAPTER 1

1. OC 6, 452.
2. *Remarques* 388.
3. *Elogia* 2, 409.
4. Lefranc, *La Jeunesse* 195.
5. Lefranc, *La Jeunesse* 34. For the Hangests see also M. Reulos, *Les attaches de Calvin.*
6. OC 5, 8; Battles and Hugo, *Commentary on De Clementia* 12–13.
7. OC 21, 121. Cf. Colladon, OC 21, 54; and Masson, *Elogia* 2, 411.
8. Thurot, *De l'Organisation* 2, 94; see also Thorndike, *University Records*; Rashdall, *Universities of Europe* 1; Renaudet, *Préréforme et Humanisme*; and the same, *L'Humanisme et L'Enseignement.*
9. See Reichling, *Das Doctrinale* LXXXVI.
10. See Reichling, *Das Doctrinale* LXXXVI.
11. *Opera omnia* 1, 514.
12. *Glosa notabilis* to *Doctrinale*, Reichling III.
13. *Comm. on I Thess.* OC 13, 525–6; CTS 234.
14. *Opera* 1, 21; see Thurot, *De l'Organisation* 2, 94.
15. For the colleges, see Renaudet, *Préréforme*; M. Godet, *Le Collège de Montaigu*; the same, *Le Congrégation de Montaigu*; Quicherat, *Histoire de Sainte-Barbe.*
16. Renaudet, *Paris de 1494 à 1517,* 7.

17. Cf. Beza 2: 'even at that early age he was wonderfully devout and a strict censor of all the faults in his fellow students'—OC 21, 121.
18. *Gargantua and Pantagruel* 4, 21.
19. OC 21, 54.
20. *Works of Ridley*, Parker Society, 189ff.
21. But we need not suppose that he read nothing but his textbooks. The library of another arts student (Jean Bouchard, who died in 1522) is surprisingly broad, containing *inter alios*, a Bible, Virgil's works, several volumes of Cicero, a Valla, and Ovid's Epistles (see Villostrada, *La Universidad de Paris* 445-6).
22. An hypothesis brought into prominence by K. Reuter, *Das Grundverständnis der Theologie Calvins*.

CHAPTER 2

1. For the University of Orléans see Fournier, *Histoire de la science du droit* t. 3; Bimbenet, *Histoire de l'Université de Lois d'Orléans*; Rashdall, *Universities of Europe* vol. 2; Doinel, *Calvin à Orléans*; Boussard, *L'université d'Orléans*; Mesnard, *Calvin, étudiant en droit, à Orléans*.
2. *Gargantua and Pantagruel* Bk. 2, ch. 5.
3. OC 21, 122.
4. For the study of law see the works listed under n. 1, and also Jolowicz, *Historical Introduction to the Study of Roman Law*; Hunter, *Introduction to Roman Law*; Savigny, *Histoire du droit romain*; Bohatec, *Calvin und das Recht*.
5. Viard, *André Alciat* 116, n.3.
6. *Corpus Iuris Civilis* I, 3a.
7. ibid.
8. OC 21, 29 and 54.
9. OC 21, 122.
10. Fournier, *Histoire* 3, 106-7; Bimbenet, *Histoire* 213.
11. Bimbenet, *Histoire* 237.
12. Fournier, *Histoire* 118.
13. OC 21, 29 and 54.
14. OC 21, 29 and 54 and 121.
15. *Remarques* 390.
16. For Bourges see Raynal, *Histoire du Berry* t. 3; Rashdall, *Universities of Europe* vol. 2.
17. For Alciati see Viard, *André Alciat*; *Biographie universelle* t. 1.
18. 'Ils furent glorieusement ouvertes', cries Raynal, carried away in 1844 by the echoes of the cheering in 1529.
19. Preface to *Ad rescripta principium*; *Opera omnia* 3, 178.
20. ibid.
21. *Une grève d'étudiants au XVIe siècle*.
22. For l'Estoile see *Biographie universelle* t. 7.
23. Breen, *John Calvin* 46.
24. OC 12, 364-5; CTS 100-1.
25. Cuissard, *L'Étude du Grec à Orléans* 93.
26. Raynal, *Histoire* 3, 308.
27. ibid.
28. Raynal, *Histoire* 3, 309.
29. *Jean Calvin* 1, 611.
30. OC 31, 19-34; CTS 1, xl-xlviii.
31. *Inst.* I. ii. 1.
32. OC 10b, 3-6; Herminjard 2, 278-82; ET 1, 5-6.

33. OC 10b, 7–9; Herminjard 2, 331–3; ET 1, 1–2.
34. OC 10b, 9–11; Herminjard 2, 346–8; ET 1, 3–4.
35. OC 10b, 15–16; Herminjard 2, 397–8; ET 1, 6–7.
36. Lefranc, *La Jeunesse* 201–2.
37. *Opus Epistolarum Erasmi* (Allen) 8, no. 2091.
38. *Remarques* 393.
39. *De clementia* I, vii. OC 5, 62; Battles and Hugo, *Commentary on De Clementia* 134 and 135. The introductions in Battles and Hugo, although not always satisfactory in their inferences and conclusions, are nevertheless full of interesting information and suggestions.
40. *Jean Calvin* 1, 216.
41. *Calvin* (ET) 29.
42. OC 10b, 20–1; Herminjard 2, 418–19; ET 1, 8–9.
43. OC 10b, 19–20; Herminjard 2, 417–18; ET 1, 7–8. That this letter was written to Loré and not (as Herminjard, with query, and OC) to Daniel, see Battles and Hugo, *Commentary on De Clementia* 387–91. Confirmation is supplied by the copy of the Commentary in the Bibliothèque Mazarine in Paris, which bears Loré's name instead of the printer's. (R. Peter's review of Battles and Hugo in *Rev. d'Hist. et de Phil. Relig.* 1971, 79–81.)
44. For the nations see Bimbenet, *Histoire*; Rashdall, *Universities of Europe* vol. 2; Kibre, *Nations in the Medieval Universities*.
45. Doinel, *Calvin à Orléans* 174–85. The two documents are printed 179–80.
46. OC 10b, 25–30; Herminjard 3, 103–11; ET 1, 11–16.
47. Sermon 14, on II Sam. 5. 13. *Supplementa Calviniana* 122.
48. OC 21, 56f. and 123.
49. OC 13, 681.
50. Lefranc, *La Jeunesse* 201.
51. *Jean Calvin* 7, 575.
52. Desmay, *Remarques* 390; Le Vasseur, *Annales* 1170.
53. OC 10b, 51f.; Herminjard 3, 348–9; ET 1, 18–19.

CHAPTER 3

For expositions of Calvin's theology in general see Niesel, *Calvin's Theology*; Wendel, *Calvin*.

1. Op. sel. 1, 22. All the references in this chapter are to Op. sel. I shall therefore give only the volume and page references.
2. 1, 21.
3. 1, 37.
4. 1, 40.
5. 1, 53.
6. 1, 59.
7. 1, 69.
8. 1, 70.
9. 1, 75.
10. 1, 76.
11. 1, 78.
12. 1, 86.
13. 1, 86.
14. 1, 87, 89, 90, 107.
15. 1, 91.
16. 1, 92.

17. 1, 98.
18. 1, 101.
19. 1, 118.
20. 1, 118.
21. 1, 118.
22. 1, 120–1.
23. 1, 121.
24. 1, 132.
25. 1, 137f.
26. 1, 139.
27. 1, 140.
28. 1, 142.
29. 1, 146.
30. 1, 163.
31. 1, 172.
32. 1, 175.
33. 1, 183.
34. 1, 202.
35. 1, 225.
36. 1, 226–7.
37. 1, 231.

CHAPTER 4

1. *Life* (Everyman Edition) 214.
2. Lefranc, *La Jeunesse* 205.
3. ibid. 210.
4. OC 31, 23–6; CTS 1, xlii–xliii.
5. For Geneva see Monter, *Calvin's Geneva*; Naef, *Les Origines*; and bibliographies in Niesel, *Calvin-Bibliographie*, 48ff. and *Calvin Theological Journal* (6/2) 172f.
6. OC 10b, 63; ET 1, 121.
7. OC 10b, 91.
8. *John Calvin* 182.
9. OC 21, 58f.
10. Op. sel. 1, 233.
11. ibid.
12. Op. sel. 1, 235ff.
13. Op. sel. 1, 237.
14. OC 10a, 7; Op. sel. 1, 370; Theological Treatises, LCC 49.
15. OC 10a, 8; Op. sel. 1, 371; Theological Treatises, LCC 50.
16. OC 10a, 9; Op. sel. 1, 372; Theological Treatises, LCC 51.
17. On I Cor. 5: 5. OC 49, 380–1; CTS 1, 185.
18. OC 10a, 11; Op. sel. 1, 374; Theological Treatises, LCC 53.
19. OC 10a, 11; Op. sel. 1, 374; Theological Treatises, LCC 52–3.
20. OC 21, 207.
21. OC 21, 217.
22. OC 10b, 83–4.

CHAPTER 5

1. OC 10b, 229; Herminjard 5, 71; ET 1, 51.
2. OC 10b, 221; Herminjard 5, 44; ET 1, 48–9.

3. OC 11, 165; Herminjard 7, 39; ET 1, 211.
4. OC 10b, 339; Herminjard 5, 291; ET 1, 111.
5. ibid.
6. See Reyburn, *John Calvin* 85.
7. OC 10b, 332; Herminjard 5, 270; ET 1, 107.
8. OC 10b, 430–1; Herminjard 6, 127; ET 1, 141. See also Herminjard 6, 163f., n. 26 and R. Peter, *Jean Calvin avocat.*
9. Herminjard 6, 163–4.
10. OC 10b, 273; Herminjard 5, 166; ET 1, 76.
11. Herminjard 5, 14.
12. Herminjard 5, 13ff.
13. OC 10b, 271; Herminjard 5, 163; ET 1, 72–3.
14. OC 10b, 340; Herminjard 5, 292; ET 1, 112.
15. OC 10b, 272; Herminjard 5, 165; ET 1, 75.
16. OC 10b, 396ff.; Herminjard 6, 52ff.; ET 1, 127ff.
17. OC 10b, 348; Herminjard 5, 314; ET 1, 117.
18. OC 11, 30; Herminjard 6, 199–200; ET 1, 151.
19. OC 1, 255–6.
20. ibid.
21. For Calvin's biblical work see Parker, *Calvin's New Testament Commentaries.*
22. OC 10b, 403. See *Calvin's New Testament Commentaries* ch. II.
23. Op. sel. 3, 6.
24. OC 14, 317.
25. See *Calvin's New Testament Commentaries*, chs VI and VII.
26. OC 10b, 352; Herminjard 5, 338; ET 1, 120.
27. OC 10b, 351; Herminjard 5, 336; ET 1, 118f.
28. OC 10b, 339; Herminjard 5, 290–1; ET 1, 110.
29. OC 10b, 361; Herminjard 5, 372–3; ET 1, 127.
30. OC 11, 114; Herminjard 6, 366; ET 1, 195.
31. OC 5, 386; Theological Treatises, LCC 222.
32. OC 11, 30; Herminjard 6, 199; ET 1, 151.
33. OC 11, 91; Herminjard 6, 325–6; ET 1, 187.
34. OC 11, 113; Herminjard 6, 364; ET 1, 194.
35. OC 11, 96; Herminjard 6, 334; ET 1, 186.
36. OC 21, 282.

CHAPTER 6

1. OC 11, 281; Herminjard 7, 249; ET 1, 260.
2. OC 10a, 31–2; Theological Treatises, LCC 72.
3. OC 10a, 20 note f; Theological Treatises, LCC 61 n. 20.
4. OC 10a, 30; Theological Treatises, LCC 71.
5. OC 10a, 30 note 1; Theological Treatises, LCC 71 n. 84.
6. OC 11, 321f.; Herminjard 7, 333–5; ET 1, 261.
7. OC 11, 377f.; Herminjard 7, 439; ET 1, 291.
8. OC 11, 377f.; Herminjard 7, 438; ET 1, 290.
9. OC 11, 417; Herminjard 8, 79; ET 1, 314.
10. OC 11, 674; Herminjard 9, 156–7; ET 1, 385.
11. OC 11, 673–4; Herminjard 9, 156; ET 1, 380.
12. Op. sel. 2, 16.
13. ibid.
14. Op. sel. 2, 17.

15. ibid.
16. ibid.
17. Op. sel. 2, 18.
18. OC 10a, 27; Theological Treatises, LCC 68.
19. OC 10a, 17; Theological Treatises, LCC 58. For Calvin's preaching see Mülhaupt, *Die Predigt Calvins*; Parker, *Oracles of God*.
20. OC 54, 8.
21. *Inst.* I. vii. 1.
22. OC 53, 266.
23. OC 25, 666f.
24. OC 51, 566.
25. OC 11, 365–6; Herminjard 7, 412.
26. OC 11, 417; Herminjard 8, 79; ET 1, 314.
27. OC 21, 302.
28. See Gagnebin, *L'incroyable histoire*.
29. OC 26, 473f.
30. OC 54, 283f.
31. OC 46, 289–90.
32. OC 46, 574. I am indebted to Mr Maurice Miles for drawing my attention to this quotation and the next.
33. OC 54, 291.
34. OC 49, 661.
35. Ges. Aufs. 3, 267.
36. OC 26, 304.
37. OC 50, 327.

CHAPTER 7

1. OC 11, 521; Herminjard 8, 298; ET 1, 353.
2. OC 21, 417.
3. OC 11, 338–9; ET 2, 42–4.
4. OC 21, 382.
5. OC 11, 355–7; ET 2, 47–8.
6. OC 21, 439–40.
7. OC 12, 504; ET 2, 92.
8. OC 13, 230–1; ET 2, 202.
9. OC 53, 254.
10. OC 12, 586–7; ET 2, 128.
11. OC 13, 516.
12. OC 21, 107.
13. OC 12, 319–20; ET 2, 29.
14. OC 21, 109–10.
15. OC 21, 109.
16. For the *Institutio*, see Warfield, *Literary History*; Pannier, *Comment Calvin a révisé* . . .
17. OC 13, 192.
18. OC 13, 192; ET 2, 248–9.
19. OC 12, 391; ET 2, 58.
20. OC 12, 216.
21. OC 12, 368.
22. OC 14, 307.
23. OC 12, 545.
24. OC 12, 546; ET 2, 108.

25. OC 12, 564–5.
26. OC 12, 632–3; ET 2, 134–5.
27. OC 12, 639; ET 2, 137.
28. For de Ecclesia, see Kingdon and Bergier, *Registres* 1, 47, 56–63, 132–4, 144–8. Hughes, *Register* 92f., 105–7, 108f., 201–6, 209–11.
29. Kingdon and Bergier, *Registres* 1, 148; Hughes, *Register* 206.
30. Kingdon and Bergier, *Registres* 1, 80–1; Hughes, *Register* 138.
31. Kingdon and Bergier, *Registres* 1, 81; Hughes, *Register* 138.
32. *Doctrine of Predestination* Note XXI, pp. 393ff. See also article *Predestination* in Richardson, *Dictionary of Christian Theology*.
33. *Inst.* III. xxi. 5.
34. Kingdon and Bergier, *Registres* 1, 122; Hughes, *Registers* 173.
35. Kingdon and Bergier, *Registres* 1, 124; Hughes, *Registers* 177–8.
36. Kingdon and Bergier, *Registres* 1, 127; Hughes, *Registers* 182.
37. OC 21, 520.
38. OC 14, 455–6; ET 2, 369–70.
39. OC 14, 509; ET 2, 377–8.
40. OC 14, 478.
41. OC 21, 547.

CHAPTER 8

1. For the considerable literature on the Servetus affair see Niesel, *Calvin-Bibliographie* 51–3.
2. OC 8, 670.
3. OC 8, 653.
4. OC 8, 674.
5. OC 12, 283; ET 2, 19.
6. OC 13, 42; ET 4, 409.
7. OC 21, 146.
8. OC 8, 837.
9. OC 8, 842.
10. OC 8, 848.
11. OC 8, 761.
12. OC 8, 786.
13. See Roget, *Histoire* 4, 91.
14. OC 8, 789.
15. OC 8, 461.
16. Op. sel. 1, 260.
17. OC 21, 698ff.
18. OC 21, 554.
19. OC 21, 560.
20. OC 21, 560.
21. OC 21, 593.
22. OC 15, 356.
23. OC 15, 617–18; ET 3, 182.
24. OC 13, 587–90.
25. For the Academy see Borgeaud, *Histoire de l'Université*; Geisendorf, *L'Université de Genève*.
26. OC 21, 687.
27. OC 10a, 21; Theological Treatises, LCC 62–3.
28. OC 42, 189f.

29. OC 42, Prolegomena side 4; CTS Minor Prophets 1, xxvii.
30. See Parker, *Calvin's Doctrine of the Knowledge of God.*
31. Dedicatory letter, *Institutio*, Lausanne 1576, fol. **ii.
32. The credit for this important textual work belongs to J. W. Marmelstein: *Etude comparative des textes latins et français de l'Institution.*

CHAPTER 9

1. *Inst.* IV. i. 2.
2. ibid.
3. *Inst.* IV. i. 3.
4. *Inst.* IV. i. 4.
5. *Inst.* IV. ii. 6.
6. *Inst.* IV. ii. 12.
7. OC 11, 217; Herminjard 7, 115; ET 1, 239.
8. OC 34, 412–13.
9. OC 34, 421.
10. OC 11, 24; Herminjard 6, 191; ET 1, 85.
11. Herminjard 9, 374 n. 18.
12. OC 10b, 432; Herminjard 6, 130–1; ET 1, 143.
13. ibid.
14. OC 11, 774–5; Herminjard 9, 374; ET 1, 409.
15. OC 12, 6ff.; ET 1, 416ff.
16. OC 9, 461–2; ET 4, 119 n. 1.
17. OC 11, 28; Herminjard 6, 196; ET 1, 89.
18. OC 12, 166; ET 2, 146.
19. OC 14, 313–14; ET 2, 333.
20. OC 14, 314; ET 2, 333.
21. OC 20, 131.
22. OC 11, 259; Herminjard 7, 197–8; ET 1, 253.
23. OC 14, 43; ET 1, 373.
24. OC 12, 401; ET 2, 63.
25. OC 12, 578; ET 2, 123.
26. OC 12, 64ff.; ET 1, 429ff.
27. OC 17, 198; ET 3, 426.
28. OC 17, 252f.; ET 3, 451.
29. OC 17, 585–6; ET 4, 60.
30. OC 17, 680–1; ET 4, 77–8.
31. OC 21, 714.
32. OC 13, 77–90; ET 2, 168–84.
33. OC 34, 602.
34. OC 34, 609.
35. See Monter, *Calvin's Geneva* 135.
36. OC 14, 492; ET 2, 375.
37. OC 14, 545; ET 2, 387.
38. OC 16, 629f.; ET 3, 361.
39. *Inst.* IV. xx. 31.
40. OC 18, 84–5; ET 4, 104.
41. OC 18, 81–2; ET 4, 107.
42. OC 18, 38–9; ET 4, 91.
43. OC 20, 8; ET 4, 305.
44. OC 19, 688; ET 4, 302.

CHAPTER 10

1. OC 17, 335; ET 3, 475.
2. OC 17, 351–2; ET 3, 473–5.
3. OC 40, Prolegomena side 2; CTS Ezekiel 1, xlvii.
4. OC 20, 253; ET 4, 358ff.
5. OC 20, 382–3; ET 4, 362.
6. OC 40, 516; CTS Ezekiel 2, 345.
7. OC 9, 888–9; ET 4, 370.
8. OC 9, 891; ET 4, 373.
9. OC 9, 891–4; ET 4, 373–7.
10. OC 20, 302–3; ET 4, 364.
11. OC 21, 815.
12. Colladon, OC 21 106.

Sources and Bibliography

The main sources of information on Calvin's life are four. First, contemporary registers; second, correspondence; third, contemporary chronicles; fourth, contemporary or near contemporary biographies.

Registers. The registers of the Cathedral Chapter of Noyon, now lost, are known only through the transcripts of some entries and by an eighteenth-century digest. Those that relate to Calvin have been reprinted in Lefranc: *La Jeunesse*. K. Müller's correction of some of the dates should be noticed (*Calvins Bekehrung*). For the later period we have the registers of the Genevan Councils and of the Venerable Company of Pastors. Extracts from the former are printed in OC 21. The latter appear as the two volumes edited by Bergier and Kingdon, and as selections in the English translation by Hughes.

Correspondence. Calvin's correspondence occupies volumes 10b–20 in OC. Much other material relating to Calvin and his circle is to be found in Herminjard's nine volumes, which, however, stop at 1544. The English translation of Calvin's own letters by D. Constable and M. R. Gilchrist was published too early to have the advantage of the valuable notes in Herminjard and OC. The quality of the translation is, moreover, poor and gives occasion to many derisory comments in OC notes.

Chronicles. These relate to Geneva and have already, as might be expected, been worked over very thoroughly. They are by the nun, Jeanne le Jussie, who lived through the early years of reform in the city, by Michael Roset, secretary to the Council, by Antoine Froment, one of the early evangelists, and by François Bonivard, the prisoner of Chillon.

Biographies. The earliest is Calvin's autobiographical sketch in the Preface to his *Psalms* (OC 31, 23ff.). This gives the barest outline of his life, intended to mark the steps which had led him to his ministry. The next three lives are related. The first by Beza (which I have referred to as Beza 1) was in French, the preface to the posthumously published *Joshua* (1564). The second, also a preface to *Joshua* (1565), was issued under Beza's name but was in fact the work of Nicolas Colladon. The third was in Latin, the *Ioannis Calvini Vita* by Beza in his edition of *Calvini Epistolae et Responsa* (1575), which I have called Beza 2. The value of these lives is that they were written by men who knew Calvin intimately (Beza probably knew him in Bourges) and who were in touch with his early friends. Colladon's account is also a primary source for the dates of Calvin's preaching and lecturing. These lives contain inaccuracies, but the scepticism about their general accuracy shown by some writers is excessive. They may safely be accepted unless they are contradicted by established evidence (and not merely by conjecture). Bolsec's *Histoire de la vie, mœurs, constance et mort de Jean Calvin* (1577), concerned only to slander his old enemy, may be disregarded. But Le Vasseur's *Annales* (1633), no less virulent, nevertheless took the trouble to consult the Noyon registers as well as some aged inhabitants of that city who could narrate tradition at only second hand. Desmay also based his *Remarques* on the Noyon registers and on 'conversations which I had with those who had seen and lived with Calvin's contemporaries' (398). His work in its entirety is said to be no longer extant and to be known only in Cimber and Danjou: *Archives curieuses*, which dates Desmay as 1621. These editors suppressed the first thirty pages 'parce qu'elles ne donnent que des renseignements peu importants sur les parents de Calvin' (387 n. 1). In fact, there is a copy of Desmay in the British Museum Library; but the early pages (as Doumergue saw and I have confirmed) contain only an essay on the Anglican liturgy. Papire Masson's very fair life of Calvin in his *Elogia varia* (1638) also makes use of the Noyon tradition.

Among later works, Doumergue, for all his faults of partisanship and lack of perspective, stands alone with his wealth of detailed information. Lefranc's *La Jeunesse* was a pioneering work which has not been superseded. His weakness is that, as a descendant of the family of Calvin's mother, he writes of Calvin too exclusively in terms of Noyon. He also pretends to more knowledge of details than we possess.

The list that follows contains only names of works mentioned in the notes. For exhaustive bibliographies see (1) to 1900, OC 59, 517–86; (2) 1901–59, W. Niesel: *Calvin-Bibliographie 1901–1959*, München 1961; (3) 1960–72, J. N. Tylenda: *Calvin Bibliography 1960–1970* and P. De Klerk: *Calvin Bibliography 1972*, both in Calvin Theological Journal; volume 6 no. 2 and volume 7 no. 2.

1. CALVIN'S WRITINGS

Ioannis Calvini Opera quae supersunt omnia. Ediderunt G. Baum, E. Cunitz, E. Reuss. Brunswick and Berlin 1863–1900. 59 volumes [Corpus Reformatorum edition].

Joannis Calvini Opera Selecta. Ediderunt P. Barth, W. Niesel, D. Scheuner. München 1926–52. 5 volumes.

Supplementa Calviniana. Sermons inédits. Neukirchen (1936) 1961ff. In progress.

Calvin Translation Society. Edinburgh 1843ff. 47 volumes.

Calvin: Theological Treatises. Translated with introductions and notes by J. K. S. Reid. Library of Christian Classics vol. XXII. London 1954.

Calvin's Commentary on Seneca's 'De Clementia'. With introduction, translation and notes by F. L. Battles and A. M. Hugo. Published for the Renaissance Society of America. Leiden 1969.

Correspondance des Réformateurs dans les pays de langue française . . . recueillie et publiée . . . par A.-L. Herminjard. Seconde Édition. 1878–97. 9 volumes.

Letters of John Calvin. Compiled from the original manuscripts and edited with historical notes by Dr Jules Bonnet. Volumes 1–2, translated by David Constable. Edinburgh 1855, 1857. Volumes 3–4, translated by M. R. Gilchrist. New York 1858 (1972 and 1973).

2. REGISTERS AND CHRONICLES

Noyon. Relevant extracts printed in Lefranc: *La Jeunesse* 193–201, and in Le Vasseur: *Annales*.

Orléans. Relevant extracts printed in Doinel: *Calvin à Orléans*.

Geneva. *Registre du Conseil*. Relevant extracts printed in OC 21. *Registres de la compagnie des pasteurs de Genève au temps de Calvin*. Edited R. M. Kingdon and J.-F. Bergier. Geneva 1962, 1964, 1969. (*Travaux d'Humanisme et Renaissance*, 55 and 107). 3 volumes. *The Register of the Company of Pastors in the Time of Calvin*. Edited and translated by P. E. Hughes. Grand Rapids 1966.

François Bonivard: *Chroniques de Genève*. Edited G. Revelliod. Geneva 1867.

Antoine Froment: *Les Actes et Gestes Merveilleux de la Cité de Genève*. Edited G. Revelliod. Geneva 1854.

Jeanne le Jussie: *Le levain du Calvinisme*. Geneva 1865.

Jean Roset: *Les Chroniques de Genève*. Edited H. Fazy. Geneva 1894.

3. EARLY LIVES

Beza 1. *Theodore de Besze au Lecteur chrestien*, as preface to *Commentaires sur le livre de Iosue*. Geneve 1564. (OC 21, 21–50.)

Colladon. *Commentaires de M. Iean Calvin sur le livre de Iosué*. Avec une Preface de Theodore de Besze, contenant en brief l'histoire de la vie et mort d'iceluy. Geneve 1565. (OC 21, 51–118.)

Beza 2. *Ioannis Calvini Vita* in *Calvini Epistolae et Responsa*. Geneva 1575. (OC 21, 119–72.)

Jacques Desmay: *Remarques sur la Vie de Jean Calvin, tirées des Registres de Noyon, ville de sa naissance* in L. Cimber and F. Danjou. *Archives Curieuses de l'Histoire de France depuis Louis XI jusqu'à Louis XVIII*, t. 5, 387–98. Paris 1835.

Jacques Le Vasseur: *Annales de l'Eglise Cathedrale de Noyon, jadis dites de Vermand*. Paris 1633.

Masson. *Cl. Viri Io. Papirii Massonis . . . Elogia Varia . . .* Paris 1638.

4. OTHER EARLY WORKS

Bayle. *The Dictionary Historical and Critical of Mr Peter Bayle*. The Second Edition. London 1734–8. 5 volumes.

Cellini. *The Life of Benvenuto Cellini written by himself*. Translated by A. Macdonell. (Everyman edition.) London 1960.

Corpus Iuris Civilis. Editio stereotypa. Edited P. Krueger, T. Mommsen, R. Schoell and G. Kroll. Berlin 1872, 1877, 1895.

Cranmer. *The Miscellaneous Writings and Letters of Thomas Cranmer*. Edited for the Parker Society by J. E. Cox. Cambridge 1846.

Das Doctrinale des Alexander de Villa-Dei. Kritisch-exegetische Ausgabe, mit Einleitung . . . bearbeitet von Dietrich Reichling. Berlin 1893.

Desiderii Erasmi Roterodami Opera Omnia . . . Lugduni Batavorum 1703–1706. 9 volumes.

Opus Epistolarum Des. Erasmi Roterodami denuo recognitum et auctum per P. S. Allen & H. M. Allen. Oxford 1934.

Jewel. *The Works of John Jewel, the Third Portion.* Edited for the Parker Society by J. Ayre. Cambridge 1848.

François Rabelais: *The Histories of Gargantua and Pantagruel.* Translated by J. M. Cohen. London 1955.

Ridley. *The Works of Nicholas Ridley.* Edited for the Parker Society by H. Christmas. Cambridge 1841.

5. SECONDARY WORKS

J. E. Bimbenet: *Histoire de l'Université de Lois d'Orléans.* Paris and Orléans 1853.

Biographie universelle (Michaud). Nouvelle édition. Paris and Leipzig 1843–7.

A. Blaise: *Dictionnaire Latin-Français des Auteurs Chrétiens.* Paris 1954.

J. Bohatec: *Calvin und das Recht.* Graz 1934.

C. Bourgeaud: *Histoire de l'Université de Genève: 1 L'Academie de Calvin, 1559–1798.* Geneva 1900.

J. Boussard: 'L'Université d'Orléans et L'Humanisme au début du XVIe Siècle' in *Humanisme et Renaissance* 5, 1939, 209–30.

Q. Breen: *John Calvin: A Study in French Humanism.* Second edition. Hamden, Conn. 1968.

V. Carrière: 'La Sorbonne et L'Évangélisme au XVIe siècle' in *Aspects de l'Université de Paris.* Paris 1949.

C. Cuissard: *L'Étude du Grec à Orléans depuis le IXe siècle jusqu'au milieu du XVIIIe siècle.* Orléans 1883.

J. Dagens: 'Humanisme et Évangélisme chez Lefèvre d'Étaples' in *Courants Religieux et Humanisme à la fin du XVe et au début du XVIe Siècle* (Colloque de Strasbourg 9–11 Mai 1957). Paris 1959.

H. Dörries: 'Calvin und Lefèvre' in *Zeitschrift für Kirchengeschichte* 44/4, 1925, 544–81.

J. Doinel: 'Jean Calvin à Orléans. Date précise de son sejour d'après des documents inédits' in *Bulletin du Société de l'histoire du Protestantisme français*, t. XXVI, 1877, 174–85.

E. Doumergue: *Jean Calvin. Les hommes et les choses de son temps.* Lausanne 1899–1927. 7 volumes.

M. Fournier: *Histoire de la science du droit en France.* t. 3, *Les Universités françaises et l'enseignement du droit en France au moyen-âge.* Paris 1892. Réimpression Aalen 1970.

B. Gagnebin: *L'incroyable histoire des Sermons de Calvin.* Geneva 1955.

A. Ganoczy: *Le jeune Calvin: Genèse et évolution de sa vocation réformatrice.* Wiesbaden 1966.

P.-F. Geisendorf: *L'Université de Genève.* Geneva 1959.

M. Godet: 'Le Collège de Montaigu' in *Revue des Études Rabelaisiennes*, t. VII, 1909. Paris. 285–305.

M. Godet: *La Congrégation de Montaigu (1490–1580).* Paris 1912.

K. Holl: 'Johannes Calvin'. 1909. In *Gesammelte Aufsätze* 3, 254ff. Tübingen 1928.

W. A. Hunter: *Introduction to Roman Law*. Revised by F. H. Lawson. Ninth edition. London 1934.

P. Imbart de la Tour: *Les Origines de la Réforme*. T.3, *L'Évangélisme (1521–1538)*. Paris 1914.

H. F. Jolowicz: *Historical Introduction to the Study of Roman Law*. Cambridge 1939.

P. Kibre: *The Nations in the Mediaeval Universities*. Cambridge, Mass. 1948.

H. Lecoultre: 'Une grève d'étudiants au XVIᵉ siècle' in *In Memoriam. Mélanges*, 67–83. Lausanne n.d.

A. Lefranc: *La Jeunesse de Calvin*. Paris 1888.

J. W. Marmelstein: *Étude comparative des textes latins et français de l'Institution de la religion chrestienne par Jean Calvin*. Groningen, Den Haag 1921.

P. Mesnard: 'Jean Calvin, étudiant en droit, à Orléans' in *Actes du Congrès sur l'ancienne Université d'Orléans*, 81–91. Orléans 1962.

E. W. Monter: *Calvin's Geneva*. New York 1967.

M. Mousseaux: *Briçonnet et le mouvement de Meaux*. Paris 1923.

J. B. Mozley: *A Treatise on the Augustinian Doctrine of Predestination*. London 1878.

E. Mülhaupt: *Die Predigt Calvins, ihre Geschichte, ihre Form und ihre religiösen Grundgedanken*. Berlin 1931.

K. Müller: 'Calvins Bekehrung' in *Nachrichten von der Königl. Gesellschaft der Wissenschaften zu Göttingen*. Göttingen 1905. 188–255.

H. Naef: *Les origines de la Réforme à Genève*. Geneva 1936.

W. Niesel: *The Theology of Calvin*. Translated by H. Knight. London 1956.

J. Pannier: 'Comment Calvin a révisé les éditions successives de l'Institution' in *Bulletin du Société de l'histoire du Protestantisme français*, t. LXXIX, 1930, 79–81.

T. H. L. Parker. *Calvin's Doctrine of the Knowledge of God*. Edinburgh 1969.

T. H. L. Parker: *Calvin's New Testament Commentaries*. London 1971.

T. H. L. Parker: *The Oracles of God. An Introduction to the Preaching of John Calvin*. London 1947.

R. Peter: 'Jean Calvin, Avocat du Comte Guillaume de Furstenberg: Éléments d'un dossier' in *Revue d'Histoire et de Philosophie Religieuses*, Nᵒ 1, 1971, 63–78.

R. Peter: 'Notes de Bibliographie Calvinienne à propos de deux ouvrages récents' in *Revue d'Histoire et de Philosophie Religieuses*, Nᵒ. 1,1971, 79–81.

J. Quicherat: *Histoire de Sainte-Barbe, Collège, Communauté, Institution*. Paris 1860. 2 volumes.

Hastings Rashdall: *The Universities of Europe in the Middle Ages*. Edited by F. M. Powicke and E. B. Emden. Oxford 1936. 3 volumes.

L. Raynal: *Histoire du Berry depuis le temps les plus anciens jusqu'en 1789*. t.3. Bourges 1844.

A. Renaudet: *Préréforme et Humanisme à Paris pendant les premières guerres d'Italie (1497–1517)*. Second edition. Paris 1953.

A. Renaudet: 'L'Humanisme et l'Enseignement de l'Université de Paris au temps de la Renaissance' in *Aspects de l'Université de Paris*, 135–55. Paris 1949.

A. Renaudet: 'Paris de 1494 à 1517: Église et Université; Réformes Religieuses; Culture et Critique humaniste' in *Courants Religieux*, 5–24.

A. Renaudet: 'Un problème historique, la pensée religieuse de Lefèvre d'Étaples' in *Humanisme et Renaissance*, 201–16. Geneva 1958.

M. Reulos: 'Les attaches de Calvin dans la région de Noyon' in *Bulletin du Société de l'Histoire du Protestantisme français*, 1964, 193–200. Paris.

K. Reuter: *Das Grundverständnis der Theologie Calvins*. Neukirchen 1963.

H. Y. Reyburn: *John Calvin, his life, letters and work*. London 1914.

A. Richardson: *Dictionary of Christian Theology*. London 1969.

A. Roget: *Histoire du peuple de Genève depuis la Réforme jusqu'à l'Escalade*. Geneva 1870–87. 7 volumes.

F. C. de Savigny: *Histoire du Droit Romain au Moyen-Age*. Translated by C. Guenoux. Paris 1839. 4 volumes.

P. Sprenger: *Das Rätsel un die Bekehrung Calvins*. Neukirchen 1960.

L. Thorndike: *University Records and Life in the Middle Ages*. New York 1949.

C. Thurot: *De l'Organisation de l'Enseignement dans l'Université de Paris au Moyen-Age*. Paris and Besançon 1850.

P. E. Viard: *André Alciat 1492–1550*. Paris 1926.

R. Villoslada: *La Universidad de Paris durante los estudios de Francisco de Vitoria (1507–1522)*. Analecta Gregoriana XIV. Rome 1938.

W. Walker: *John Calvin, the Orgainzer of Reformed Protestantism 1509–1564*. New York 1906 and 1910.

B. B. Warfield: *The literary History of the Institutes of the Christian Religion*. Philadelphia 1909.

F. Wendel: *Calvin. The Origins and Development of his Religious Thought*. Translated by P. Mairet. London 1969.

Index 1

Calvin's Life

Index 2

Calvin's Writings

Index 3

Calvin's Doctrines

Index 4

Geneva

Index 5

Names